Britain and France in Two World Wars

Britain and France in Two World Wars

Truth, Myth and Memory

EDITED BY ROBERT TOMBS AND EMILE CHABAL

B L O O M S B U R Y
LONDON · NEW DELHI · NEW YORK · SYDNEY

Bloomsbury Academic

An imprint of Bloomsbury Publishing Plc

50 Bedford Square	1385 Broadway
London	New York
WC1B 3DP	NY 10018
UK	USA

www.bloomsbury.com

Bloomsbury is a registered trade mark of Bloomsbury Publishing PLC

First published 2013
Reprinted 2013 (twice)

British Library Cataloguing-in-Publication Data
A catalogue record for this book is available from the British Library.

ISBN: HB: 978-1-4411-6933-4
PB: 978-1-4411-3039-6
ePDF: 978-1-4411-0635-3
ePUB: 978-1-4411-6619-7

Library of Congress Cataloging-in-Publication Data
A catalogue record for this book is available from the Library of Congress.

Typeset by Deanta Global Publishing Services, Chennai, India
Printed and bound in Great Britain

CONTENTS

ACKNOWLEDGEMENTS

This book is the outcome of a conference held at St John's College, Cambridge, in September 2011. The conference was made possible by generous financial support from the Fellows' Research Fund of St John's, from the French Embassy in London and from the Prince Consort and Trevelyan Fund of the Cambridge History Faculty; and by an advance on royalties provided by the publisher. The editors would like to express their thanks to all of them.

CONTRIBUTORS

Sébastien Albertelli, is an *agrégé* and teaches history and georgraphy at the Lycée Voltaire, Paris. He is the author of *Les services secrets du général de Gaulle: Le B.C.R.A. 1940–1944* (Éditions Perrin, 2009).

Martin S. Alexander, Professor of International Relations, Aberystwyth University, is the author of *The Republic in Danger. General Maurice Gamelin and the politics of French defence, 1933–39* (Cambridge University Press, 1993).

Philip Bell is the author of *France and Britain, 1900–1940* (2 vols, Longman, 1996).

Robert Frank, Professor at Université de Paris I Panthéon, is the author of *La hantise du decline: le rang de la France en Europe, 1920–1960* (Belin, 1994).

Elizabeth Greenhalgh, research fellow at the School of Humanities and Social Sciences, University of New South Wales at the Australian Defence Academy, author of *Victory through Coalition: Britain and France during the First World War* (Cambridge University Press, 2005).

John Keiger is Director of Research in the Department of Politics and International Studies, University of Cambridge, and author of *France and the Origins of the First World War* (Macmillan, 1983) and *Raymond Poincaré* (Cambridge University Press, 1997).

William Philpott, Professor of the History of Warfare, Department of War Studies, King's College, London, author of *Bloody Victory: The Sacrifice on the Somme and the Making of the Twentieth Century* (Little Brown, 2009).

David Reynolds, Professor of International History, Cambridge, is the author of *In Command of History: Churchill Fighting and Writing the Second World War* (Penguin, 2004) and of *The Long Shadow: The Great War and the 20th Century* (Simon and Schuster, 2013).

Gary Sheffield, Professor of War Studies, University of Birmingham, is the author of *Forgotten Victory: The First World War: Myths and Realities* (Headline, 2001), and *The Chief: Douglas Haig and the British Army* (Aurum, 2011).

Olivier Wieviorka, Professor at the École Normale Supérieure de Cachan, is the author of *Normandy: The Landings to the Liberation of Paris* (Harvard University Press, 2010) and of *Divided Memories: French Recollections of World War II from the Liberation to the Present* (Stanford University Press, 2012).

Jay Winter, Charles J. Stille Professor of History, Yale University, is the author of *Remembering War: The Great War between Historical Memory and History in the Twentieth Century* (Yale University Press, 2006).

Akhila Yechury, Lecturer in Asian History, University of Edinburgh, has published articles on the French territories in India.

EDITORS

Robert Tombs, Professor of French History, Cambridge, is the co-author of *That Sweet Enemy: The English and the French from the Sun King to the Present* (Heinemann, 2006).

Emile Chabal, research fellow in French Political History, St John's College, Cambridge, is the author of articles on contemporary French politics, Franco-British relations and France's imperial legacy.

Two Great Peoples

Robert Tombs

Our two ancient peoples, our two great peoples, remain linked together. They will both succumb or else they will win together.
Charles de Gaulle, 8 July 1940[1]

The General's declaration, which could be applied to the whole period from 1914 to 1945, can probably not be read today without inspiring at least a tinge of irony. This is less, I think, because his implication of an equal and reciprocal partnership had been belied by France's disastrous defeat than because the relationship between the 'two great peoples' has so often been fraught with resentment and misunderstanding. So it has remained in the historical record, not least because of de Gaulle's own wartime and post-war intransigence, which features prominently in his memoirs.

In wider 'popular memory' – that of people with at most a passing interest in historical detail – the Franco-British relationship hardly exists, or else exists as one of disagreement, rivalry and perhaps more or less good-humoured banter. The media in both countries are happy to indulge in *schadenfreude* and mockery at the expense of the other. Politicians are readier to point to the failures than the successes of their cross-Channel neighbour and to use those failures as proof of their own superior policies. The ubiquitous French use of the term 'Anglo-Saxon' – a rare example in Western political discourse of an ethnic term being used to convey political and social messages – shows the existence of a widely accepted stereotype that is at least ambivalent and more often negative. Nicolas Sarkozy, admittedly for a time an admirer of Britain's apparent economic success, reverted to type following the 2008 financial crisis in casting Britain as 'the Other', embodying what France must avoid: 'Frankly, when you see the situation . . . in the United Kingdom, you don't want to be like them.'[2] British politicians, who are capable of at least equal negativity, take for granted that France, especially in European politics, represents the opposite pole from Britain. Although defence collaboration is now unprecedentedly close, as formalized in the Defence and Security Co-operation Treaty (November 2010), this often evokes public surprise and scepticism, as if France and Britain had never been allies before. One MP expressed the view that 'We need to recognise that France has never and is never likely to share the same strategic priorities as the UK. There is a long track record of duplicity on the French part. When it comes to dealing with allies, we should never be under any illusion.'[3]

It might be said that these attitudes are derived from history. Undoubtedly they are. But which history? We would probably all agree that there is no such thing as 'straight' history, in which past events directly shape later attitudes. But there are certainly versions of history that are more distorted than others, and help to create and perpetuate prejudices and suspicions. This book aims to lift the veil on certain key episodes over the last century which have undoubtedly shaped subsequent British and French attitudes towards each other through the way in which they have been remembered, interpreted or simply forgotten – forgetting can be as significant as remembering.

The question of 'memory', as it is conveniently though problematically called, is an important element of this book. What we really mean by the term is discussed by Jay Winter (p. 175). In brief, at this distance in time, we are rarely thinking of personal memories based on experience, though immediate family traditions are significant. Nor are we mainly thinking of history, if by this we mean a systematic and in principle a critical analysis of the past – though there is certainly a two-way interaction between history and memory. Rather, by 'memory' we mean the combination of diverse cultural actions and artefacts – involving places, ceremonies, museums, memorials, speeches, oral traditions, images, fiction, films, documentaries and writings – which seek to preserve and transmit ideas and emotions about the past.[4]

The year 2004 was an important year for memory. It combined the 60th anniversary of D Day, the centenary of the *entente cordiale* and the 90th anniversary of the outbreak of World War I. In both France and Britain, in well-meaning attempts to marshal memory to create amity, ceremonies great and small proclaimed friendship between former allies and reconciliation with former enemies, and recalled what Britain and France had endured together. Yet an opinion poll that same year showed that among the words the French most commonly chose to describe the British were 'isolated', 'insular' and 'selfish'. The British were no more generous, commonly describing the French as 'untrustworthy' or 'treacherous', and nearly one in three considered them 'cowardly'.[5] Here, clearly, are the distorted traces of a hard and often bloody century, and probably above all of a certain 'memory' of World War II in the Anglophone countries.

Clearly, there are aspects of memory that resist present-day attempts to mould them into officially approved and edifying shapes. But memory also bears the traces of earlier and different official moulding, most effective at times of particular crisis or under the influence of dominating personalities – in this context, most obviously de Gaulle and Churchill. The French are largely unaware that British forces played a major part in the liberation of France in 1944 – a point taken up by Olivier Wieviorka and Robert Frank.

The British, for their part, have long forgotten (if they were ever aware of) the French soldiers who died defending Dunkirk and thus permitting the successful evacuation of British and Allied troops. The widespread press coverage of the 60th anniversary of Dunkirk in 2010 made, as far as I could see, no reference to the French at all – one of the things that prompted this book. The full story is thoroughly investigated by Martin Alexander in Chapter 4.

These distortions of memory are doubtless unconscious, but that does not mean that they are accidental. For example, in the days after Dunkirk, politicians and the media emphasized purely British heroism as 'totemic of an indomitable Albion', in Martin Alexander's words; and the theme of 'Britain alone' became an important part of the memory of 1940. As for French memory of the Liberation, that too has been shaped by the needs of patriotic myth-making. The role of the French people themselves in bringing about their own liberation was a central theme of the Gaullist legend.

From the British perspective, interpretations of events at the time and since were affected by long-term assumptions about France's historic trajectory, seen as one of growing weakness, even decadence. William Philpott places a 'meta-narrative of French decline' in the later stages of World War I. He shows that assumptions about French military weakness were present in the writings of Field Marshal Haig and other senior figures. Haig was eager to claim victory for his own army and downplay the role of the French – a line followed by much subsequent British history. But there seem to have been more general prejudices about the French nation and its supposed decline which, as William Philpott and Elizabeth Greenhalgh show, were not based on the actual performance of the French army, which to the very end of the war played an essential role and even a predominant one in the final victory. Gary Sheffield shows that a belief in French 'decadence' (which, to be fair, was widely shared in France too) was strengthened by the defeat of 1940, and again seemingly confirmed by France's long and disastrous retreat from empire after 1945. In both countries, there has been an exaggerated belief in both their own and each other's decline.[6]

....

This difficult relationship between France and Britain is an essential explanatory element in twentieth-century history. It cannot be said that it has been a neglected subject: there have been many monographic studies, some of the most important of them by contributors to this volume; many collections of detailed articles; and some attempts to synthesize the findings of research. The present book consists of interpretative essays by leading scholars, organized around key moments of the Franco-British relationship during the two world wars, accompanied by reflections on the memory of those events in both countries. The 'key moments' were chosen both because of their importance at the time and because of their prominence in subsequent historical memory. There is of course no direct or simple connection between event and memory. The more complex relationship between history, commemoration and memory – in which Britain and France differ significantly – is itself a subject of historical study.[7]

The Franco-British relationship has often been antagonistic, and that antagonism did much to shape their sense of their own history and identity. Yet actual enmity between them is now nearly two centuries in the past – a longer period of peace than either has enjoyed with all but one other Great Power.[8] Since Waterloo, they have been allies in the Crimean War, cooperated in several minor imperial expeditions and even tried to be 'cordial', both in the 1840s and in the 1900s. They have long shared liberal values, have had important economic interests in common and from 1815 to 1945 were the most (semi-)democratic of the major European States. But they were also colonial competitors in Africa and Asia, and continued to nourish a sense of deep cultural difference, much of which stemmed from a sense of historic rivalry.[9]

This created a legacy of mistrust, arguably more on the British side. It began as a conviction that the French had not accepted the verdict of Waterloo. Palmerston expressed it in 1840 with characteristic bluntness, diagnosing

> a spirit of bitter hostility towards England growing up among Frenchmen of all classes and all parties; and sooner or later this must lead to conflict . . . I do not blame the French for disliking us. Their vanity prompts them to be the first nation in the world; and yet at every turn they find that we outstrip them in everything. It is a misfortune to Europe that the national character of a great and powerful people . . . should be as it is.[10]

Palmerston was not wholly wrong: there were vocal elements in France that were bitterly Anglophobic, and that did indeed aim to destroy the 'treaties of 1815'.[11] Palmerston's suspicion was widely shared in Britain, as shown by the huge popular response to the Volunteer movement in the 1860s, catalysed by an exaggerated fear of French invasion. But this generalized suspicion made it very difficult to recognize when French governments were being friendly. Palmerston did cooperate with France, for example in the Crimea, but always charily. Well after his death, instinctive suspicion of France was enough to cause the cancellation of the Channel Tunnel in 1883, despite the patent weakness and vulnerability of France's position after the 'Terrible Year' of 1870–71.

Both countries were prompt to indulge in emotional and self-righteous recriminations. The majority in Britain, from the Queen downwards, were committed Dreyfusards, and indignantly denounced French injustice and lack of political integrity.[12] French opinion was equally vehement over the Boer War, and French volunteers went to fight for the Boers. The foolish and pointless Fashoda incident in 1898 had even led to talk of war. However, by this time, British worries about French enmity could only arise if France was allied with another Power, and particularly with Russia, whose expansionism in Asia was the main strategic worry of British statesmen. As long as Salisbury and his generation were in power, this was something to be lived with: 'We know that we shall maintain against all comers that which we possess, and we know, in spite of the jargon about isolation, that we are amply competent to do so.'[13] But soon pessimism in Britain was 'an all pervasive and quintessential characteristic'[14] of official thinking on future world affairs, and it turned out to be a dangerous one.

When in 1900 Germany began building battleships for the North Sea, British policy began a reorientation towards France and Russia, the first major fruit of which was the Entente Cordiale of 1904, originally motivated by British fear that Germany might establish a naval presence in Morocco.[15] As J.F.V. Keiger shows in Chapter 1, the Entente led France and Britain into a dangerously ambiguous relationship which ended in a war and an alliance in circumstances that neither country had chosen or expected. As Keiger summarizes it, 'Britain saw the Entente as largely backward-looking: a settlement of past imperial disputes; France saw the Entente as a forward-looking process towards alliance' (p. 30). Both views encouraged a British rapprochement with Russia. Whether different policies could have prevented the outbreak of war in 1914 remains a controversial and doubtless insoluble question. It has often been argued that the uncertainty of the Anglo-French Entente contributed to the dangerous instability in Europe, which both created fears and encouraged risks. It was probably politically impossible for Britain to commit itself more definitely to France, as Paris wanted. It would probably have been politically impossible for any conceivable French government to weaken its relationship with Russia in order to please Britain. So neither government had much room for manoeuvre. Judgement really depends – as analysis of the causes of the war always has – on whether Germany is seen as the principal source of danger or as in some sense a victim of what its rulers claimed was 'encirclement'. If it happened to be the former case, France and Britain, whatever they did, were really on the sidelines in 1914 in a conflict over south-eastern Europe. On the other hand if it happened to be the latter case, Britain's crab-like rapprochement with France and subsequently Russia was adding to the danger.

Keiger points to important intellectual and cultural barriers to clear understanding between the two governments before World War I. There were other important differences between the two countries. France's governing elite, especially after 1880s, was far less patrician than the British, whose politicians', diplomats' and soldiers' attitude to their French counterparts was often frankly snobbish. Even as late as 1940, it is striking to read in British officers' memoirs how concerned they were to find out whether French officers were 'gentlemen'. The French, for their part, tended to patronize the British as amateurish, naïve, ignorant, even half-hearted. As a source of instinctive friction and mistrust on both sides – especially when aggravated by existing national stereotypes – social and cultural differences were far from negligible. Elizabeth Greehalgh (p. 76) gives an example of a not unfriendly declaration by the French writer Georges Bernanos in 1942 referring to the British in World War I as like 'lords of the manor' whom the French assumed were not fully engaged in the conflict; and she shows that attitudes like this (often in much more accusatory language) were commonplace. One might point out that the British Expeditionary Force (BEF) had the lowest proportion of prisoners to total casualties of any of the major armies – a sign of its willingness to keep fighting.[16] But of course perceptions are at best tenuously connected with realities.

In 1940, the French, drawing on their First World War memories, certainly treated their British counterparts with some condescension: 'it is for us to give them moral support, to organize the strategy of the campaign, and to provide the necessary planning and inspiration,' said the French Commander-in-Chief General Maurice Gamelin.[17] Gamelin believed that '1914–18 has shown that one must always keep large French forces alongside the . . . British. Whenever these were removed, they had to be rushed back in times of crisis.' He deployed the strongest element of France's strategic reserve, the 7th Army, on to the BEF's left, to counter a possible German advance into Holland, but also to discourage any British rush for the ports.[18] This was to prove a catastrophic move. When disaster duly came, one obstacle met by Churchill in trying to persuade the French government to continue the struggle was the hostility of Marshal Pétain and General Weygand, clearly influenced by their experiences in 1918, which Elizabeth Greenhalgh analyses in Chapter 3. 'You, the English, were done for [in March 1918],' said Pétain to Churchill. 'But I sent forty divisions to rescue you. Today it's we who are smashed to pieces. Where are your forty divisions?'[19]

The shared efforts and sacrifices of World War I had clearly not removed – to put it mildly – the traditional ambivalence of the Anglo-French relationship, but it would be an error to see this as wholly abnormal. As Gary Sheffield reminds us, an alliance is not a friendship, but a business relationship in which costs and benefits are inevitably calculated. The length of World War I, which took most people – though not all – by surprise, meant that the British had to engage far more than originally expected in not only one but in several land campaigns, instead of confining themselves to supplying mainly naval and financial support to their allies, as some had originally expected – though of course they did these things too. Both William Philpott and Elizabeth Greenhalgh remind us of the asymmetry of France and Britain during the war, creating an inevitable asymmetry of historical memory. It took at least 2 years for Britain to create a substantial army, and the effects of its naval blockade, though immediately felt in Germany, took years to have a seriously disabling effect. France's other ally, Russia, proved far less formidable than expected. So France had to bear the brunt of the land war with Germany. The battle of the Somme saw Britain taking a major part in the war in the West, while the French army was assailed at Verdun. The growth in Britain's military power relative to that of France made relations between the two difficult – comparable, perhaps, to the similar process between Britain and the United States in World War II.

Generals, politicians, ordinary soldiers and historians on both sides showed an equal tendency to claim the lion's share of glory, and even to deprecate their allies' efforts, particularly in 1917–18. Many in Britain – including senior soldiers and politicians – believed that France was exhausted and barely capable of an active part in the last phase of the war. Given the French army's huge losses, this was a not implausible belief, and it was linked with their own confidence in growing British military strength. But, as contributions to this book show unambiguously, the French army was still active and formidable. On the French side, it was difficult for even highly placed and well-informed French soldiers or politicians to appreciate the economic and naval effort being made by the British, and this caused considerable bitterness: as one French officer put it unanswerably, British coal miners and sailors 'aren't getting killed'. But without their efforts, the war could not have been pursued. The French, notes Elizabeth Greenhalgh, 'simply did not appreciate the difficulties in convoying American troop transports across the Atlantic' (p. 73). Paradoxically, the year of victory in 1918 caused particular tensions and generated conflicting memories. William Philpott calls these 'limited, false and self-serving impressions of each other's sacrifice in their common struggle' (p. 58), yet they rapidly became established in memoirs and official histories. The resentful notion of the British being willing to 'fight to the last Frenchman' remained sufficiently familiar to be resurrected by German and Collaborationist propaganda during World War II.

The public memory of World War I from the 1920s onwards has also taken very different forms in France and Britain. There are at least three elements in this difference. First, as already noted, memory reflects to some extent the way in which the war was fought – its asymmetry. Each side remembered and commemorated its own particular epics and tragedies. This was perhaps inevitable, and even natural, given the scale of the sacrifice and the sense of loss. In any case it seems to be a characteristic shared with other participants. For Canada, Australia, New Zealand and the United States the war has remained prominent in national memory, but it seems to be strongly associated with particular episodes: Vimy Ridge, Gallipoli, Saint Mihiel, etc.

Second, the significance of the war, as several of our authors emphasize, was fundamentally different in France, and has remained so in what Jay Winter terms 'common and often unspoken assumptions about what the war was about, what it meant'. For the French, it was a war to liberate national soil. For Britain and the other Anglophone countries, the war's meaning was more complex: a 'war to end war', a war against militarism, a war for strategic security, a war for the preservation of the empire. Perhaps such 'abstractions', as David Reynolds terms them, were inherently more ephemeral; but in any case, the disappointments of the interwar period and the returning threat of war in the 1930s caused them to evaporate, making World War I appear a futile sacrifice. The war was increasingly remembered in Britain as a monument of waste, a fresco of inexplicable images of horror. Hence, Winter suggests, in Britain the war discredited or destroyed the traditional vocabulary of military and patriotic glory, but not in France. Retrospective revulsion and rejection of World War I continued in Britain, and even increased after the 1960s as it came to embody the horror of 'war' in the abstract, and to carry other symbolic (and many historians would say tendentious) messages too, concerning class division and military incompetence. This phenomenon has inspired its own literature.[20] In Britain World War I can be lamented, denounced and even mocked in a way that would be unthinkable in France, where says Winter, it 'can never be a laughing matter'.

The third element that distinguishes British memory of World War I from that of other European countries is that it remains the worst disaster in modern British history, whereas elsewhere it has been overtaken and obscured by the far worse experiences of the 1940s. For all these reasons, the experience of World War I and its traces in subsequent culture from 1918 to the present day have been vastly different in France and Britain. Several of our authors point out that this is not solely a matter of general cultural trends, but also of differences in academic historiography which have meant that many British specialists in First World War military history have no easy access to adequate material on the French army, not least because French academic historians neglect the purely military history of World War I in favour of its cultural and political dimensions.

The most serious political consequences of conflicting Franco-British memory were felt in the interwar period. Britain's Foreign Secretary, Lord Curzon, stated in December 1921 that 'a combination of Great Britain and France would be so strong that no other likely combination could successfully resist it'.[21] But of course no such combination materialized until it was too late. In the simplest terms, French policy was more national: suspicious of Germany as the source of past and perhaps future aggression, and more reliant on traditional methods of maintaining security – military strength and alliances. This arose from the simple fact, suggests David Reynolds, that the war had been fought for the defence and liberation of the national soil, and this primal cause influenced post-war thinking about physical territorial security. 'France sought to prevent a repetition of 1914,' says David Reynolds, 'whereas the British wanted to move on from 1919.' They wanted to believe, in Lord Balfour's words, 'that Germany was repentant, that her soul had undergone a conversion and that she was now absolutely a different nation.'[22]

Hence, British policy was more 'international' and inclined to conciliation or appeasement of Germany. Moreover, Britain wished to concentrate on imperial rather than on Continental security, and the main threat to that security, the German fleet, was lying at the bottom of Scapa Flow. If there was a new rival, it seemed during the early 1920s to be France. But at a more idealistic level, the war had come to be seen in Britain and other Anglophone countries as a disastrous product of the general system of nationalist rivalry, trade competition and antagonistic diplomacy. The leading Labour politician Philip Snowden could, thus, convince himself in 1936 that the 'damned French are at their old game of dragging this country behind them in the policy of encircling Germany.'[23] One should not, however, draw the dividing line too starkly. Appeasement views were held elsewhere, including very strongly on the political Left in France. As Philip Bell reminds us, the conviction that there should 'never again' be war was passionately held on both countries. On the other hand, some British politicians realized that France was still a pillar of British security – 'thank God for the French army', in Churchill's words. Important differences did exist between the two sides of the Channel. But the real and perilous difference was that on the other side of the Rhine, where a powerful body of opinion had never accepted the fact of defeat and the peace terms of the Treaty of Versailles.

Either stronger deterrence or more generous conciliation might have worked better than the contradictions and uncertainties of policy that emerged, and which neither deterred nor conciliated Germany. The Paris peace conference and the drafting of the highly controversial treaty of Versailles produced ill-tempered wrangling over debts, reparations and trade, as well as a disastrous divergence over the way in which to manage the post-war world. The United States and Britain both refused to ratify a security guarantee promised to France. One of the reasons, says John Keiger, was memory of the confused outbreak of war in 1914: 'in the 1920s British politicians were wary of striking up a new agreement with Paris, let alone an alliance' (p. 42). France during the 1920s tried and failed to control Germany unilaterally; the 1930s, after the Nazi seizure of power, saw a forlorn attempt, mainly led by Britain, at appeasement, which continued until the outbreak of war in 1939. Elizabeth Greenhalgh suggests a human analogy for the post-war antagonism: 'Just as marriages often fail after a tragedy such as the loss of a child, so too the nations that had managed to win victory in 1918 found it too difficult to maintain the relationship after that victory had been sealed by a peace treaty' (p. 74).

But after 1938, and the sudden realization after Hitler's flouting of the Munich agreement that appeasement was not enough, there came a rapid rapprochement, with the British realizing that a close alliance of France and Britain – even an economic and perhaps political union of the two states – was necessary.[24] Not all French statesmen were convinced by this sudden conversion. The former prime minister Édouard Daladier told the American ambassador that 'he fully expected to be betrayed by the British' and added that 'this was the customary fate of allies of the British.'[25] Viscount Halifax, the Foreign Secretary, accepted in November 1939 that many in France thought that 'war has come upon them again owing to our having taken the teeth out of the Versailles settlement, and having ever since shown a sentimental spinelessness in dealing with Germany.'[26] The events of 1940 – especially the Dunkirk evacuation and the attack on the French fleet at Mers-el-Kébir – caused many Frenchmen to agree with either or both of these views, which became staples of collaborationist propaganda.

World War II remains the dominant event in modern history and a crucial episode in forming instinctive French and British views of each other and their places in the world. As several contributors emphasize, the 1940 disaster casts a very long shadow. As early as Marshal Pétain's doleful wireless broadcast of 16 June – ascribing France's defeat as inevitable due to 'too few arms, too few children, too few allies' and also to the French people's 'spirit of pleasure' which had overcome the 'spirit of sacrifice' of 1914–18 – France's defeat was seen as proof of catastrophic national moral decline. The Labour politician Hugh Dalton, newly appointed Minister of Economic Warfare, agreed: the French 'are too much attached to their mistresses, and their soup, and their little properties,' he wrote. 'We see before our eyes nothing less than the liquification of France.'[27] Conversely, Britain's continuing resistance was seen as proof of renewed historic virtue.

Many historians have deconstructed these ideas and prejudices. Britain's decision to fight in 1940, though it undeniably showed impressive national unity, was far from desperate or quixotic: it was based on superior economic, naval and air power, the support of the empire and access to world resources.[28] France's 'strange defeat'[29] in 1940 had little to do with national character or deep-seated economic or military failings: the French armed forces were strong, well equipped and determined. Rather, the May 1940 attack by Germany was a desperate gamble that the military ingenuity of the Wehrmacht enabled to succeed.[30] Martin Alexander provides in Chapter 4 a powerful analysis of Dunkirk and its meanings, so central to British memory, and so significant a cause of divergence with memory in France. He shows how much Britain owed to the French army and how little French soldiers' conduct bears out the 'decadence' theme that was so long the orthodoxy, and which their own commanders did much to propagate in an attempt to exculpate themselves.

But whatever the revisions of modern historical research, there can be no doubt of the baleful ramifications of 1940, which Robert Frank and David Reynolds discuss in a long-term context. It ended the rapprochement between France and Britain that had begun really only in 1938. More profoundly, it marked a parting of the ways. This seemed immediately clear to some on both sides, however different their conclusions were. Pierre Laval, now Vichy prime minister, thought that

> England's day has passed. No matter what happens now, she will lose her empire . . . She will not gain a foothold in Europe again. She left it forever when she reembarked at Dunkirk . . . Everything that doesn't end up by being Russian will be American.[31]

Lord Halifax thought it very unlikely that Britain would in future revive the Entente Cordiale and would rather embark on a 'special association' with the United States.[32] Although the Free French, the BBC,[33] the Resistance and the Liberation created strong feelings of solidarity, and an attempt to renew the pre-war alliance with the Treaty of Dunkirk (1947), Frank and Reynolds agree that there had been a long-term change. For Britain, says Reynolds, 'these efforts were always subordinate' to an Atlantic alliance (p. 201). From the 1950s onwards, France developed its own 'special relationship' with Germany. It has become commonplace to explain divergent British and French attitudes to European integration as a consequence of their different experiences of the war. Though this is a useful half-truth, it risks obscuring the similarities of the two countries' post-war policies. Both were equally determined to maintain their status as imperial powers and after decolonization as great powers. It is this, of course, which explains both their frequent rivalry since the late 1950s and their developing defence relationship since the 1990s.

Akhila Yechury and Emile Chabal sketch out the world war that this European war inevitably became. Britain was involved more widely than any other combatant, and the Free French too were from the beginning engaged in it. Charles de Gaulle proved his breadth of vision by realizing as early as 1940 that Western Europe was not the decisive point of the conflict. However, he overestimated the independence of the French empire, which he saw as an essential dimension of Free-French independence and of France's rehabilitation. But the Vichy regime too saw the empire as a trump card, and it retained actual control of most of it. This led the British and American governments to make approaches to powerful Vichy figures or men thought to be better placed than de Gaulle to win over cautious colonial officials. This partly explains de Gaulle's notorious quarrels with Churchill, aggravated by the mutual suspicions of de Gaulle and President Roosevelt. He caused unnecessary friction with his Allies by clinging to imperial sovereignty in Saint-Pierre et Miquelon and in Syria. As Robert Frank shows, antagonism continued after the Liberation, as de Gaulle, determined to assert an equal status for France, quarrelled violently with the British government over Syria. However, London was in reality France's only effective supporter in world politics, wishing to rehabilitate France as a European and colonial power. Even during the war itself, de Gaulle's meagre influence over France's colonies had been largely owing to British backing. But however frail the French empire had become, it played a crucial part in the Gaullist myth: 'Thanks to its empire, France is a victorious power,' intoned the Guyanese Radical politician, Gaston Monnerville. This conviction – or bluff – would lead to grave post-war conflicts in the empire and at home. It only ended when de Gaulle, in power again from 1958, realized that the empire had ceased to be viable. This too had an Anglo-French aspect, suggest Yechury and Chabal: it was 'a recognition that the two-century battle between France and Britain for control of the world stage' was no longer relevant.

Of course, for most French people, this world war essentially played out at home, and this is their predominant memory, with Occupation, Collaboration, Resistance and Liberation the centrepieces. Britain contributed to the last two. How far it did so, and how its contributions are remembered, have formed an important but changing part of mutual perceptions, not without effect on the post-war relations of the two countries. Sébastien Albertelli assesses British participation in the Resistance in detail, especially through the efforts of the Special Operations Executive [SOE]. He shows how the inherent difficulties and complexities of trying to organize and run a resistance movement from overseas provided many occasions for friction (e.g. over arms deliveries, codes and security procedures). On top of that came the attitude of de Gaulle who considered control of the Resistance movements an important source of legitimacy and resented what he saw as British interference. He adopted a consistent policy of intransigence in dealing with the British: 'you have to bang the table,' he told his subordinates, 'they back down.'[34] Whether or not this was really the best approach, it was one that de Gaulle used repeatedly, including after he returned to power in 1958, for example over NATO and Europe, and it constitutes an important element of the Gaullist myth.

In particular, Gaullists were suspicious of the wholly British-controlled 'F-Section' of SOE, and after D Day, de Gaulle was quick to order its agents out of France. These lingering concerns were reflected in the story of M.R.D. Foot's 1966 history of SOE in France, which told the detailed story of British involvement in organizing and arming the Resistance. On its release, it was bitterly attacked by Gaullist politicians as anti-French and only published in France 40 years later, in 2008.[35]

The Liberation, comprising the Normandy landings, the battle for Normandy, the landings in Provence and the general combat with German forces in France, shows how far memory can change or indeed be altered. From the beginning, public relations were an important element. As always, de Gaulle was very aware of the political implications of military events, and his outrage at being excluded from the preparations for D Day, and his fear that the Americans might try to elbow him out of power and treat France as a defeated country, are famous. Yet the Allies were in one significant way willing to give the Gaullists pride of place: General Leclerc's 2nd Armoured Division – the famous '2e DB' – was brought over specially from England, avoiding the Normandy carnage, to liberate Paris, and it then went on to do the same for Strasbourg. The arrival of French troops in the capital was an act of immense symbolic importance in restoring French pride, and it was carefully orchestrated by de Gaulle, who arrived to take over the levers of the State. At the Hôtel de Ville he proclaimed that 'Outraged, broken and martyred Paris' had been 'liberated by itself, liberated by its people with the aid of the armies of France, with the support and aid of the whole of France, fighting France, the only France, the true France, the eternal France'.[36]

It is scarcely deniable that the huge part played by Britain in the Liberation has been generally obscured, even forgotten – perhaps increasingly so as the generation that lived through that great event disappears, leaving memory to be created by official pronouncements, ceremonies, museums and popular media such as films, television and non-academic history. In France, far more than in Britain, the State consciously attempts to shape historical memory, and the teaching of history in schools is given high priority by public and politicians.[37] Anniversary celebrations may be used by politicians for domestic or diplomatic purposes. Olivier Wieviorka points out (p. 138) that while the D-Day memorial ceremonies of 1984, 1994 and 2004 all acknowledged the British presence, in 2009, Sarkozy downplayed their contribution as part of a charm offensive towards President Obama. The following year Sarkozy, in London for the 70th anniversary of de Gaulle's BBC broadcast on 18 June 1940, paid a glowing tribute to British support for de Gaulle in 1940, saying that it had helped to save French honour and made resistance possible. It is as if the British role was confined to that of early support for the Free French. Marginalization of Britain's part in World War II is far from being a French phenomenon, however. One apparently influenced by it is the present prime minister, David Cameron, who declared in July 2010 that 'we were the junior partner [to the USA] in 1940.'

In reality, as Olivier Wieviorka states, 'the liberation of France would have been impossible without the efforts and sacrifices of the British', without whom D Day could not have been launched (p. 149). Britain's naval, air and ground forces in Operation Overlord were superior to those of the United States, and its losses in the Battle of Normandy were far heavier. This is clearly not how D Day is now remembered in France – or, to be sure, in Britain or America. As Wieviorka remarks, 'the memory of the D-Day landings has gradually been Americanised', largely due to films, television and popular history. Opinion polls have long shown that the French, irrespective of age, sex and class, attribute a negligible role in France's liberation in 1944 to the British – a point taken up by Robert Frank (p. 185). But is there more here than a general Americanization of memory?

Historians, including contributors to this volume, take somewhat different views. Robert Frank argues that there is a particular difficulty for the French: 'British successes have continued to hold up a mirror to French humiliations' (p. 186). But Olivier Wieviorka argues that French memory is to some extent a reflection of reality: Britain's part in the battle for Normandy and the subsequent Liberation was limited by the numbers and perhaps by the morale of its troops, and he links what he judges the 'dismal performance of British forces on the battlefield' with Britain's global decline – a view that would be widely accepted in a Britain long conditioned by 'declinism'. This shows the complexity of the issues involved in trying to confront 'history' and 'memory', and the way in which detailed historical interpretation is inevitably influenced by more general assumptions. We may see a parallel here with British interwar views of France, when, as Gary

Sheffield reminds us, a belief in French decline retrospectively affected judgement of the French army's performance during World War I.

I am grateful that such a distinguished group of scholars have been willing to contribute to this book, and to participate in the conference that preceded and prepared it.[38] The Franco-British relationship has often been soured by distortion, myth and ignorance, often with damaging, and sometimes with grave, consequences. Yet it has long been, and it remains, one of the most 'special' relationships the two countries have. My hope is that not only students and specialists but also readers with a general interest in Franco-British relations will find it valuable to have authoritative reflections on these key moments in our shared history. They will conclude, I believe, that we owe each other far more than we generally recognize. The General, *en fin de compte*, was not far wrong.

Notes

1   BBC broadcast following the Mers-el-Kébir attack, in Crémieux-Brilhac, Jean-Louis, *La France libre: de l'appel du 18 juin à la Libération* (Paris: Gallimard, 1996), p. 65.

2   Comment during television discussion 'Face à la crise', broadcast on several channels, 5 February 2009 (my translation).

3   Bernard Jenkin, M.P. quoted in *The Guardian* (2 November 2010). Admittedly, most political comment was more favourable.

4   French scholars of course were among the pioneers of such studies, perhaps most famously in Pierre Nora, ed. *Les Lieux de mémoire* (3 vols, Paris: Gallimard, 1984–1992).

5   *Libération*, 5 April 2004.

6   On 'declinism' in both countries, see Frank, Robert, *La hantise du déclin: Le rang de la France en Europe, 1920–1960: Finances, défense et identité nationale* (Paris: Belin, 1994); Tomlinson, Jim, *The Politics of Decline: Understanding Post-war Britain* (Harlow: Longman, 2000).

7   For a thorough comparison, see Waldman, Abby Lisa, 'The role of government in the presentation of national history in England and France, c. 1980–2007' (Cambridge PhD, 2011).

8   Britain and Vichy France, however, had undeclared armed clashes. For details, see Smith, Colin, *England's Last War against France: Fighting Vichy, 1940–1942* (London: Phoenix, 2009). America, of course, is the only major Western State France has never fought against (though it came close in the 1860s), and Britain not since the War of 1812.

9   An attempt to discuss these general themes is Tombs, Robert and Isabelle, *That Sweet Enemy: The French and the British from the Sun King to the Present* (London: Heinemann, 2006); *La France et le Royaume-Uni: Des ennemis intimes* (Paris: Armand Colin, 2012).

10 Bourne, Kenneth, *Palmerston, The Early Years 1784–1841* (London: Allen Lane, 1982), p. 613.

11 See Darriulat, Philippe, *Les Patriotes: la gauche républicaine et la nation, 1830–1870* (Paris: Le Seuil, 2001).

12 Tombs, Robert 'Lesser breeds without the law: the British establishment and the Dreyfus affair, 1894–1899,' *Historical Journal* 41 (1998) 495–510.

13 Steiner, Zara S., *Britain and the Origins of the First World War* (London: Macmillan, 1977), p 23.

14 Brown, Judith M. and Louis, W.R., *Oxford History of the British Empire*, vol. 4, *The Twentieth Century* (Oxford University Press, 1999), p. 50.

15 Walsh, Sebastian, 'Britain, Morocco and the development of the Anglo-French entente' (Cambridge PhD, 2011).

16 Ferguson, Niall, *The Pity of War* (London: Penguin, 1998), p. 295.

17 General Gamelin, quoted in Bloch, Marc, *Strange Defeat* (London: Oxford University Press,1949), p. 74n.

18 Letter of 6 February 1940, quoted in Rocolle, Pierre, *La guerre de 1940* (2 vols, Paris: Armand Colin, 1990), vol. 1, pp. 282–3.

19 11 June 1940, quoted in Charles de Gaulle, *Mémoires de guerre* (3 vols, Paris: Plon, 1954), vol.1, *L'Appel*, p. 70 (my translation).

20 For example, Bond, Brian, *The Unquiet Western Front: Britain's Role in Literature and History* (Cambridge University Press, 2002); Todman, Dan, *The Great War: Myth and Memory* (London: Hambledon Continuum, 2005).

21 Quoted in Alan Sharp and Keith Jeffery, '"Après la guerre finit, Soldat anglais parti …": Anglo-French relations, 1918–25', in Erik Goldstein and B.J.C. McKercher (eds), *Power and Stability: British Foreign Policy, 1865–1965* (London: Frank Cass, 2003), 119–38, at p. 120.

22 Lentin, Anthony, *Lloyd George and the Lost Peace: From Versailles to Hitler* (Basingstoke: Palgrave, 2001), p. 81.

23 Adamthwaite, Anthony, *Grandeur & Misery: France's Bid for Power in Europe 1914–1940* (London: Arnold, 1995), p. 203.

24 Bell, P.M.H., *A Certain Eventuality: Britain and the Fall of France* (Farnborough: Saxon House, 1974).

25 Conversation with American ambassador, quoted in Jackson, Julian, *The Fall of France: The Nazi Invasion of 1940* (Oxford: Oxford University Press, 2003), p. 70.

26 Quoted in Gates, Eleanor M., *End of the Affair: The Collapse of the Anglo-French Alliance, 1939–40* (London: Allen & Unwin, 1981), p. 61.

27 Dalton, Hugh, *The Second World War Diary of Hugh Dalton, 1940–45*, ed. Ben Pimlott (London: Jonathan Cape, 1986), p. 48.

28 See, for example, Edgerton, David, *Britain's War Machine: Weapons, Resources and Experts in the Second World War* (London: Penguin, 2012); Peden, G.C., *Arms, Economics and British Strategy: From Dreadnoughts to Hydrogen Bombs* (Cambridge University Press, 2007).

29   The title of Marc Bloch's famous and influential analytical essay, *L'Étrange défaite*, written in 1940.

30   Jersak, Tobias, 'Blitzkrieg revisited: A new look at Nazi war and extermination planning,' *Historical Journal*, 43 (June 2000), 565–82; May, Ernest R., *Strange Victory: Hitler's Conquest of France* (London: I.B. Tauris, 2000); Tooze, Adam, *The Wages of Destruction: The Making and Breaking of the Nazi Economy* (London: Allen Lane, 2006).

31   Quoted in Lukacs, John, *The Last European War: September 1939–December 1941* (London: Routledge, 1977), p. 407.

32   Frank, *La hantise du déclin*, pp. 260–1.

33   See Cornick, Martyn, 'Fighting myth with reality: the fall of France, Anglophobia and the BBC', in Valerie Holman and Debra Kelly, eds, *France at War in the Twentieth Century: Propaganda, Myth and Metaphor* (Oxford: Berghahn, 2000); and Stenton, Michael, *Radio London and resistance in occupied Europe: British political warfare 1939–1943* (Oxford University Press, 2000).

34   Crémieux-Brilhac, *La France libre*, p. 161.

35   Foot, M.R.D., *SOE in France* (London: HMSO, 1966). There were sensitivities in Britain too: see Murphy, Christopher J., 'The Origins of *SOE in France*', *The Historical Journal*, 46, 4 (2003), 935–52.

36   Speech at the Hôtel de Ville, 25 August 1944 (my translation).

37   For details, see Waldman, 'The role of government in the presentation of national history', passim.

38   Conference held in Cambridge, September 2011. Its full discussions can be found at http://sms.cam.ac.uk/collection/1183660.

PART ONE
The First World War

Introduction

Gary Sheffield

Building and maintaining a coalition, and fighting a coalition war, is difficult, complex and demanding. This reality is the context in which the three chapters under discussion need to be set. The problems highlighted by John Keiger, William Philpott and Elizabeth Greenhalgh were not unique to France and Britain in the era of First World War. Similar if not identical challenges can be found in the histories of many other coalitions. The same themes emerge time after time. Coalitions are often marriages of convenience, marked by acute suspicion of partners. The Second World War relationship between Britain and the Free French stands out as an example of a particularly awkward alliance, and the relationship between the Britain and Prussians during the 1815 Waterloo campaign demonstrates that such situations were not a purely twentieth-century phenomenon. Some coalitions are only held together by shared hostility to a third party, and collapse when the enemy is defeated. The sheer speed with which what Churchill termed the 'Grand Alliance' of the UK, USA and USSR against Nazi Germany broke into the two hostile camps of the Cold War is an extreme example, but there are plenty of others, including the disintegration of the anti-German coalition at the end of the Great War.

As Paul Kennedy has observed, coalitions are not friendships. They are business arrangements in which the interests of individual states often come into conflict. Likewise national interests and the interests of the wider coalition are sometimes incompatible. Such problems can only be overcome by negotiation and compromise, hammered out at endless meetings. It is not surprising that the papers of senior figures within a coalition are full of the details of such assemblies.[1] Fighting in coalition is rarely, if ever, a smooth process. We know a very great deal about the Anglo-American coalition of 1941–45. It has had its wirings laid bare, and historians have pitilessly exposed the tensions and disputes between the partners. Reading some of the work on this coalition, it sometimes takes an effort to remember that it was highly successful in delivering victory. Much the same could be said about the Franco-British coalition of 1914–18.

John Keiger reminds us that Britain and France formally became allies only in September 1914, when the war had already been going on for a month. That it took so long to formalize the alliance, after French and British troops actually began to fight along each other against a common enemy, is symbolically appropriate, given the complicated Anglo-French relationship from the *Entente Cordiale* of 1904 onwards. This is sometimes erroneously referred to as 'an alliance', but it fell well short of that. Keiger describes this relationship as 'a dialogue of the deaf', characterized by 'misunderstanding of each other's policies, strategies and perceptions'. The essential mistake was the French belief that the loose agreement of 1904 could be converted into a fully fledged alliance with the British. Underpinning this belief was the assumption that Britain equally shared France's fear of Germany and would therefore be amenable to 'an insurance policy'.

This mutual incomprehension led to the situation on 2 August 1914, which would have been ludicrous had it not been so serious: Paul Cambon (the French ambassador in London) was outraged by his belated realization that the Asquith government did not regard Britain as having an obligation to support France, while the British cabinet, despite the existence of military agreements of which many of its members had until recently been unaware, continued to maintain that it had a free hand in foreign policy. The impasse was, fortunately for the two countries' relationship, broken by the Germans, whose invasion of neutral Belgium gave the British a cause to rally behind, and no less importantly posed a significant threat to British maritime security.

There is little doubt that John Keiger's analysis is correct, and further that what he calls 'cultural crossed wires' were at the root of these misunderstandings of what the Entente was actually *for*. So, in some cases, were personalities. Of the critical figures in the British decision-making elite, neither Sir Edward Grey nor H.H. Asquith ever fully appreciated what their French counterparts wanted out of the agreement, or, more importantly, what they believed the British were committed to. On the French side, Paul Cambon, a key figure in the creation of the *Entente Cordiale,* never quite understood the country to which he was ambassador from 1898 to 1920, or the people with whom he dealt. Cambon believed that London, like Paris, was motivated by the search for security against German aggression. In his case, a little knowledge was a dangerous thing. He appreciated that Britain had, historically, sought to oppose powers that sought hegemony in Europe by participating in a coalition to restore the balance of power. Since 1688, successive French regimes – especially that of Louis XIV, the Revolutionaries of the 1790s and Napoleon – had been the object of British suspicions. Indeed, during the period 1793–1815 Britain had been Revolutionary and Napoleonic France's most constant foe. Cambon assumed that the emerging threat of Germany in the first decade of the twentieth century fitted neatly into this pattern, and he was right – in theory.

Keiger, however, points to Britain's nuanced view of the advantages of an agreement with France, not least that it might lead to an agreement with France's ally Russia, which would be advantageous in Imperial terms; that for many in the post-1906 Liberal governments, domestic concerns had priority over the international scene; and Cambon failed to understand the nature of British cabinet government, which meant that the pro-neutrality views of key ministers in the Liberal administration carried real weight. Cambon and other French leaders read far too much significance into the military and naval negotiations between the two states, although one can hardly blame them for doing so.

One might broaden Keiger's critique. France, not Germany, was regarded by many as Britain's natural enemy at the beginning of the twentieth century. The memory of a state of almost constant war between 1688 and 1815 could not be effaced overnight, and if the Crimean War of 1853–56 was an example of a military alliance between Britain and France, that had rapidly been succeeded by the 'panic' of 1859 in which fear of invasion by Napoleon III had prompted the formation of the Rifle Volunteer movement. If Franco-British rivalry in Europe, and naval rivalry, had gradually declined, it intensified elsewhere: Fashoda had occurred only 6 years before the signing of the *Entente Cordiale*.

Religion was also perhaps a factor in the idea of France as Britain's natural enemy. Linda Colley's work on the creation of a British identity, which convincingly argued that war against Catholic France was a factor in bringing together Protestant England and Scotland, is of relevance here.[2] By contrast, Germany (or at least Prussia) was regarded as Protestant. Moreover there were intimate family ties between the Royal families of Britain and Germany, while republican France had an alien political system (and a recent history of political instability). In contrast to long-standing British suspicions of France, Germany had been regarded as a friendly state until very recently. Arguably, although the undoubted growth of antagonism with Germany was serious, it had failed to displace France completely from its privileged, if unwanted, position of Britain's hereditary enemy.

From many perspectives the pre-1914 Franco-British entente was unsatisfactory. It has even been suggested that it contributed to the outbreak of war by failing to send a strong, deterring signal to Germany that Britain would stand by France in the event of a general war. In truth, the entente was about as much as the British market would bear. Senior French figures, especially Cambon, must take a share of the blame for failing to understand this, and for only hearing what they wanted to hear. Senior British figures, especially Grey, must also take a share of the blame for failing to understand French beliefs and desires concerning their relationship with London. It would not have taken much for the Franco-British agreement to have collapsed in August 1914, and if that had occurred, the consequences would have been of the utmost gravity.

If anything, once France and Britain began actively to cooperate in alliance, the challenges increased, and the two stimulating papers by Elizabeth Greenhalgh and William Philpott bring some clarity to the debate. Over the last few years, these two historians have made major contributions to our understanding of the Anglo-French military relationship, and the role of the French army more generally, in First World War. Their exchanges in the pages of *War in History* helped to ignite a previously largely dormant debate. Dr Greenhalgh's books on coalition warfare, and Foch, and Prof Philpott's books on the Franco-British relationship and the Somme have done much to correct the Anglocentricism that undoubtedly existed in the literature. Other scholars of the Western Front who do not work on the French dimension, including this author, have benefitted greatly from their analysis and archival work. Indeed, along with American scholars Robert Doughty and Michael Neiberg,[3] Greenhalgh and Philpott can justly claim credit for a quiet revolution in the Anglophone historiography of First World War. It is indeed interesting, as Philpott comments, that it is Anglophone rather than French historians that have been putting in the spadework on the French army.

In some ways, what they have done is remind us of what the British chose not to remember. As Philpott reminds us, the reality was that in 1914–15, when Britain was raising and training a mass army and, in his dry phrase, 'adventuring against Turkey',[4] French soldiers were fighting and dying in very large numbers on the Western Front. Verdun is probably the only 'French' battle to have any resonance among lay people in Britain.[5] The popular success of Alistair Horne's *The Price of Glory*, published in 1964 during a boom in popular writing on First World War, possibly has something to do with that. British efforts in 1915 were small scale, but it is Loos, and not any of the major French offensives, that survives in the British popular memory. Such national chauvinism is not unique to First World War. For all the efforts of both scholarly and popular authors in recent years, the importance of the Soviet Union and the Red Army in determining the outcome of Second World War is consistently underplayed in Britain and the United States.

The presence of Marshal Foch's statue outside Victoria Station in London, unveiled in 1930, is testimony to one-time popularity in the United Kingdom of the generalissimo of 1918. So is the fact that when in the 1920s the popular novelist P.G. Wodehouse chose to put into Bertie Wooster's mouth words of praise about a plan, he said that 'Foch might have been proud of [it]'. Foch, note, not Haig; and this was at a time when the British Field Marshal's reputation was riding high.[6] While in the years after his death in 1928 Haig's standing collapsed to such an extent that it is comparable to the fate suffered by Neville Chamberlain's reputation in 1940, Foch was simply forgotten.

Two reasons (at least) suggest themselves as explanations for this British historical amnesia, and the reshaping of memories. The first is an understandable, if regrettable, tendency to concentrate on 'our boys'. The fate of the British soldier in the Great War has been a national fixation, certainly since the 1960s, and it has been the role of both allies and enemies to be reduced to supporting actors in this drama of a supposedly futile war. Second, the French nation and army of 1914–18 are condemned to live in the shadow cast backwards from 1940. Philpott refers to a British 'image of France as a womanly nation, weak, decadent, in decline and a drain on, not a support to, its British ally' (p. 8). This transformed over the years into an Anglo-American image of 'cheese-eating surrender monkeys' and imputations of cowardice when France refused to participate in the 2003 Iraq War. This is in sharp contrast to the image of France before 1870. Under Napoleon, France was, as the leading military power in Europe, a national embodiment of aggressive militarism; and as suggested above, even under the less impressive leadership of his nephew, Napoleon III, France was regarded as a threat to Britain. Perhaps the defeats in the Franco-Prussian War of 1870–71 began the process of change in attitudes, but British fears of French power into the late nineteenth century suggest that we should not push that argument too far.

The suddenness of the French defeat in May–June 1940, combined with the supposedly 'miraculous' escape of the British Expeditionary Force (BEF) from Dunkirk and Britain's 'Finest Hour' which began immediately afterwards, powerfully reinforced a sense of French decadence. Traditional anti-French feeling, never very far below the surface, reappeared in a different guise. Neither the effectiveness of Juin's French Corps in Italy nor the considerable French army that took the field from late 1944 onwards was able to efface this 'womanly' image. In the 1950s and early 1960s, Dien Bien Phu and later the loss of Algeria reinforced Anglo-American prejudices. While interwar Anglophone historiography began marginalizing the French effort in the Great War, 1940 and what followed powerfully reinforced it.

Given the important work by Anglophone historians in recent years, there is no longer any excuse for dismissing or ignoring the military effectiveness of the French army in the latter part of the war. Philpott's work has been particularly effective in presenting an apparently familiar topic, the Battle of the Somme, in a new light by emphasizing that this battle was very much an allied effort. It is fair to say that while his views on the respective competence of the French and British armies have raised some eyebrows, it has also initiated a very healthy and productive debate. In his chapter, Philpott argues that 'a lack of inquisitiveness on the part of British scholars' has led to the persistence of inaccurate views of the French army in the Great War. There is certainly some substance to this, but other factors also need to be taken into account.

In an ideal world, transnational, comparative history would be the norm, but in the real one, the British army of 1914–18 is a big enough topic easily to absorb a scholar's efforts. After all, there were and are numerous misconceptions about the British experience that need correcting, and this has understandably been the focus of British and Dominion historians. There are obvious problems of language, but given that most historians have at least a smattering of schoolboy/girl reading French (and of course, access to the internet), being linguistically challenged is probably less important than the difficulties of getting physical access to French archives, or even being able to find a copy of the French official history. My experience is that far from being uninterested in the French army, many Anglophone scholars of the British army, without the time or possibly language skills to do archival work in France, were frustrated by how little published material there was on the French army, let alone material that was translated into English. That is why the works of Philpott, Greenhalgh *et al* have been so welcome and influential: at last, scholars are producing the sort of work on the French army that have been appearing on the British and Dominion forces for many years.

Similar comments could be made about the historiography of the German army. So far, however, the French army of 1914–18 lacks an equivalent of Jack Sheldon, a retired British army officer who has produced a valuable series of books that contain German primary sources for the various battles (personal accounts, sections from regimental histories and the like).[7] If someone were to 'do a Sheldon' for the French army, it would be a small but significant step towards the integration of the French experience into the mainstream of Anglophone understanding of the Great War. Perhaps the centenary of the outbreak of the war in 2014 be a good time to start?

Elizabeth Greenhalgh's chapter is a typically stimulating piece, and her points about the tensions within the coalition are well made. As noted above, the problems she highlights were not unique to the British and the French in First World War; and similar challenges can be found in the history of many other coalitions. Although she does not say so explicitly, in First World War the problems between the senior partner, the French and their British ally were exacerbated by the fact that by the end of the war, Britain and France were roughly equal in power. In 1914, the respective size of the armies on the Western Front was such that the imbalance of power in the relationship was starkly evident, even if the likes of Sir John French resented it. The recruitment and subsequent deployment of the British mass citizen army (Kitchener's Army and the Territorials, later topped up by conscripts) did not alter the fact that France remained the senior partner. But by 1916 and certainly by 1918, the French were no longer, as it were, as senior as before. One of the roots of Douglas Haig's uneasy relationship with successive French commanders was the belief that not enough respect was being paid to him as commander in chief of a large and independent army, the military expression of a proud and powerful empire, and that the French did not give the BEF sufficient credit for its achievements.[8] William Philpott's apposite comments about the mutual incomprehension of the French and British about each other's military efforts, sacrifices and achievements are of relevance here.

All this suggests that it is in many ways easier if there is a dominant 'framework nation' that provides undisputed (if resented) leadership of a coalition. During the Cold War in Europe, this role in Nato was carried out by the United States, which provided the Supreme Allied Commander Europe (SACEUR); the British who recognized the facts of life about the relative power within the alliance, settled for the position of Deputy SACEUR. Disputes and rivalries were not eliminated, but they were conducted within a clearly recognized hierarchy that reflected national power. A similar arrangement was never on the cards during First World War.

Field Marshal Sir Douglas Haig features prominently in both Elizabeth Greenhalgh's and William Philpott's chapters. Both authors' comments about the extent to which Haig's diaries have shaped the perceptions of Anglophone historians regarding the French army are well made. After the war Haig's gripes were exacerbated by his belief that it was the British, and not the French, who inflicted the decisive blows on the German army in 1918. Whether or not this was true or fair is another matter – but this is a case where perception jostles with reality for importance. It is not surprising that the British official history should follow Haig's version of the events of March 1918, given Sir James Edmonds' view of his role as official historian, his relationship with Haig and the very nature of 'official history'.

As Elizabeth Greenhalgh ably demonstrates, national perceptions colour views of the same event. Take for instance her reference to the fact that the Third Battle of Ypres ('Passchendaele') in 1917 was regarded by the French as a 'duck's march'. From another perspective it can be seen, at least in part, as an attempt to achieve a fundamental British war aim, the clearance of the Channel coast; moreover, it was a campaign that, arguably, came closer to success than is often realized, although that is a controversial view among historians.

In Haig's case the cliché 'familiarity breeds contempt' is all too accurate. His views on the French generals were influenced by differences in class and culture and perhaps religious prejudice. I would, however, stress that Haig was well aware of the importance of his role, as C-in-C of the BEF, in maintaining the alliance. Thus while Greenhalgh's comments on Haig's dismissive attitudes to the French at Mont Kemmel and downplaying of Foch's counterstroke at Second Marne are pertinent, we should draw a distinction between what Haig said and wrote (letting off steam in his diary)[9] and what he actually did. He could certainly be an awkward and prickly coalition partner (as could French, Pétain, Joffre, Nivelle, Pershing and Foch); and the scarring experience of the Nivelle affair should not be underestimated. But on the whole his performance as a coalition commander was creditable. It was no easy thing to juggle national interests with the wider interests of the coalition.

That Haig was ungrateful for French assistance and reluctant to acknowledge French successes is regrettable, and of course Haig felt that the French had behaved towards him in a similar way. But all this was really of little consequence. It is the very stuff of coalition warfare. If, however, he had behaved in such a way as to undermine the effectiveness of the coalition, or even if he had behaved in a similarly tactless and cavalier fashion towards his allies as Bernard Montgomery was to do a generation later – that would have been a serious, and potentially disastrous, matter. One is tempted to say that Haig's moans against his French allies and their complaints against him cancel each other out.

Some specific points in Elizabeth Greenhalgh's chapter are worthy of comment. My reading of the evidence is not that in March 1918 General Headquarters (GHQ) intended to abandon the extreme south of the British line – it was hoped that with French aid it would not come to that – but it is certainly true that there was a clear recognition that if ground had to be given up, that was the place to do it, rather than further north, where the Channel ports might be threatened. I also think that words such as 'collapse' are misleading as applied to the BEF in the 1918 German spring offensive. As the losses of prisoners and guns indicate, Gough's Fifth Army in particular endured a torrid time, but the setback was local and tactical rather than operational or strategic; Gough's left did quite well on 21 March, but Butler's III Corps, holding the weakest position with insufficient numbers of troops, suffered badly. But had the Fifth Army truly collapsed, the Germans might well have won a decisive victory.

The term 'Hundred Days' came in for some criticism. It is of course correct that there has been a dearth of modern scholarly books in English on the Second Battle of the Marne, but that is generally true of all battles of the Hundred Days, (as I will continue to call it) including Amiens (ditto). While it does imply an Anglocentric perspective, the 'Hundred Days' remains a useful term. Its use does not (in least in my case) imply an acceptance of the view that 'the French army was too exhausted to do any real fighting in the last offensives'. In fact, there is no reason why this evocative definition should not be extended to encompass Second Marne.

There are many reasons why the British should have seen Amiens rather than Second Marne as the crucial battle, some being better than others. They include the parochial rationale that it was the first battle in the changed strategic situation in which the BEF played a major role; that it was the first major Allied offensive (as opposed to counter-offensive); and (arguably) that while Second Marne repelled the German offensive and seized the initiative, at Amiens, the Allies were able to exercise the initiative to much greater effect.

Elizabeth Greenhalgh's section on logistics and the maritime dimension is particularly interesting on the invisibility of the war at sea to the French. As she argues, geography was indeed important. It shaped the strategic culture and much else of a maritime island with the world's greatest fleet that protected it from invasion. It similarly shaped the culture of a land power with vulnerable frontiers that had suffered invasion, defeat and occupation within living memory. As with geography, so with history. We have seen that the Entente Cordiale was a marriage of convenience, not love. The (possibly apocryphal) stories of British soldiers in August 1914, who believed that they were off to fight the French, not the Germans, illustrate that French and British did not view each other as natural allies. More importantly, the formative years of senior commanders in both armies had been spent by regarding the other as a potential enemy rather than as an ally. This lethal combination of geography and history gave the Anglo-French coalition a peculiarly difficult character and made a post-war divorce, to continue Greenhalgh's analogy of marriage, all the more likely. As I argued above, coalitions tend by their very nature to be formed to cope with a specific threat and break up when the threat has vanished. This one was no different.

For all that, we should not lose sight of the fact that the coalition was successful – unlike its successor in 1940. The relationship between Foch as Generalissimo and Haig as C-in-C BEF had its rocky moments (a saying at GHQ was that Haig had to fight three foes – 'Boche, Foch and Loygeorges')[10] but must ultimately be judged a success. Coalition warfare is an immensely difficult business, and between 1914 and 1918, the French and the British conducted it well enough to help bring about victory.

Notes

1 Gary Sheffield, 'Not the Same as Friendship: The British Empire and Coalition Warfare in the Era of the First World War', in Peter Dennis and Jeffrey Grey (eds), *Entangling Alliances: Coalition Warfare in the Twentieth Century* (Canberra: Australian Military History Publications, 2005), pp. 38–9.

2 Linda Colley, *Britons: Forging the Nation 1707–1837* (London: Yale University Press, 1992).

3 Robert A. Doughty, *Pyrrhic Victory: French Strategy and Operations in the Great War* (Cambridge, MA: Harvard University Press, 2005); Michael S. Neiberg, *The Second Battle of the Marne* (Bloomington, IN: Indiana University Press, 2008).

4 'The Gallipoli campaign does not figure prominently in French perceptions of or historical studies about the First World War', David Dutton, 'Docile Supernumerary: A French Perspective on Gallipoli', in Jenny Macleod (ed.), *Gallipoli: Making History* (London: Frank Cass, 2004), p. 86. The contrast with the centrality of Gallipoli to the British memory of the war, let alone the Australian and New Zealand versions, is stark.

5 For instance, *Western Front*, a 1999 television series written and presented by Prof Richard Holmes (whose doctoral thesis was on the French army of the Second Empire) devoted one out of six episodes to Verdun; the others dealt mainly with British themes.

6 Quoted in Gary Sheffield, 'Finest Hour? British Forces on the Western Front in 1918: An Overview', in Ashley Ekins (ed.), *1918, Year of Victory: The End of the Great War and the Shaping of History* (Wollombi, NSW: Exisle, 2010), p. 43.

7 For example, Jack Sheldon, *The German Army at Cambrai* (Barnsley: Pen & Sword, 2009).

8 See, for example, Gary Sheffield, *The Somme* (London: Cassell, 2003), pp. 141–2; *idem, The Chief: Douglas Haig and the British Army* (London: Aurum, 2011), pp. 289–90.

9 For a Second World War example of a British general much involved in running a coalition using his diary for a similar purpose, see Alex Danchev and Dan Todman (eds), *War Diaries 1939–45: Field Marshal Lord Alanbrooke* (London: Weidenfeld & Nicolson, 2001).

10 Headlam diary, 22 February 1923, in Jim Beach (ed.), *The Military Papers of Lieutenant-Colonel Sir Cuthbert Headlam 1919–1942* (Stroud: History Press, 2010), p. 147.

CHAPTER ONE

Crossed Wires, 1904–14

John Keiger

On 3 August 1914 Germany declared war on France; the following day, Britain declared war on Germany. But it was only on the following 5 September that, by the Treaty of London, France and the British Empire formally became allies, along with the Russian Empire. The political and military alliance that France had sought, arguably since the signing of the Entente Cordiale in 1904, became a reality. But why did Britain become France's ally effectively on 4 August 1914 and why had France sought a British alliance? How have the French and British remembered this 10-year process and what have they forgotten about it?[1] This chapter will describe what France and Britain each desired from the Entente, the impact of cultural and personal misunderstandings, the progressive militarization of the Entente and finally how the Entente has been remembered.

To a large extent the French have remembered their 1914–18 alliance with Britain as the natural outcome, or even extension, of the 1904 Entente Cordiale, even though that agreement was not an alliance, nor even a treaty and it contained no political or military commitment in the event of war, nor even a statement of general policy on friendlier relations. Instead, the Entente Cordiale was a hotchpotch of documents whereby Paris and London settled numerous outstanding colonial differences across the globe. And yet the French have remembered the period from 1904 to 1914, exceptions notwithstanding, through rose-tinted spectacles as a natural progression from engagement to marriage. In so doing they have erased or at least underplayed the anguished position of the British government in agreeing to discuss the possibility of joint military and naval deployments with France from 1906 in the event of war with Germany, and have overlooked the frequent French disappointment with Britain that verged on a total break in 1914. In truth, the 10-year genesis of the eventual British commitment to France was marked by controversy, prejudice and cross-cultural misunderstandings on both sides of the Channel. The low point came on 2 August 1914 when the French Ambassador in London, Paul Cambon – unable to secure the commitment from the Liberal Foreign Secretary Sir Edward Grey that Britain would come to France's aid if attacked by Germany, which he believed existed and which Grey was adamant did not – asked 'whether the word "honour" should not be struck out of the English vocabulary'.

Both states at the time had different interpretations of the same narrative. How did this misunderstanding of each other's policies, strategies and perceptions come about? Why had Britain and France been engaged in a dialogue of the deaf during the previous decade? Historians still argue about the nature and extent of the British commitment to France prior to 1914. But in the end, the differing perceptions of that commitment in London and Paris lay with cultural crossed wires rather than with actual degrees of commitment.

British reluctance to be tied to France in the event of war was almost as old as the Entente itself. As Grey wrote in a private letter to the Prime Minister, Herbert Asquith, on 16 April 1911:

> Early in 1906 the French said to us 'will you help us if there is a war with Germany?' We said 'we can't promise [,] our hands must be free.' The French then urged that the Mil[itar]y Authorities should be allowed to exchange views – ours to say what they could do – the French to say how they would like it done, if we did side with France – Otherwise, as the French urged, even if we decided to support France, on the outbreak of war we shouldn't be able to do it effectively. We agreed to this.[2]

As late as 2 August 1914, Asquith was convinced that Britain still had no commitment to France. He recorded in his diary that 'We have no obligation of any kind either to France or Russia to give them military or naval help'.[3] This was not the French Ambassador's view.

Britain may have wished to 'have its cake and eat it' by drawing the benefits from the Entente without accepting the subsequent responsibilities it implied, but the French too wanted *le beurre et l'argent du beurre* in sealing the Entente Cordiale and then seeking to inveigle Britain into a commitment that she was not ready to give. Britain saw the Entente as largely backward-looking: a settlement of past imperial disputes; France saw the Entente as a forward-looking process towards alliance. The motivation for France's policy was simple: an almost 40-year fear of Germany. That of Britain was more complex, varying according to different factions in government, party, parliament, ministry and public. There was the historical instinct of not wishing any one state – by this time, Germany – to dominate the continent of Europe, and also the need to placate Russia and France for imperial reasons. France's fear of Germany led her, or her Ambassador in London, to push relentlessly for an alliance; Britain's balancing of complex motives made her reluctant, evasive and even duplicitous. In many ways it was an inconvenient engagement, an 'Uneasy Entente'[4] and thus likely to give rise to misunderstandings.

It is unclear whether Paris or London looked at the historical precedents to Franco-British military cooperation prior to 1905, but it is unlikely. Yet had either side dusted off the files, they would have discovered previous episodes of joint Franco-British military expeditions, such as 1860 in China or the Middle East, and the practical consequences of differing national interests and the lessons to be learnt.[5] It is helpful to look at what either side hoped to obtain from these Entente arrangements. What were their ideal objectives? This leads to the question of why they eventually did become allies – out of necessity or folly? We now know with hindsight that the Franco-British Entente did become an alliance for the course of the war and that its contribution was indispensible to the Allies winning the war. The public on both sides of the Channel were either never aware of, or have forgotten, the difficulties that beset the arrangement and the extent to which in August 1914, the Entente came close to collapse.

National requirements from Franco-British collaboration, 1905–14

Though sharing similar commitments to democracy and the rule of law, Britain and France did not share many vital strategic interests. But they were willing to put their differences to one side in the interests of their own idea of what the Entente represented to them. That they did not take sufficient cognizance of what the other party desired was clear at the time and even more so with hindsight. So what did each hope to achieve from the Franco-British agreement?

What the French sought from the outset of the signing of the Entente Cordiale was for it to become an alliance. As the French Foreign Minister of the time Théophile Delcassé wrote to a senior French Foreign Ministry official about the Entente settlement: 'This liquidation should lead us, and I desire that it shall lead us, to a political alliance with England'. The second reason flowed from the first: 'If we could lean both on Russia and on England, how strong we should be in relation to Germany'.[6] What France craved was protection and security from an increasingly powerful Germany whose Bismarckian policy had ensured that France remained isolated and vulnerable for 20 years until the Franco-Russian alliance of 1892–94. Third, in the light of her security reliance on Russia, France was relieved to have the support of another great power, politically more acceptable to the

French public, and one likely to limit her uneasy dependence on Russia. An added advantage was that the French, like the British, benefited from the reduction in imperial tensions which had been a heavy drain on national resources.

Paul Cambon's wishful thinking led him to believe that Britain sought the same thing from the arrangement as France did, namely, an insurance policy against a too powerful Germany. Writing to his brother in 1910 about the British he affirmed: 'Hostility to Germany is implacable because it is born of fear'.[7] He saw Britain's strategy as the traditional one of the balance of power whereby London was willing to side with any power likely to counterbalance a dominant one on the continent of Europe. But the diagnosis was too reductionist. For sure, this worry did motivate British politicians during these years, but it did not do so for all of them all of the time. In truth most members of the Liberal government from 1906 to 1914 were more interested in domestic reform than in international affairs, and reform required finance, which for many equated to saving on military expenditure. For this reason many in the Cabinet, notably the radicals, preferred an arrangement with Germany, as the Haldane Mission of 1912 demonstrated.[8] Furthermore, Cambon did not appear to understand that even if for some in London the logic of countering German power on the continent by an arrangement with France was compelling, it was also a tenet of British policy, defined by Palmerston, Gladstone and others, that Britain should not contract herself to other powers for some future hypothetical scenario.

Thus British objectives for the Entente were more complex than those perceived by Cambon. According to Keith Wilson, a powerful lobby in British governing and military circles, notably Grey, wanted the agreement to act as a stepping stone to the securing of an agreement with Russia on Asia that would maintain cordial relations with her and thereby ensure the security of India. According to Wilson, 'Because Russia was the ally of France, and because Great Britain needed to be on the best possible terms with Russia for her own selfish imperial reasons, the British took advantage of the French connection with Russia to establish a purely imperial one of their own'.[9]

The Entente was also the opportunity, according to Wilson, for Britain not to be isolated internationally from the two powers that could do her interests, above all those of the British Empire, much damage: Russia and France. When Asquith was told on 28 July 1914 by King George V that he had informed Prince Henry of Prussia that Britain would remain neutral in any conflict, he pointed out a danger: 'Russia says to us: "If you won't say you are ready to side with us now, your friendship is valueless, and we shall act on that assumption in the future"'. Shortly afterwards, Cambon warned in comparable terms: if those in France who counted on British assistance were let down 'those in favour of an alliance with Germany at the expense of Britain could feel justified' – France would look on at the ruin of the British

Empire 'without a movement of sympathy'.[10] At stake for Britain was the safety of the British Empire and more. As the pro-Russian Permanent Under-Secretary at the Foreign Office since 1910, Sir Arthur Nicolson, put it:

> It is difficult not to agree with M. Sazonov [the Russian Foreign Minister] that sooner or later England will be dragged into the war if it comes . . . Should that war come, and England stands aside, one of two things must happen:
>
> **a** Either Germany and Austria win, crush France and humiliate Russia. With the French fleet gone, Germany in occupation of the Channel, with the willing or unwilling cooperation of Holland and Belgium, what will be the position of a friendless England?
>
> **b** Or France and Russia win. What would then be their attitude towards England? What about India and the Mediterranean?[11]

Thus using the Entente to block Germany was not the sole preoccupation of the majority of the British establishment.

The French should have suspected that something was not right in the relationship from the way their views and those of the British were not aligned on the nature of the Entente. That astute observer of Franco-British relations and niece of Jules and Paul Cambon, Geneviève Tabouis, put her finger on the problem: 'From the very moment of signature, the Foreign Office sought to minimise the extent of the *Entente*, while the Quai d'Orsay took pains to make the very most of it'.[12] They also failed to detect anything untoward in the secretiveness with which the British surrounded the Franco-British military and naval talks, which were 'never known by more than four ministers at any one time before the autumn of 1911, and never espoused by more than five ministers (out of twenty) at any one time thereafter'.[13] Winston Churchill, First Lord of the Admiralty, may indeed have reminded Grey that Britain had all the duties of an alliance and none of the advantages, but Churchill's view was not accepted by key figures including Grey himself and Asquith. Critics have suggested that the absence of a formal alliance denied Britain the opportunity of restraining French decision makers while at the same time failing to deter Berlin.[14] Thus on both sides political and cultural misunderstandings confused positions: for Frenchmen such as Cambon, British support was to be expected, while the likes of Grey and Asquith resisted the idea that Britain was being progressively lured into a moral commitment to France.

Because the outcome of the Entente process was eventually a success, in that France and Britain did become allies for the war's duration and were victorious, there has been a tendency in France and Britain subsequently to overlook how the relationship could have gone startlingly wrong. Britain could have decided in the end to stay neutral, leaving France to confront

Germany with only Russia by her side. Historians such as Niall Fergusson, retrospectively taking the side of the Cabinet radicals opposed to Britain siding with France or going to war, have claimed that Britain would have been much better off remaining neutral.[15] But this is to ignore, as Sir Arthur Nicolson put it above, what the consequences of such a policy would have been for Britain in the aftermath of war whatever its outcome.

So how might the difficulties inherent in the Franco-British Entente up to 1914 be explained?

Cultural crossed wires

There were several levels of potential misunderstanding between Paris and London over the nature and purpose of the Entente. These ranged from different cultural approaches to more down-to-earth differences between personalities, and most notably the protagonists in the Entente drama, the British Foreign Secretary Sir Edward Grey and the French Ambassador in London, Paul Cambon.

Of peoples

'That the British are pragmatic, empirical, and practical, the French juridical, deductive, and systematic, that the British are what they like to call "outward-looking" where the French are "continental" . . . are platitudes that have all at one time or another helped to explain as well as to complicate the uneasy Franco-British relationship, so ill-named *Entente cordiale*. Yet when issues are actually in dispute, the importance of these and other recognized incompatibilities in the field of foreign policy is often underestimated, as is the importance of the cumulative effect of a long history of misunderstandings'.[16] So wrote that authority on France in the post-war years, Dorothy Pickles, outlining the differing intellectual and cultural approaches to foreign policy making. She went on to state that 'one of the most important factors in Franco-British misunderstanding is the British preference for cautious empiricism, and dislike of specific commitments in fields of general principle – above all of "fixed resolutions for eventual probabilities"'.[17]

The Prime Minister William Gladstone explained this trait of British diplomacy in a letter to Queen Victoria on 17 April 1869:

> England should keep entire in her own hands the means of estimating her own obligations upon the various states of facts as they arise; she should not foreclose and narrow her own liberty of choice by declarations made to other Powers, in their real or supposed interests, of which they would claim to be at least joint interpreters; it is dangerous for her to assume alone an advanced and therefore isolated position, in regard to European

controversies; come what may it is better for her to promise too little than too much; she should not encourage the weak by giving expectation of aid to resist the strong, but should rather seek to deter the strong by firm but moderate language from aggression of the weak.[18]

The differing cultural practices were further outlined by Pickles in noting that 'French Governments, with their Cartesian preferences for precision, and for progression from the general to the particular, have fought for precise statements of principle, and for commitments and guarantees, with a passion and a consistency comprehensible only in the context both of their political insecurity and of their juridical and systematic approach to international relations'.[19] Had British politicians and officials understood more clearly France's overwhelming need for an alliance with Britain, and France's juridical way of proceeding, Britain might not have been so naively seduced into a perceived moral commitment by July 1914. Similarly, for France a better understanding of Britain's position and ways of proceeding might have clarified their respective positions and reduced mutual confusion about the issue of commitment. As the diplomat son of Sir Arthur Nicolson, Harold Nicolson, noted on French diplomacy: 'The concentration, again, of the French mind upon a particular line of policy prevents them on occasions from observing events which lie outside their immediate and intense focus'. This is a reflection on Paul Cambon's weakness: consumed by an intense concentration on achieving an alliance, he often did not see the trees for the wood, such as strenuous opposition in cabinet to a formal alliance with France.

Of personalities

Other than the general national cultural framework seen to be governing approaches to foreign policy in the two states, there was also the difference in the intellectual framework of individuals involved in the policy-making process. Harold Nicolson described in particular the faults of British statesmen in the early part of the twentieth century: 'There is considerable ignorance, not so much of foreign conditions, as of foreign psychology; there is unbound optimism; there is a dislike of facing unpleasant possibilities in advance'.[20] The classic example of this was Sir Edward Grey. His direct experience of foreign countries was extremely limited. He had never set foot in France before April 1914 and spoke no foreign languages. In many ways he conformed to the German Chancellor Prince Bulow's impressions of the English politician recorded in his diary following a visit to Windsor:

> The English politicians do not know the Continent well. They do not know much more about conditions on the Continent than we know about conditions in Peru or Siam. Their general ideas, according to

our standard, are somewhat naïve. There is something naïve in their unconscious egotism, but they have also a certain credulity. They are not prone to suspect really evil intentions. They are very quiet, rather indolent and very optimistic.[21]

Grey was patient, wary, persistently evasive, but also naive in his dealings with the French Ambassador. He was willing to relate to Cambon's personal views about potential British support for France that he never shared with his Liberal Cabinet members,[22] and which Cambon perceived as commitment forgetting the importance of collective Cabinet decision making. Moreover, both men shared a particular practice that could not have aided the Entente in moments of difficulty: absenteeism from London often at moments of importance such as during the later stages of the July Crisis, with Grey fly-fishing or bird watching in remote parts and Paul Cambon habitually back in Paris.

Just as Grey might be characterized as the archetypal English politician, Paul Cambon had many of the traits of the archetypal Frenchman. He was convinced of the superiority of French culture and, despite being a diplomat, was more at home in Paris than abroad. Indeed, for all its longevity from 1898 to 1920, Paul Cambon did not enjoy his posting in London, although he drew considerable satisfaction from his achievements there. This in itself became part of the problem: thinking as he did of himself as the instigator and the guarantor of the Entente, he became complacent about its strengths and blinded to its weaknesses. He never came to terms with the climate, spoke insufficient English, socialized little and spent as much time as he could in Paris, as his own son Henri recorded: 'He returned to Paris very frequently, if not every week, at least once every fortnight'. His apartment in Paris became 'a sort of material and moral refuge away from the London fog and the melancholy he developed there'.[23] This may also explain why he came to rely too heavily on the views and opinions of the Permanent Under-Secretary of State at the Foreign Office, Sir Arthur Nicolson, with whom he had entertained good relations since their simultaneous posting to Constantinople. He wrongly supposed that Nicolson was the voice of Grey and the British government. But Nicolson was a persistent advocate of closer ties with France (and Russia) and certainly did not represent the increasingly powerful views of the more pro-German Foreign Office grouping around Sir William Tyrell, Grey's private secretary.[24] Consequently, Cambon did not have the full picture of interests competing for Grey's attention, not all of whom were so enthusiastic about close relations with France. Cambon's partial view derived from Nicolson, whose pro-French views were not shared by members of the Cabinet like Lord Loreburn (Lord Chancellor) or Lord Morley and by the radical wing of the government.[25] Nor was Franco-British mutual understanding fostered by the fact that, according to Paul Cambon's son, during their diplomatic meetings Grey spoke English and Cambon French, both paying attention to articulate clearly. If, as Henri

Cambon noted in respect of Grey, 'many nuances must have escaped him', then it would be fair to deduce that many must also have escaped Paul Cambon.[26]

For a diplomat, albeit not by training as he had come to the career via the French prefectoral corps rather than the Quai d'Orsay, Paul Cambon did appear to underestimate a key concept of British constitutional practice: the role of collective cabinet government in British policy and decision making. For that reason, as will be shown below, he underestimated the significance of cabinet opposition to war and the role of Parliament in the final decision in 1914. That acute observer of French and British diplomatic practices, Harold Nicolson, quoted in this respect what the Foreign Secretary Lord Palmerston once wrote to the British Ambassador in Russia:

> It is not usual for England to enter into engagements with reference to cases which have not actually arisen, or which are not immediately in prospect; and this for a plain reason. All formal engagements of the Crown, which involve the questions of peace and war, must be submitted to Parliament; and Parliament might probably not approve of an engagement which should bind England prospectively to take up arms in a contingency which could not as yet be foreseen.[27]

How then did the British and French experience and understanding of their Entente differ? How did cultural misunderstandings develop up to the July Crisis?

Militarization and more misunderstanding in the Entente

From the British perspective no better definition of the Entente could be given than that of the senior Foreign Office official, Eyre Crowe: 'The fundamental fact of course is that an Entente is not an alliance. For purposes of ultimate emergencies it may be found to have no substance at all. For an Entente is nothing more than a frame of mind, a view of general policy which is shared by the governments of the two countries, but which may be, or become, so vague as to lose all content'.[28] Crowe's statement of 2 February 1911 was a plea in favour of a more precise commitment to France by way of a defensive alliance, something that Grey was unwilling or unable to endorse.[29] But from the French perspective what gave the Entente alliance-like potential were the Franco-British secret military staff conversations that had begun in early 1905. The militarization of the Entente firmly embedded misunderstanding by confusing military and political commitment. Although not intended to bind the two governments, Paris saw in them firm and concerted British military support that in French eyes certainly appeared a step closer to an alliance. The conversations were intended to map out possible joint action should the two countries have to go to war side by side. Although initially conceived as only a temporary measure to provide for the contingency of conflict with Germany following the First Moroccan Crisis of 1905 and the subsequent 1906 Algeciras conference to settle international interests in Morocco, they became a key feature of Franco-British relations, allowing the Entente to be construed as a forward-moving process, as the French had always wanted. Although the military conversations diminished from 1906 to 1910 Cambon continued to believe in Britain's commitment to France. This was clear during the diplomatic tension created by the Franco-German Casablanca crisis in November 1908. Shortly afterwards the Military Correspondent of *The Times*, Lieutenant Colonel Charles à Court Repington, wrote to Lord Esher: 'You see Cambon has already given Clemenceau [the French prime minister] a formal assurance that he can count on us, and there is a risk that he may now go to Grey and ask for something more definite than Grey can possibly give'. Repington believed Cambon's diplomacy to be 'clumsy' and noted: 'I have a less exalted opinion of his diplomacy than before'.[30] To be fair to Cambon, although the British military attempted to disabuse the French of any commitment fearing that the staff negotiations might bind Britain more tightly than was in British interests, politicians such as Haldane, Asquith and Grey were, according to Esher's account, more supportive.[31]

Although on the back burner from 1906 to 1910 the Franco-British military conversations flourished when Brigadier-General Henry Wilson became Director of Military Operations in August 1910. Nevertheless, as late as August 1911, Wilson was obliged to admit to the Committee of Imperial Defence that he had no precise details of French war plans. Prompted by the 1911 Agadir Crisis, the new Chief of the French General Staff General Joffre gave a greater place to Britain's assistance than his predecessors did. However, when Joffre presented his new Plan XVII to the Defence Council in April 1913, he was far more realistic than Cambon in assuming that he could not count on British assistance, precisely because the British had not given any undertaking in writing or otherwise and that consequently relying on British land forces was imprudent.[32] Grey continued to repeat to Cambon that the secret talks – so secret that until 1912 most of the British Cabinet were unaware of their existence and would probably never have approved them – in no way bound either country to come to the other's assistance in the event of war. The British were saying one thing and apparently doing another. But Cambon did not appear to understand, or chose to ignore, the implications of such warnings and the constitutional and political rationale that lay behind them, and preferred instead to work by stealth for an alliance in all but name.

The consequence of seeing things as Cambon wished to see them would, in the longer term, be a major source of frustration, misunderstanding and disappointment for his masters in Paris. Blind faith in Britain's support as relayed by Cambon led to French incomprehension at Lord Haldane's 1912 mission to Germany to discuss an agreement to limit naval rivalry. Again Cambon did not appear to grasp the seriousness of a potential agreement that might have committed Britain to neutrality should Germany be at war with another power. In the end it was the British Ambassador in Paris, the Francophile Sir Francis Bertie, who brought to the attention of the French government a fuller understanding of the implications of the Haldane Mission, warning that Paul Cambon had not fully understood what was at stake. Even Sir Arthur Nicolson could not understand how Cambon could have been so unmoved by the Haldane talks.[33] Strong representations from the French, supported by Bertie, in the end contributed to Britain abandoning the Haldane initiative. Paul Cambon correctly, but naively, summed up his philosophy in dealing with Britain when he told the French Premier and Foreign Minister, Raymond Poincaré: 'her friendship is precious to us and whosoever requires that friendship must respect her confidence'.[34] Even when there was a possibility that the talks could be renewed with the appointment of a new German ambassador to London, Cambon brushed anxiety aside and professed 'an imperturbable confidence' in the Entente.[35]

Cambon pressed on with his single-minded quest to secure a greater British commitment. In the exchange of what became known as the Grey-Cambon letters of November 1912, Paris and London agreed that the French should concentrate their main naval forces in the Mediterranean, while Britain would transfer part of its Mediterranean fleet to the North Sea. Franco-British naval talks begun in early 1908 had lapsed and then been revived at the time of the Agadir Crisis in November 1911 for the disposition of the two countries' respective fleets. Now with Britain increasingly pressed financially and threatened strategically in the Mediterranean by the expansion of the Austro-Hungarian and Italian fleets and by the expansion of the German fleet, an opportunity arose for France to capitalize on Britain's vulnerability. As Samuel Williamson has pointed out, 'What Morocco had once been to the entente the Mediterranean now became'.[36]

Though the British continued to insist that such an arrangement in no way bound Britain to side with France in a conflict, agreeing only to consult in the event of a potential conflict, it certainly gave France a strong moral claim to British support should war break out as her Channel coasts now relied on the Royal Navy for protection. The Grey-Cambon letters were a further example of differing cultural approaches and attitudes that not for the last time would lead to misunderstandings between the two countries. In the negotiations which Paul Cambon opened in April 1912, Britain insisted throughout in pragmatic mode that such an arrangement on mutual fleet dispositions could be merely verbal, as it did not commit either side to assist the other in the event of a conflict. There were signs of the potential for misinterpretation as early as July when Grey told Cambon that a naval agreement would not prejudice the freedom of decision of either government to commit to assist the other in the event of war. Grey insisted: 'It was necessary to be clear about this'. He stressed that there was no formal Entente between France and Britain. But Cambon was quick to retort that there was a moral Entente 'which might however be transformed into a formal "Entente" if the two Governments desired, when an occasion arose'.[37] Cambon's dogged pursuit of a formal agreement met with Grey's pragmatic analysis of the Entente: 'It was now what it had been for several years past, why could it not be left as it was?'[38] The misunderstanding over the British commitment to side with France was verging on the surreal by Cambon's requirement that it be committed to paper. Writing down the present state of affairs while otiose for Grey was a necessity for Cambon. In London's view if Britain refused to commit herself to France, the fact that she signed a piece of paper in the form of an exchange of letters stating that there was no commitment did not alter that state of affairs. The legalistic Frenchman believed that what was committed to paper had greater force because it had the sanctity of text; it was a French cultural trait of cherishing form over substance, the reverse of the British approach. But the First Lord of the Admiralty, Winston Churchill, warned of where all this was leading: 'Everyone must feel who knows the facts that we have all the obligations of an alliance without its advantages and above all without its precise definitions'.[39] But Churchill's view did not predominate in government, just as Cambon's optimism about a British commitment was not shared by all on the French side.

By September 1912 cultural dissonance was ever more in evidence. Paul Cambon, on his own initiative, proposed a formula whereby on fear of an aggression by a third power or a threat to peace, the two governments would consult and search for a means of avoiding it. Grey replied that 'this was what would happen under the existing conditions'. Cambon 'agreed that this was so in fact, but said that there was no written understanding'.[40] In this strange display of Chinese whispers Grey was insisting that the existing *de facto* case would be no different from the written *de jure* case, while Cambon was maintaining the contrary. That difference of interpretation would be at the heart of the Grey-Cambon letters and thus of the mutual incomprehension that was so much in evidence in August 1914.

Grey, knowing that he had to do something to placate the French, finally gave in and accepted the formula whereby the two states should consult in the event of a threat to peace. When Asquith saw it he made the supercilious but telling remark: 'I don't see any harm in Cambon's formula; indeed it is almost a platitude'.[41] On 22 and 23 November Sir Edward Grey and Paul Cambon exchanged letters, Grey's in English, Cambon's in French, fittingly symbolizing their different cultural standpoints. These set down that although in recent years British and French military and naval experts had consulted together, it had always been understood that this did not restrict the freedom of either government to decide at any future time whether or not to assist the other by armed force and that the dispositions of the French and British fleets were not based on an engagement to cooperate in war. But if either government had reason to expect an unprovoked attack by a third power or something that threatened the general peace, it should discuss with the other whether both governments should act together to prevent aggression, preserve peace and decide on measures to be taken. If action was necessary the plans of the general staffs would be taken into consideration.[42] For the French the military agreements had become the Entente's defence arm, while the British believed they had maintained Gladstonian independence for 'a contingency that has not arisen and may never arise'.[43]

For the French the letters shored up the Entente Cordiale short of an alliance. In complete contrast to Asquith's description of them as 'a platitude', Poincaré – steered by Cambon – recognized 'the great value of these documents'.[44] The British cabinet for its part did not believe it had incurred any obligation as a result of the exchange of letters, and even the radicals thought the letters were definite written recognition that the irregular staff talks, about which they had now been informed, did not commit the British government. The Colonial Secretary Lewis Harcourt even spoke of 'our unfettered policy and discretion'.[45] For this reason there was no real crisis within the cabinet in 1912: that would come in 1914. Even if historians like Zara Steiner believe that the government's freedom had been compromised, it is still safe to say that its freedom was not as fettered as Paul Cambon believed, or would have had Paris believe. It is also fair to say that Cambon had misunderstood or had chosen to ignore the nature and power of radical opposition to siding with France; he was guilty of overconfidence in Britain's loyalty to France and as a result misled his political masters. At the beginning of August 1914 he appeared to take little account of the difficulties faced by the Liberal government threatened as it was with collapse. While Asquith and Grey hinted at resignation if France were not supported, up to five members of the cabinet were ready to resign if she was.[46] Liberal back-bench opinion was strongly anti-war, as were the trade unions, the Labour Party, the Free Churches, the City of London, large swathes of public opinion down to the dons of Cambridge University.[47]

It is no surprise that Cambon should describe 2 August 1914 as 'the day through which I passed the darkest moments of my life'.[48] But for the French historian of Britain, Élie Halévy, although the Entente meant preparations complete to the last detail for concerted military action if the parties to it found themselves at war, and the Grey-Cambon letters meant that instead of waiting for war, the two governments would concert beforehand, there was no agreement to make war. Britain reserved her freedom to the last moment.[49] Samuel Williamson describes that moment as 'this nadir in the history of the prewar entente'.[50] The ultimate question as to what Britain's attitude would be in the event of war, as Sir Edward Grey had emphasized repeatedly, was dependent on the cabinet, Parliament and public opinion. And so it was still on 1 August 1914, barely two days before France was at war with Germany. Then it was that Cambon insisted that Britain had a moral obligation to defend France's northern coastline because France had transferred its fleet to the Mediterranean. But still Grey insisted that a decision to side with France rested with Parliament. That day the French ambassador spluttered to Sir Arthur Nicolson, 'They are going to ditch us. They are going to ditch us'.[51] George Lloyd, a Conservative backbencher who was in contact with Cambon about the Opposition's position, told Leo Amery: 'The French regarded themselves as completely betrayed and were in an awful state of mind'. Cambon had told George Lloyd: 'if we stood out and the French won they would gladly do everything to crush us afterwards'.[52] These examples show, as Philip Bell points out, 'how near Britain and France came, during the war crisis of 1914, to a complete and probably fatal break. If Britain had stood out of a war', asks Bell, 'could such a breach ever have been healed?'[53] In the final hour the Entente was not saved by France or for France, but by the German invasion of Belgium. In remembering how France and Britain did enter the war as allies, this was something that, in France at least, tended to be forgotten.

Remembrance of alliance past

A combination of lack of candour about the nature of the Franco-British relationship, the absence of a certain cultural awareness and the presence of personalities with differing mental maps conspired to produce, over several years, a Franco-British dialogue of the deaf that could have been fatal for either country in 1914. Although not for the war's duration, it did have consequences after the war in the 1920s in how the process of military staff talks, naval agreements and Franco-British relations were remembered. Both sides interpreted the experience differently. For some British politicians, officials and members of the public, particularly those seduced by the arguments of the 1920s, fuelled in part by German propaganda, that France and Raymond Poincaré had an important share of responsibility in the origins of the war, negative lessons were learnt of the pre-war relationship with France. Many in the 1920s were convinced that London had become committed to Paris and had rejected better relations with Berlin before the war as a result of a 'policy of stealth and subterfuge', partly at the hand of France.[54] Consequently, in the 1920s British politicians were wary of striking up a new agreement with Paris, let alone an alliance, in order to allow her greater freedom, in part to develop better relations with Weimar Germany and not become inveigled into what some saw as a new French bid for hegemony in Europe. Similarly, in the 1930s following Hitler's reoccupation of the Rhineland, British proposals for Anglo-French-Belgian open military staff talks provoked hostility among military planners who believed the 1905 Franco-British conversations had restricted the options for the British Expeditionary Force in 1914.[55]

In 1920s' France the pre-war experience of British hesitancy led politicians and diplomats to press all the more strongly for a formal alliance. The fact that the decade-long relationship had culminated in the alliance and the joint war effort put a more positive glow on renewing the alliance because it demonstrated what could be achieved by it. Thus in retrospect the Entente Cordiale became the starting point for an ever-closer union with Britain and the reference point for future improved relations with London. Drawing a veil over what might have come to pass if Britain had not finally come down on France's side, French politicians and the public concentrated on the victorious outcome. Clemenceau was willing to make serious sacrifices in order to achieve that; for example, the concessions he made to acquire the still-born 1920 security guarantee by the United States and Britain. Even then throughout the rest of the 1920s the French were again at serious pains to convince London of the necessity of renewing the alliance and were still hankering for one until war came again in 1939. Refreshed by positive Franco-British Second World War cooperation the Entente Cordiale emerged more appealing still in Paris, ushering in the first peace-time Franco-British alliance with the carefully named but quickly eclipsed Dunkirk Treaty of 1947. It was not long before the unfortunate 1956 Suez experience led the French to take the European route rather than continued reliance on London. But when it came to the centennial celebrations of the Entente Cordiale in 2004 little of the difficult experience of that decade 1904–14 clouded the French memory. As the French Foreign Minister Dominique de Villepin noted in the foreword to a volume celebrating that centenary: 'the great revolution that the Entente began was to ensure that our century of shared diplomacy has been marked by only "friendly disagreements"'.[56] How different the picture would have looked had it not been for Belgium.

Notes

1 Works on the Entente Cordiale are numerous, but classic texts are:
   C. M. Andrew, *Théophile Delcassé and the Making of the Entente Cordiale* (London: Macmillan, 1968); P. J. V. Rolo, *Entente Cordiale: the Origins and Negotiation of the Anglo-French Agreements of 8 April 1904* (London: Macmillan, 1969); on the militarization of the agreements, see Samuel R. Williamson, *The Politics of Grand Strategy. France and Britain Prepare for War, 1904–1914* (Cambridge, MA: Harvard University Press, 1969).

2 TNA, FO 800/100 cited in Annika Mombauer (ed.), *The Origins of the First World War: Diplomatic and Military Documents* (Manchester: Manchester University Press, 2013).

3 Christopher Andrew and Paul Vallet, in Richard Mayne, Douglas Johnson, Robert Tombs (eds), *Cross-Channel Currents. 100 Years of the Entente Cordiale* (London: Routledge, 2004), p. 30.

4   Dorothy Pickles, *The Uneasy Entente. French Foreign Policy and Franco-British Misunderstandings* (Oxford: Oxford University Press, 1966).

5   On the underutilization of foreign ministry historical branches, see M.S. Alexander and J.F.V. Keiger, 'Limiting Arms, Enforcing Limits: International Inspections and the Challenges of Compellance in Germany post-1919, Iraq post-1991', *The Journal of Strategic Studies*, 29, 2 (April 2006) 348–50.

6   G.P. Gooch, quoted in P.M.H. Bell, *France and Britain 1900–1940. vol. I: Entente and Estrangement* (London: Longman, 1996), p. 32.

7   Paul to Jules Cambon, 26 Feb 1910, quoted in Bell, *France and Britain*, vol. I, p. 40.

8   On the differences in British governing circles regarding Germany and the Haldane Mission, see Zara Steiner, *Britain and the Origins of the First World War* (London: Macmillan, 1977), pp. 94–109 and *passim*.

9   Keith Wilson, *Problems and Possibilities. Exercises in Statesmanship 1814–1918* (Stroud: Tempus Publishing, 2003), p. 188.

10 Ibid., p. 202.

11 Ibid., pp. 205–6.

12 Geneviève Tabouis, *Perfidious Albion-Entente Cordiale* (London: Thornton Butterworth, 1938), p. 109.

13 Wilson, *Problems and Possibilities*, p. 184.

14 Samuel R. Williamson, *The Politics of Grand Strategy. Britain and France Prepare for War, 1904–1914* (London: Ashfield Press, 1990), p. 366.

15 Niall Ferguson, *The Pity of War* (London: Penguin, 1998).

16 Pickles, *Uneasy Entente*, p. 1.

17 Ibid.

18 Quoted in Harold Nicolson, *Diplomacy* (London: Thornton Butterworth, 1939), p. 137.

19 Pickles, *Uneasy Entente*, p. 5.

20 Nicolson, *Diplomacy*, p. 142.

21 Ibid., p. 140.

22 See Bell, *France and Britain*, vol. I, pp. 38–42.

23 Un diplomate [Henri Cambon], *Paul Cambon, Ambassadeur de France* (Paris: Plon, 1937), p. 182.

24 Zara Steiner, *Britain and the Origins*, pp. 181–6. On the power of Tyrrell see the views of the more attuned German Ambassador in London, Prince Lichnowsky, cited in Élie Halévy, *A History of the English People in the Nineteenth Century*, vol. 6, *The Rule of Democracy (1905–1914)*(2nd edn, London, Ernest Benn, 1961), p. 631.

25 Williamson, *Politics of Grand Strategy*, pp. 144–5. Williamson gives other accounts of Paul Cambon's inability to fully comprehend Grey's position, pp. 144–7.

26 [Henri Cambon] *Paul Cambon, Ambassadeur*, p. 234.

27 Nicolson, *Diplomacy*, p. 136.

28 Keith Wilson, *Policy of the Entente. Essays on the determinants of British foreign policy 1904–1914* (Cambridge: Cambridge University Press, 1985), p. 37.

29 Steiner, *Britain and the Origins*, p. 184.

30 Repington to Esher, 20 January 1909, no. 69, in A.J.A. Morris (ed.), *The Letters of Lieutenant-Colonel Charles à Court Repington CMG Military Correspondent of The Times 1903–1918* (Sutton Publishing, 1999), p. 150. I am grateful to Dr Elizabeth Greenhalgh for providing me with this information and reference.

31 According to Esher's *Journal,* 12 Nov 1908, vol. II, p. 359, quoted in ibid, p. 307, n. 88.

32 Bell, *France and Britain*, vol. I, p. 49.

33 For details of Paul Cambon's lack of grasp of the seriousness of the Haldane Mission, see John F.V. Keiger, *France and the Origins of the First World War* (London: Macmillan, 1983), pp. 106–10.

34 Paul Cambon to Poincaré, 7 February 1912, *Documents Diplomatiques Français*[DDF] 3ᵉ série, vol. I, nos. 628, 629.

35 Paul Cambon to Poincaré, 8 May 1912, DDF 3e serie, vol. II, no. 419.

36 Williamson, *Politics of Grand Strategy*, p. 263.

37 Grey-Carnegie (Plenipotentiary Minister, British Embassy, Paris) 22 July 1912, *British Documents on the Origins of War, 1889–1914 [BD]* vol. VII, no. 400.

38 Grey-Carnegie, 26 July 1912, ibid., no. 402.

39 Cited in Keith Hamilton, 'Great Britain and France, 1911–1914', in F.H. Hinsley (ed.), *The Foreign Policy of Sir Edward Grey* (Cambridge: Cambridge University Press, 1977), p. 334.

40 Grey to Bertie, 19 September 1912, BD, vol. VII, no. 410.

41 Asquith to Grey, 11 October 1912, BD, vol. VII, no. 412.

42 Paul Cambon to Poincaré, 23 November 1912, DDF, 3e serie, IV, annexes 1, 2; Grey to Cambon, 22 November 1912, BD, X no. 416; Cambon-Grey, 23 November 1912, ibid, no. 417.

43 Grey to Cambon, 22 November 1912, BD, X no. 416.

44 Poincaré to Paul Cambon, 25 November 1912, DDF, 3e série, IV, no. 562.

45 Steiner, *Britain and the Origins*, p. 104.

46 Robert and Isabelle Tombs, *That Sweet Enemy. The French and the British from the Sun King to the Present* (New York: Alfred A Knopf, 2007), p. 465.

47 J.F.V. Keiger, 'Britain's "union sacrée" in 1914', in Jean-Jacques Becker and Stephane Audoin-Rouzeau (eds), *Les sociétés européennes et la guerre de 1914–18,* (Paris: Publication de l'Université de Nanterre, 1990), pp. 39–52.

48 Keith Eubank, *Paul Cambon Master Diplomatist*, (Norman: University of Oklahoma Press, 1960), pp. 181–2.

49 Halévy, *History of the English People*, vol. VI, pp. 630–2.

50   Williamson, *Politics of Grand Strategy*, p. 353.

51   Bell, *France and Britain*, vol. I, p. 57.

52   Ibid.

53   Ibid.

54   Williamson, *Politics of Grand Strategy*, p. 371.

55   Ibid.

56   Dominique de Villepin. 'Foreword', in Mayne et al., *Cross Channel Currents*, p. xv.

CHAPTER TWO

Unequal Sacrifice? Two Armies, Two Wars?

William Philpott

English parishes and French communes alike mark their Great War sacrifices. French civic memorials, inscribed '*pour la patrie*', customarily stand in front of *mairies*: such monuments are representative of the national struggle against the invader and an acknowledgement that this was a war in which France's citizen-soldiers did their duty. Their statuary endorses this: as often as not, a *poilu* in martial pose guards the village square, rifle and bayonet at the ready; sometimes he holds aloft a laurel wreath of victory. They also acknowledge the loss: '*à nos morts*' many record, the names of the community's fallen sons listed on the plinth or in the church nearby. English memorials, frequently sited in churchyards and surmounted by a simple cross, also list the names of the dead. 'For king and country' some say; many more bear Kipling's national epitaph 'their name liveth for evermore'. Beneath their lists of Great War dead there is customarily a shorter list, '1939–1945', a reminder that the effort made for king and country – and, although never stated, in practice for France and Britain's other allies, 'brave little Belgium' prominent among them – turned out to be nugatory. In the conflict that by its end had morphed into a 'war to end wars' each nation sacrificed its young men willingly in the common cause. Yet as time passed the reasons for this sacrifice receded, alongside the memory of shared effort. British and French memory has long since bifurcated into two national strands of history representing trauma and loss. Joint endeavour is overlooked.

Confronted with the varying motifs of the war effort of 1914–18 and its aftermath, established in the monuments and rituals of remembrance, societies and historians seem thereafter to have struggled with their attempts to find meaning in that conflict. It is, Annette Becker and Stephane Audoin-Rouzeau suggest, 'the weight of the dead on the living', increased by the dead of the twentieth century's later wars and genocides, which has robbed that war of meaning for future generations.[1] In practice, World War I remains a living war, its history and meaning shifting with each subsequent generation. The historian faces the difficult task of attempting to position the war experience within the shifting framework of the history of the conflict. A closer analysis of the historiography of World War I by Jay Winter and Antoine Prost has identified that the war's history has passed through three configurations: military and diplomatic, social and cultural and social.[2] We might anticipate a fourth as the war's centenary passes, although whether that will be an effective (and much-needed) synthesis of the three that have gone before or the development of a new way of viewing the war remains to be seen. What Winter and Prost themselves suggest, however, is the need to move beyond 'national boundaries of interpretation' to an agreed European synthesis of the war's history and meaning. To date, 'the first rule that seems to govern . . . historiography is that every nation has its own Great War'.[3] We should bear this in mind when considering why the efforts of allies in the common cause have been neglected or skewed as historical narratives have shifted through their generational configurations.

We should expect that two nations sharing the same war, indeed on many occasions fighting the same battles, have taken different meaning from it. We can accept this as inevitable, because societies have different histories, cultures and traditions which give meaning to events as they pass. For France, invaded, occupied and devastated, the psychological and physical impact of war would always be deeper than on an island empire, relatively untouched, proximate yet safe from invasion.[4] Similarly defending one's national soil in practice and fighting for the defence of 'hearth and home' at a distance as British Tommies were doing in foreign fields[5] evoke different responses and feelings. It perhaps makes meaning easier to find and more straightforward in France's war than in Britain's. It also suggests that even when lined up against a common enemy they were already fighting rather different wars, which undoubtedly also facilitates the process of forgetting the role of allies with different agendas in defining national narratives. Add to that the impact of the war itself on separate societies, as well as the refractive effect of divergent later histories, and we should not be surprised that Britain and France remember their war differently. What their memories share is a shift from the sense of national endeavour, a hard-fought struggle and ultimately hard-won victory, to a sense of disillusion: from 'heroic sacrifice' to 'futile slaughter'.[6] To explain this, we need to contrast the histories of their military experience, while drawing parallels and explaining differences.

. . . .

In 1916, as the British Empire's armies commenced their first major trial of strength with the enemy on the Somme, Lord Esher, Britain's unofficial representative in Paris, could write to the commander-in-chief of the need to keep the French press up to date with the actions of the British army.[7] Since the opening of the German attack on Verdun the French press had been filled with accusations of British inaction while France sacrificed its young men in the allied cause: France was already composing its own narrative of heroic efforts and half-hearted assistance. Eighty years later Paddy Griffith could rightly remark when considering the British army's tactical progression, 'most of the serious fighting . . . was left to our French allies, with whom we were often on terms of such cordial hostility that their absolutely vast contribution has never to this day been fairly laid before the British public'.[8] Not much had changed in the intervening years to reconcile the perspectives and histories of the two belligerents. Cleary the lack of understanding and appreciation of the two armies' mutual effort and shared experience is deep rooted.[9] Recently, some attention has been paid on both sides of the Channel to monumental battles, human stories that transcend national boundaries: there are several English-language works on Verdun, and more recently a couple of French-language studies of the Somme.[10] The often fraught working of the Anglo-French alliance has been dissected with a certain relish, if only by Anglo-Saxon historians.[11] Indeed, recently France's war effort has been rediscovered (by an American scholar);[12] and (although it took more than 90 years) the present author has finally restored the French army to its central role in the planning and conduct of the coalition's greatest battle, on the Somme.[13] But the problem of military history remains its parochialism. Britain remembers its battles, argues about its generals, debates strategic might-have-beens, and above all, investigates and celebrates the ordinary men who went to war in foreign fields. France has its own monumental battles and political conflicts to consider, as well as the deeper traumas of invasion, occupation and military, social and economic crises. What has gone before suggests that there are common themes to war history, if until very recently mutually exclusive narratives.

In order to identify how and why, three interrelated influences must be identified. First there is war experience itself. This was shared up to a point: both armies suffered heavy losses in notorious battles on the western front; both mobilized their populations to fight a new sort of war; both were gripped by political divisions and civil–military crisis as the war was prolonged; both expended lives and treasure, and were forced subsequently to address the question 'was it worth it?' The primary contrast in war experience, although one which was eroded as the war went on, lay in the contrasting nature of the British and French military systems. In August 1914 divided Britain united behind a just cause, rallied its empire and called on men and women to 'do their bit': voluntarism thereafter defined the British way in warfare even if the exigencies of modern warfare obliged a switch to continental-style conscription fairly early on.[14] For France, it was the obligations and rights of the mobilized republican citizen-soldier which underpinned the mindset of combatants and the methods of the state in a war in which metaphysical French honour and practical French security were at stake, underwritten by a certain implacable spirit of revenge.[15] If nations have different value systems, different social and political structures and different purposes for waging war, it should not surprise if they have divergent histories and memories.

This war history itself is the second influence on the construction of the narratives of national and common endeavour and loss. How was the story of the war constructed: by whom, and with what purpose? How was the war presented to subsequent generations, and has the central story shifted down the years? Where has history transmuted to myth and why? This relates to the third influence, that of war memory, closely intertwined with but distinct from its history; not the stuff of academic argument and periodic scholarly revision, but well-established popular perceptions and rituals. It engages with how we remember and commemorate the war these days: a complicated sociocultural phenomenon which Jay Winter has termed 'historical remembrance'.[16] This theme is explored in another chapter in this collection, so here, experience and history will be the focus.

The two nations came to the 1904 Entente Cordiale and the ensuing war with different experiences and perspectives. For France, with an established security policy based on alliances and arrangements for mutual military aid, British support was another element of its insurance policy against Germany.[17] With its long-established traditions of 'splendid isolation' in diplomacy, balance of power politics in relation to the European continent and military and naval independence, close diplomatic alignment, economic integration and military cooperation with the awkward neighbour across the Channel would naturally prove problematic for Britain, as John Keiger relates above. This occasioned mutually suspicious – yet not antipathetic – perspectives before war broke out. Although 'my enemy's enemy is my friend' was an appropriately pragmatic approach as German power waxed, Fashoda, where the two imperial rivals had come close to blows in 1898,[18] was still a recent raw memory. Military and political leaders had spent their formative years as rivals, and for the British, fear persisted of French dominance if they were not reined in; for the French, anxiety about British reliability, commitment and effort emerged.

Nevertheless Britain did send France its army – commanded by the appropriately named Sir John French – when war broke out. This small professional army, composed of long-service volunteers led by experienced officers, and practised in colonial campaigns, acquitted itself well in the field in 1914. Its historians represent that it did much to save France, overlooking that in reality France did most to save itself (and that Russians did a lot more than British, and Belgians about the same!). Britain's regular Expeditionary Force was the first sacrifice in the allied cause, selling itself dearly in the first prolonged attritional battle around Ypres in autumn 1914: the fact that it fought shoulder-to-shoulder with Frenchmen who on many occasions saved British troops from disaster is largely overlooked.[19] Although the professionalism of the pre-war regular army imbued the wartime levies, Britain's army is remembered not as a professional force, but as an amateur citizen army. While conscription raised the majority of the force, it is the many volunteers who answered Secretary of State for War Lord Kitchener's call in 1914 and 1915 and formed the armies that bore his name who personify British effort and sacrifice. 'Your country needs you', his finger-pointing poster famously proclaimed, a sentiment echoed in the epitaph on many monuments to the fallen. It was this splendid army which was sacrificed in the allied cause: well aware of its mission to master the German army in battle, as well as the nature of the war it was engaged in. To subsequent less patriotic or deferential generations this army was slaughtered for no particular cause or result; and not by an enemy determined to hold their ground at all costs, but by its own flawed and callous commanders. The shifting interpretations of 'history' in time turned an army of citizens led by soldiers (whose real war experience was one of enthusiastic, intelligent amateurs learning military skills from the surviving cadres of the regular army) into 'lions led by donkeys': unwitting and increasingly unwilling victims of outmoded methods and outdated values.

The history of this army, or of the conscripts who filled its depleted ranks from 1916, has never been told in France. What there was, in the 1920s, was 'A French Indictment' by no less a figure than General Victor Huguet, France's pre-war military attaché and liaison officer to British headquarters in 1914–15.[20] In his memoir of British pre-war and early war effort, he prefaced this record of ready assistance with a warning:

> This will be but one more of the many war books that will already have appeared. Yet it will not have been profitless if it helps to a better understanding of the English character, the special conditions of English life, the needs of her political policy [sic] and as a result, the principles on which we ought to base our relationship with her.[21]

Written only a few years after the war, it had clearly not taken long for recriminations to obscure the spirit of 1914:

> In war books, novels, everywhere, the war of 1914–18 is represented as the struggle between England and German superiority and the victory as an English victory. The name of France must be mentioned since it was on her soil that the greater number of big military operations took place; but her own part in it, as well as the great deeds of her Army are intentionally passed over in silence, and there is no question to-day of the comradeship in arms which for four years united the two peoples.[22]

Clearly for Huguet, who wrote his text in 1922, differences over the peace and the post-war treatment of defeated Germany had sundered the allies very quickly, with Albion reverting to her perfidious ways once France's sacrifice had secured its objective: that was 'the resumption of business', against which 'exultant and solemn avowals' to its erstwhile ally counted for nothing.[23]

The parameters of the selfish rationale behind British military policy were set early on, and have established a narrative of tardy, half-hearted military support for France. The slowness of British mobilization, Kitchener's reluctance to send troops to France where he would surrender strategic control and initiative to his French allies and above all, his diversion of resources from the Western Front to speculative and ultimately abortive operations at the Dardanelles were grounds for French pique, then and later. The real basis of such a thesis, however, lay in the unequal sacrifice that resulted. While the British were training, equipping and adventuring against Turkey, France was sacrificing its sons in battle with the German army. That France's biggest offensives took place in 1915 with only limited and relatively ineffective British support is hardly remembered in Great Britain: or at least as we shall see, these battles are remembered as murderous follies, not the early faltering steps on the road to Anglo-French victory. Kitchener himself always predicted that the war would only start in earnest in 1916 once British strength made itself felt on the principal front:[24] there perhaps lies the root of the French complaint that the British always saw it as a war between their empire and Germany. France's heavy casualties in 1915, added to those of 1914 (which together totalled more than Britain would lose in the whole war), set up an imbalance of effort and loss which sustained French suspicions of British commitment at the time, and subsequently undermined a realistic appreciation of British effort. If the battles of 1915 served some purpose, they taught the French army appropriate offensive methods for the trench-locked front; they were always much more effective than their British allies in future battles, although British military history has never acknowledged that simple truth. Another positive outcome, which the French would have trouble acknowledging, was that it actually saved many raw British troops from slaughter in battles in which military tactics and material were inadequate to realize the operational ambitions of higher commanders. As these started to be reconciled during 1916, when command ambitions were reduced and methods and military technology improved, Kitchener's hesitancy in 1915 at least left the western allies with a fresh army able to take the field and a greater share of the military burden as war weariness eroded the *poilus'* fighting capacity.

France's conscript army fought a rather different war and has a distinctly patchy history. This might be due to the nature of the history profession itself. Military history has no place in French universities, and in British universities it was until recently a marginal subject. British and Commonwealth historians of war tend to focus on Anglo-Saxon subjects and historians of

France generally tend to avoid military subjects – except the revolution and Napoleon and the trauma of France's Second World War schism. Militarily, the 'strange defeat' of 1940 has attracted much more sustained analysis than the apparently unexpected victory of 1918.[25] This might also be due to the fact that the military conduct of France's war generated fewer controversies, and less critique, than Haig's campaign or its alternatives. Those Frenchmen who did engage with events on the battlefield were generally ex-soldiers themselves, who drafted between the wars many detailed, thoughtful and interesting studies of France's military operations. But these were almost universally written in a dry, 'staff-history' style, intended to educate soldiers for wars to come rather than to engage the public with the conduct of a war just gone. Today only the most dedicated military historians mine this wealth of synthesis and professional reflection.

Instead, the predominant history we have of France's army is intellectual, social and cultural; military history such as it is focuses on the themes of high command, strategy and civil–military relations. What was its ideology and doctrine? Why did it apparently fare so badly against the German army? What was it like to fight a trench war, and how did this impact on French troops? If there is a prevailing theme it is why did war weariness set in with its consequent 1917 mutinies, apparent 1918 lassitude and eventual 1940 capitulation at the behest of the superannuated 1918 leadership? This is certainly the framework of the only English-language history of France's wartime army: its title, borrowed from Stanley Kubrick's influential yet skewed film, *Paths of Glory*, being indicative of the cultural baggage which weighs upon an engagement with the history of the French army.[26] Behind all this for the British lies an image of France as a womanly nation, weak, decadent, in decline and a drain on, not a support to, its British ally.

A negative image of France and its army – predicated mainly, and speciously, on the failure of its method and leadership, rather than on the lack of courage of its rank and file – was formed in early histories of the war which furnished the framework of perceptions for subsequent British engagement with the military actions and attributes of its former ally. I have written elsewhere of the scabrous pen-picture which Winston Churchill left of Joffre's battles in his popular and influential history–memoir *The World Crisis*. Therein a catalogue of 'sweeping rhetorical generalisations about faulty methods and losses . . . establishes Joffre and Foch's culpability relentlessly rather than cogently'.[27] 'History will be kind to me for I intend write it', Churchill famously quipped. Unfortunately those to whom Churchill chose to be unkind remain unjustly tarred with his scorn and feathered with his *bons mots*. Why he chose to be unkind to Joffre one can only speculate. After resigning from the Cabinet, for a short while in 1915 and early 1916 he shared the trench-front trials of the ordinary infantryman as a Western Front battalion commander. Therefore he came away from the war with the soldier's revulsion against the horrors and losses of industrial war, which (like a number of subsequently influential junior officers with a limited perspective but trenchant opinions) he married to an armchair general's critique of higher strategy. Unlike Prime Minister Lloyd George who later embarked on a systematic undermining of his own commander-in-chief's reputation, with Douglas Haig still alive and respected in the 1920s, Churchill chose to transfer his soldier's bitterness onto an easier, and easily discredited, foreign target. It sits strangely with his actual views of the French army. While at the front he acquainted himself with it, notably with one of its most effective field commanders, General Emile Fayolle, and was proud to sport an Adrian helmet given to him as a present. Indeed even after criticizing its early performance in the Great War, Churchill was accustomed to 'thank God for the French army' as the prospect of a second confrontation with Germany loomed. Perhaps the real issue was that Joffre's attritional strategy was pursued at the expense of his own strategic ambitions at the Dardanelles in 1915, and by representing it as murderous folly, he might salvage a little of his own tarnished reputation.

Only in the last decade have English-language scholars begun to engage systematically with Joffre and his army's early campaigns, presenting a much more positive picture of the insight and acuity of the allies' strategic director in the first half of the war, as well as the developing military effectiveness of the forces he led.[28] For many years the scholarly verdict on the French army, Douglas's Porch's conclusion that on the battlefield the French delivered 'a courageous but unintelligent performance',[29] has held the field, *faute de mieux*. Scholarship in the English language, with a few important French contributions, may in future overthrow such a judgement.[30] Admittedly Porch, an American scholar of the pre-war French army, had little evidence on which to make any judgement when he engaged with the subject in the 1980s. But a reading of his assessment makes it clear that he projected his conclusions on pre-war weakness (grounded in unresolved doctrinal disputes and civil–military tensions as much as practical preparations) into wartime experience,[31] no doubt under the shadow of earlier English judgements of Joffre and his successors. Porch relied heavily on Guy Pedroncini's study of Philippe Pétain's command from 1917, until very recently the only full study of a senior French commander.[32] Pétain, however, has attracted interest in England more for his notorious later career than on account of his success as a World War I commander. Yet, as an antidote to the perception of 'incompetence and slaughter' established by Churchill which pervades understanding of the earlier years of the war, Pétain's later army at least has received recognition as a better equipped, led and effective force. Nonetheless, according to the prevailing Anglo-Saxon narrative, it was past its best after 1917, a dispirited mob, accustomed to defeat and in need of the support of its more virile British allies. If any theme of the latter half of the war has attracted attention, it is that of morale, and more specifically mutiny. Verdun, a battle examined by a number of English scholars with feeling if with limited insight, starts the process of decline. Their focus on the traumas of the early, defensive phase of the engagement, and the bitter psychogeographic legacy of the shattered hills beyond the Meuse,[33] rather than on the successful counteroffensive of late 1916, unbalances understanding of the French army's defining battlefield experience, transmuting a hard-won victory into a psychological defeat. From there it is only one tragic step to widespread mutiny: Robert Nivelle's failed April 1917 assault at the Chemin des Dames.[34] Pedroncini also addressed the theme of the mutinies.[35] His work has been echoed in English-language studies, regrettably under the shadow of Kubrick.[36] Vast dimensions of the French army's activities remain unknown, notably the autumn 1915 Champagne offensive, the largest of the early trench war, and its defensive and offensive battles in 1918; and until very recently the Somme, a 'British' battle which it turns out that Foch directed and in which the French army came to play the predominant role![37]

Behind this meta-narrative of French decline one finds a prominent, if not entirely surprising, figure. If not deliberately setting out to shape historical memory himself, the British commander-in-chief, Field Marshal Sir Douglas Haig, nevertheless left its draughtsmen an effective tool – the copious war diary he composed daily as he fought alongside the French in a none-too-friendly and demanding joint campaign. I have elaborated the nature of and reasons for Haig's narrative of French decline elsewhere, but it is worth reprising it briefly here.[38] His story of British rise and French decline defines the shifting relationship in English eyes between the armies in the field after 1915. A brave but ill-managed and inadequately equipped French army sacrificed its best men in futile offensives in the early years of the war, leaving it to the fresher, more virile British empire to step in, confront the Germans in France and Belgium, and take the lead in driving them out. The focal point of this narrative is 1 July 1916 – the focal point for most British narratives of the war – when Britain's New Armies attacked, prematurely and disastrously, because without their effort the French would have been beaten at Verdun and the war lost. This is the rationale Douglas Haig developed in his own mind while the conflict continued, and he set it down for posterity in the pages of his diary. This source, edited by Robert Blake in 1952 and used before and since for studies of the coalition and Haig's own actions, has stood in for any realistic assessment of what the French army actually achieved and was capable of – including, for example, its striking success on 1 July 1916 and steady forward progress astride the river Somme thereafter while the British got bloodily stuck further north. In Haig's rationale, the British are later obliged to fight at Ypres in 1917 because after their mutinies the French could not fight themselves. French participation in that battle, and their recapture of the Verdun heights and Chemin des Dames ridge in two very effective offensives in the late summer and autumn, are conveniently overlooked by Haig. In 1918, he shows the British saving themselves when the German army goes on the offensive – promised French assistance is too little and too late. And the beating of the German army begins at the Battle of Amiens, 8 August 1918, where the

British Fourth Army smashes in the German front. To quote the respected British historian John Terraine on Amiens:

> The rôles of the armies were now reversed: after their heavy losses in the battles of Champagne . . . the French would not be the leaders. A strongly reinforced British Fourth Army would be doing most of the work, with the French supporting.[39]

Interestingly the main incident that Terraine mentions of the French role in the battle is the defeat of some French Colonial units by an unsilenced German machine gun. This is the only point of detail Haig himself considers worthy of note from his meeting with General Debeney, the supporting French army commander, on 8 August, adding to the evidence Haig was always quick to record of the need to 'help the French'.[40] But the two French armies advancing to the south in the associated and equally effective battle of Montdidier (8–11 August), while completing the 'black day of the German army', rather challenge the British grand narrative; as indeed do further French successes, with and without British support, in the advance to victory. As Haig explained it, on 9 August 'the French met with no opposition owing to the determined advance of the British in front of their left'.[41] This subsequent phase of operations in 'the Anglo-French offensive *par excellence*'[42] is conveniently overlooked in the standard works – probably because it is hardly mentioned by Haig himself. But if the usual measure of victory is compared, between 8 and 11 August, the British Fourth Army took 12,000 prisoners and 450 guns, the French armies 10,000 and 300. You will not find that latter figure in any English-language history, but it is indicative of the shared nature of offensive operations in 1918. This example tallies with other Haig-derived representations of French military performance, in which French efforts are downplayed and deliberately misrepresented. Elizabeth Greenhalgh's examination of the fighting at Mont Kemmel elsewhere in this book examines one such event whose history was subsequently skewed by Haig's own perspective.

Why did Haig develop this narrative of French decline and British rise? A man who after a disagreement with *generalissimo* Foch as their armies pushed together to victory, could reassure himself '*the British Army has defeated the Germans this year*',[43] and dwell on the fact that the British press were praising his allies' success rather than his own,[44] had clearly developed a deep resentment of his coalition partners after 3 years of close collaboration. From early meetings with Joffre to concert joint offensive plans, Haig had formed the impression that the French commander wanted the British to do all the work, wearing out the enemy in a series of attritional battles while French strength was husbanded to win the final victory. This resentment and suspicion of French motives, leavened by a genuine fear that the French army was in irreversible decline after Verdun, sat heavily on Haig ever after. It allowed him to form the opinion early on that 'there is no doubt to my mind but that the war must be won by the Forces of the British Empire',[45] while justifying his own offensive strategy which was continually challenged at home. As I have suggested elsewhere, it made Haig and his army central to the conduct of the war; but it also gave Haig a moral imperative – to save France by defeating Germany.[46]

Whatever lay behind Haig's evaluation of the two armies' effectiveness, the commander-in-chief's rationale became, by default, the official version, forming a framework of analysis for subsequent military histories and encouraging a separation rather than an integration of British and French war experiences.[47] There has been a lack of inquisitiveness among British historians, illustrated by the example from Terraine above: accepting Haig's self-serving perceptions as 'history' rather than re-examining the events about which Haig is making brief, subjective comments, or exploring the mindset of the man recording them. It is crass to think that the British army won the war despite the French, rather than to accept that the war was won because of and with them. Haig certainly and quite understandably felt piqued if his own and his army's efforts were denied. When threatened with relegation to the fifth carriage of the British victory parade ('more of an insult than I could put up with, even from the Prime Minister'[48]), he asserted: 'The real truth, which history will show, is that the British Army has won the war in France'.[49] Haig certainly seems to have convinced himself of this, but the fact that British historians have been happy ever after to echo the commander-in-chief's dudgeon at foreigners is more difficult to understand. It may nonetheless be speculated that this was a necessary national narrative then and since; essential for coming to terms with the traumas of the war, and justifying the moral and material effort and sacrifice which Britain made, not just the specific war policy of the commander-in-chief. A century later however, if we accept the judgement of Winter and Prost that the war's historiography should now move away from national histories to a shared history, a military narrative integrating the roles and sacrifices of the two armies, unequal though they may have been, would clearly be a good place to start.

It would be gratifying to think that in France, greater, or more positive, attention was given to their allies' 4-year military effort for their liberation, but that does not seem to be the case. A Frenchman only needs to travel through northern France – perhaps on the Eurostar which now links Paris to London – to see the physical evidence of British sacrifice in the hundreds of cemeteries and memorials in the Somme and Artois. Yet the battlefields themselves seem owned by British school parties seeking the graves of martyred poets, and the mourners of a lost generation. The *tourisme de mémoire* now developing in the Somme and Artois seems to be something to attract the pound to France's sleepy farming communities rather than an activity for the people of France themselves. It should not surprise us that engagement with allied sacrifice does not happen in a nation whose national war museum, the Invalides, gives an account of liberation in 1944 that downplays the Anglo-American landing in Normandy in June 1944 and explains the expulsion of the Nazis through a landing of French and American forces in Provence in August! Forgetfulness would be too forgiving an explanation, patriotism excusable, politics plausible, chauvinism probable.

We can find the roots of this chauvinism – on both sides in fact – in the official histories produced between the wars. Here Winter and Prost's problem of the overtly national historical perspective is writ largest – yet surprisingly these important and influential works are not discussed in their survey of the war's evolving history. These monumental studies of military operations and wartime policy have little time for allied efforts: it seems as if both armies had no interest in, and felt there was nothing to learn from, the other's military experiences. In the British official history French contributions to coalition battles are relegated to short chapter appendices, and generally treated with less depth than the enemy's role in battles. In the French history British actions get cursory treatment. For example General Rawlinson's costly attack on 1 July 1916 gets a paragraph: in the British history, it gets a whole volume! Indeed the French can skew things just as much as the British. Their official account of the Third Battle of Ypres, the one major offensive in which Haig really took charge, becomes the 'offensive Franco-Anglais' in Flanders.

Much more could be said of how and why the British and French have formed such limited, false and self-serving impressions of each other's sacrifice in their common struggle against Germany. What has been established here is that the narratives fashioned by participants such as Huguet and Haig have become by default the history of the ally's military effort: really these are impressions and opinions which, on deeper examination, bear little relation to the actual history. However, they have persisted for nearly 100 years, which does no credit to historians on either side of the Channel.

If the British and French narratives of the Great War have something in common, these histories have different roots and objectives. This should not surprise us, and whether anything can, or should, be done about this deserves fuller consideration. It seems appropriate to offer certain reflections to those who might attempt to do so. We should not use impressions formed by participants as the basis for our historical narratives: herein lies the roots of myths and misrepresentations. We should read each other's histories and try to empathize with each other's *mentalité* and experience. Above all we must recognize that these two armies, although different in ethos and social base, fought the same war for the same reasons in roughly the same way, in cooperation, and successfully. If in the early years while Britain was mobilizing its resources France made a proportionately greater sacrifice, and if at the end of the conflict British losses had not matched those of its ally, this should be judged as a consequence of events, not as a symbol of unwillingness or self-interest on one side or asininity and lassitude on the other. The Western Front was not two armies fighting separate wars side by side. They faced the same challenges and we will never properly understand them or their war unless we consider them both together. It does not do history any service to be forgetful. For historians to be uninterested, lazy and credulous does not reflect well on our profession.

Notes

1   Audoin-Rouzeau, S. and Becker, A., *Understanding the Great War* (London: Profile Books, 2002), pp. 1–9.

2   Winter, J. and Prost, A., *The Great War in History: Debates and Controversies, 1914 to the Present* (Cambridge: Cambridge University Press, 2005), pp. 6–31.

3   Ibid., p. 193.

4   Gregory, A., *The Last Great War: British Society and the First World War* (Cambridge: Cambridge University Press, 2008), p. 2.

5   For a discussion of the importance of this belief in motivating British (and German) troops see Watson, A., *Enduring the Great War: Combat, Morale and Collapse in the German and British Armies, 1914–1918* (Cambridge: Cambridge University Press, 2008), pp. 48–53.

6   Particularly in Britain when contrasted with the 'good war' against Nazism, although France's Second World War collapse also undermined the sense of national achievement of the earlier conflict. See Gregory, *Last Great War*, pp. 2–4.

7   Esher to Haig, 28 June 1916, in Blake, R. (ed.), *The Private Papers of Douglas Haig, 1914–19* (London: Eyre & Spottiswoode, 1952), pp. 150–1.

8   Griffith, P., *Battle Tactics of the Western Front: The British Army's Art of Attack* (London: Yale University Press, 1994), p. 11.

9   For a recent discussion of this see Philpott,W., 'France's Forgotten Victory', review article, *The Journal of Strategic Studies*, 34, 6, (2011), 901–18.

10 See for example, Horne, A., *The Price of Glory: Verdun 1916* (London: Macmillan, 1962); Ousby, I., *The Road to Verdun* (London: Jonathan Cape, 2002); Miquel, P., *Les Oubliés de la Somme, juillet–novembre 1916* (Paris: Tallandier, 2001); Denizot, A., *La Bataille de la Somme, juillet–novembre 1916* (Paris: Perrin, 2002).

11 Notably, Philpott,W., *Anglo-French Relations and Strategy on the Western Front, 1914–1918* (Basingstoke: Macmillan, 1996); Greenhalgh, E., *Victory Through Coalition: Britain and France during the First World War* (Cambridge: Cambridge University Press, 2005).

12 Doughty, R., *Pyrrhic Victory: French Strategy and Operations in the Great War* (Cambridge, MA: The Belknap Press of Harvard University Press, 2005).

13 Philpott, W., *Bloody Victory: The Sacrifice on the Somme and the Making of the Twentieth Century* (London: Little, Brown, 2009).

14 See such works as Beckett, I. and Simpson, K. (eds), *A Nation in Arms: A Social Study of the British Army in the First World War* (London: Tom Donovan, 1985); Simkins, P., *Kitchener's Army: The Raising of the New*

Armies, 1914–16 (Manchester: Manchester University Press, 1988); Holmes, R.,*Tommy: The British Soldier on the Western Front, 1914–1918* (London: Harper Collins, 2004); Messenger, C., *Call to Arms: The British Army, 1914–1918* (London: Weidenfeld and Nicholson, 2005). For the role of voluntarism on the home front, see Gregory, *Last Great War*, pp. 70–111.

15   See Smith, L., *Between Mutiny and Obedience: The Case of the Fifth French Infantry Division during World War One* (Princeton, NJ: Princeton University Press, 1994).

16   Winter, J., *Remembering War: The Great War Between Memory and History in the Twentieth Century* (New Haven, CT: Yale University Press, 2006).

17   Philpott, W., 'Managing the British Way in Warfare: France and Britain's Continental Commitment, 1904–1918', in Neilson, K. and Kennedy, G. (eds), *The British Way in Warfare: Power and the International System, 1856–1956* (Farnham: Ashgate, 2010), pp. 83–100.

18   It is still recalled in France, where a centenary conference was organized in 1998. Chassaigne, P. and Dockrill, M.L. (eds), *Anglo-French Relations, 1898–1998: From Fashoda to Jospin* (Basingstoke: Macmillan, 2001).

19   Beckett, I., *Ypres: The First Battle* (London: Longman, 2004) for the first time tells the story of the multinational battle.

20   Huguet, General V., *Britain and the War: A French Indictment*, trans. Cotton Minchin, H. (London: Cassell & Co, 1928). The accusatory subheading did not appear in the original French edition, *L'intervention militaire brittanique en 1914* (Paris: Berger-Levrault, 1928).

21   Ibid., vii.

22   Ibid., p. 211.

23   Ibid., pp. 210–11.

24   Robinson, H.P., *The Turning Point: The Battle of the Somme* (London: Heinemann, 1917), p. 1.

25   For a fuller discussion see Philpott, 'France's Forgotten Victory'.

26   Clayton, A., *Paths of Glory: The French Army, 1914–18* (London: Cassell, 2003). Kubrick's film revived a 1935 book by Humphrey Cobb, imprinting an earlier Great War interpretation upon a later generation. Stephen Spielberg's 2011 film of Michael Morpurgo's 1982 story *War Horse* looks set to repeat that anti-historical trick.

27   Philpott, *Bloody Victory*, p. 607.

28   Doughty, *Pyrrhic Victory*, and Prete, R., *Strategy and Command: The Anglo-French Coalition on the Western Front, 1914* (Montreal and Kingston: McGill-Queen's University Press, 2009), the first of three projected volumes on Joffre's command.

29   Porch, D., 'The French Army in the First World War', in Millett, A.R. and Murray, W. (eds), *Military Effectiveness, Vol. 1: The First World War* (London: Unwin Hyman, 1988), 190–228, p. 225.

30   Recent doctoral work in the Department of War Studies, King's College London, should be noted: House, S., 'The Battle of the Ardennes, 22 August

1914: An Operational Study' (2011); Krause, J., 'The Second Battle of Artois and the French Army's Evolution in Spring 1915' (2011); T. Gale, 'La Salamandre: The French Army's *ArtillerieSpéciale* and the Development of Armoured Warfare in the First World War' (2011).

31 See Porch, D., *The March to the Marne: The French Army, 1871–1914* (Cambridge: Cambridge University Press, 1981).

32 Pedroncini, G., *Pétain: Général en Chef, 1917–18* (Paris: Presses Universitaires de France, 1974).

33 See Ousby, *Road to Verdun.*

34 In fact the only full treatment of that battle to date examines it somewhat sympathetically. Spears, E.L., *Prelude to Victory* (London: Jonathan Cape, 1939).

35 Guy Pedroncini, *Les Mutineries de 1917* (Paris: Presses Universitaires de France, 1967).

36 Williams, J., *Mutiny, 1917* (London: Heinemann, 1962).

37 Philpott, *Bloody Victory*, esp. pp. 217–9 and 346–7.

38 Philpott, W., 'Sir Douglas Haig's command? The image of alliance in Douglas Haig's record of the war', *The Douglas Haig Fellowship Records*, 15 (2011), pp. 3–13

39 Terraine, J., *To Win a War: 1918, the Year of Victory* (London: Papermac, 1986).

40 Ibid., and Haig Diary, 8 August 1918, Blake, *Private Papers*, p. 323. In passing, this is one example of Haig altering the text of his diary to make the French appear in a less favourable light. His original diary stated Debeney was 'pleased with himself' despite the defeat of the Colonials, Sheffield, G. and Bourne, J. (eds), *Sir Douglas Haig: War Diaries and Letters, 1914–1918* (London: Weidenfeld & Nicholson, 2005), p. 440. The later transcription, in Blake, *Private Papers*, p. 323, recorded Debeney as 'much distressed and almost in tears' because of that event.

41 Haig diary, 9 August 1918, Sheffield and Bourne, p. 441.

42 Philpott, *Bloody Victory*, p. 526.

43 Haig diary, 24 October 1918, Haig's emphasis, Blake, *Private Papers*, p. 336.

44 Ibid., 17 October 1918, p. 332.

45 Ibid., 14 January 1916, p. 125.

46 Philpott, 'Sir Douglas Haig's command?'

47 It is the narrative thrust of the earliest, Haig-authorized history of Haig's campaign, Dewar, G. and Boraston, J., *Sir Douglas Haig's Command, 1915–18* (London: Constable & Co., 2 vols, 1922).

48 In passing, the tensions between commander-in-chief and prime minister informed two sides of a historical debate which has defined British writing on the war ever since. Recent shifts towards a coalition paradigm of modern warfare are finally starting to redress this Anglocentric bias in our understanding of the war.

49 Haig diary, 30 November 1918, Blake, *Private Papers*, p. 346.

CHAPTER THREE

1918: The Push to Victory

Elizabeth Greenhalgh

The balance sheet at the start of 1918

As the 'troubled year' 1917 turned into what became the final year of the war, it was clear that the failed attempts at peace negotiation meant that it would be a fight to the finish. That fight would be carried out by a different coalition of powers. Russia fell out of the war and the extortions of the Treaty of Brest-Litovsk forced upon the new Soviet government showed what a German peace would be like. Naval blockade could not prevent Ukrainian cereals and Roumanian oil from resupplying the Central Powers. The United States had joined the Entente as an associated power in April 1917, which compensated for the Russian defection. American military strength took an agonizingly long time to develop, however. At the beginning of 1918, there were only 175,000 American troops in France; and most of their weapons – tanks, guns, aircraft, and munitions – were supplied by Britain or, principally, by France.

The previous 3 years of the conflict had shown clearly where the fault lines in the Franco-British alliance lay. They concerned manpower policies, the resources to be devoted to shipping and the allocation of the manpower resources of the newly 'associated' power, the United States. Underlying these was the fact that France was invaded and occupied, whereas island Britain was not.

The most significant difference in manpower policies between the two countries lay in conscription. France's Third Republic had always conscripted, and Britain did not until 1916. This difference threw casualty rates into greater prominence. Provisional figures for France, drawn up in November 1918 before the return of prisoners of war, show that between 2 August 1914 and December 1917, 1,481,000 were killed or they disappeared or were taken prisoner.[1] In addition were the (merely) wounded: 4,002,062 wounded, ill and gassed soldiers were evacuated from the front lines between 1914 and 1917.[2] The British had taken severe losses too, but it seemed to the French that their casualty rates reflected lack of experience or, worse, sheer incompetence. If British bravery on the Somme in 1916 (Britain's first large-scale engagement in France) had been applauded, yet the British went their own way in Flanders (a duck's march through the mud) and seemed to show that purely British rather than Allied policies were predominant. Numbers of troops and length of front came to dominate Franco-British relations in 1918, at the level of both the politicians and the respective high commands.

Comparing conscription policies in both countries is a very crude measure of military effort. Britain's Royal and merchant navies have to be counted as well. The Chief of Staff of the French Army in Paris claimed in 1918: 'The truth is that the British are not putting their manpower in the fighting line; they are putting them in the Navy, which isn't fighting, and in the coal mines and sending them on nice ships all over the world, but they aren't getting killed'.[3] Yet British merchant mariners *were* being killed, as the losses in tonnage reveal. Britain's merchant shipping deficit, being the net loss of destruction over building, reached almost 2.5 m tons during 1917.[4] These losses meant that over the winter 1917–18 there were great shortages of coal and wheat. At one point in December 1917 the French Army was reduced to 2 days' supply of wheat and flour.[5] The fact that a large portion of French territory, rich in mineral resources and industrial capacity, was occupied by the invader, together with almost the whole of Belgium, rendered the manpower and shipping questions just described even more acute. The shipping question was further complicated by the Americans. It had been hard enough shipping supplies to Russia with Arctic conditions and frozen ports, but the transport of American troops across the Atlantic required not only converted liners and other transports, but also flotillas of destroyer escorts. When American troops did arrive in large numbers, the questions of where and how and with whom they would serve caused difficulties and disagreements.

These considerations underlay the annual tussle over getting the British to extend their front. When Georges Clemenceau became prime minister he collected some French Army statistics. In December 1917 the British held a front of 150 km with 39 divisions, whereas the French held 580 km, using 64 of their 108 divisions for that purpose. According to a French staff study, a more equitable sharing based on the number of divisions in line would require the British to hold 280 km and the French 500 km.[6] Meanwhile London's war cabinet committee on manpower decided that the military's demands for manpower should have lower priority than the naval and air services, shipbuilding and food production.[7]

The first German offensive against British lines in Picardy on 21 March 1918 revived these points of contention. To great acclaim in the American press, Pershing offered the help of American troops to Pétain on 25 March and again, three days later, to the new supreme Allied commander, General Ferdinand Foch. The American people, Pershing declared, "would consider it a great honor for our troops to be engaged in the present battle ... the greatest battle of history".[8] Yet the fact remained that the German pressure was being exerted against British lines in Picardy, and that the American base was in Lorraine in eastern France. Moreover, the total American strength on 31 March 1918 was only 318,621, distributed in six divisions.[9] It was a drop in the ocean of the German crisis.

The fact that a large portion of French territory, rich in mineral resources and industrial capacity, was occupied by the invader, together with almost the whole of Belgium, rendered the manpower and shipping questions just described even more acute. The French were defending their own homes and the British Expeditionary Force was as much an invader as the enemy. Liaison officer Edward Louis Spears never realized fully until war's end 'how irksome the presence of so many allies on their soil' was to the French. 'It came to me as somewhat of a shock', Spears wrote, 'when a French officer, a very great friend of our country, explained to me what an immense feeling of relief it would give him to see the back of us, when France and American-filled Paris would at last be French again. At first I was hurt and thought this ungrateful, but presently I understood what a humiliation it had been to have so many foreigners, richer, who had suffered so much less, so many of whom tended to behave as masters, swarming all over the country'.[10] (Spears would live to experience the 'over-paid, over-sexed, over here' American troops in Britain in World War II.) Furthermore, when American troops began landing at Saint-Nazaire in large numbers in 1917, the same resentments surfaced. By October the sale of strong alcohol to the doughboys had been prohibited following scenes of drunken fighting and looting.[11]

The arrival of the Americans put greater pressure on the Franco-British alliance than was ever caused by the Russian one. The Eastern and Western Fronts had to be coordinated, but were distant, whereas the American presence in France demanded space, supplies and patience. Yet there could be no question that Allies were a necessity rather than a folly at this stage of the war, the start of the war's final year. Indeed they were absolutely vital, but the alliance was beginning to show signs of strain. Paradoxically, the year in which the greatest cooperation occurred – both strategic and logistic – also saw the greatest misunderstandings. Perhaps the huge crisis which imposed that high level of cooperation caused resentment that such cooperation had been required. Given all the problems and difficulties and resentments, it is not surprising that each ally should have remembered what fitted with national sentiment and should have forgotten the relative contributions to the alliance. The following three case studies will illustrate how the resentments of crisis created the post-war narrative of the final year of the war, instead of the real achievements which, after all, did culminate in victory.

German spring offensives, March–July 1918

The first German offensive against British lines in Picardy on 21 March 1918 revived existing points of contention. France's Commander-in-Chief, General Pétain, had had little previous contact with British troops. He had not been alongside the British at Loos in 1915 or on the Somme in 1916. He disapproved of Haig's 1917 Flanders campaign, believing that a British extension of their front would have been more helpful in supporting the French Army. Pétain's attempts to ease French manpower shortages by amalgamating American troops and persuading the British to extend the length of their front dominated his actions during the winter of 1917–18.

If Pétain had little prior knowledge of the British Army, Haig's views of the French Army and its new commander-in-chief were fixed. Already by April 1915, Haig had decided that the French leaders were 'a queer mixture of fair ability (not more than fair) and ignorance of the practical side of war'. After becoming commander-in-chief, he declared: 'Some Frenchmen find it hard to conceal their jealousy of Great Britain. They hate to think that the British Army is on French soil saving France!!'[12] David Lloyd George's sneaky scheme in Calais in February 1917 to subordinate Haig to French command for the next offensive was deeply resented. Indeed, Haig believed that the French, being 'a decadent race', were always 'bound to fail in an offensive'. 'I never thought much of them and I have had a great deal to do with them since the beginning of the war', he told his Scottish Presbyterian chaplain as the French offensive wound down.[13] There had been considerable opposition to Pétain's appointment in May 1917, orchestrated by General Sir Henry Wilson, on the grounds that Pétain represented 'squatting' rather than fighting, and that he favoured waiting for the tanks and the Yanks. Nevertheless, to his surprise, when Haig met Pétain, he found him 'clear-headed and easy to discuss things with'. On 18 May Haig found him 'businesslike, knowledgeable, and brief of speech. The latter a rare quality in Frenchmen!'[14]

Two factors had forced the commanders-in-chief to work together in the winter of 1917–18: French demands, supported by Lloyd George, to extend the British Expeditionary Force's (BEF's) front and the necessity to plan for the expected German offensive in the west after the Treaty of Brest-Litovsk relieved the Central Powers of the need to fight on the Eastern Front. These two factors shaped the events of 1918, especially during the German offensives between March and July. The fact that the two commanders-in-chief reached an agreement on the extension of the BEF's front and on schemes for joint support in the event of a German attack owed less to a good mutual working relationship than to a desire to thwart the plans of the Supreme War Council (SWC). This Council had been set up as a first step towards unified command, and its Executive War Board under General Ferdinand Foch was established to create an allied general reserve. Haig and Pétain refused to provide troops for such a reserve, and they ignored the SWC's decision about the limit of the British extension by agreeing their own.

This then was the situation on 21 March 1918 when the first of Germany's spring offensives against the Allies began: the British and French commanders-in-chief had no experience of collaboration in an emergency; Haig had a low opinion of both Pétain and the French Army; the only collaboration that had occurred had the purpose of defeating Foch's attempts to collect troops for a general reserve; both had resisted making plans for a 1918 campaign and had shown their contempt for the SWC by not communicating such plans as they had drawn up; the British extension of their front had been carried out only under political pressure and the trench defences were so incomplete that one is forced to the conclusion that it was intended to abandon that sector of the front if seriously attacked. Furthermore, the German planning for the offensive included deception to make the French believe that they were being attacked further east. The French would not rush to help the British, so the Germans estimated, until they were sure of their own front.[15]

The historiography of that German attack, Operation Michael, has been remarkably consistent in accepting Haig's version of events.[16] The slightly doctored later typescript of his diary describes Pétain as slow to help the sorely pressed British Fifth Army, as covering Paris instead of maintaining contact with the retreating British, and as being 'in a funk' so that Haig was forced to call on British politicians to come to France and impose 'some plucky general who would fight', namely General Ferdinand Foch. Thus Haig's noble offer to subordinate himself to a French general became the dominant theme, rather than the British collapse, or the retreat to the Channel ports (against instructions that maintaining contact with the French took priority over the ports), or the request for 20 French divisions to cover that retreat.

Since Pétain was not slow to help – indeed he saw the danger before Haig did, thus countering the enemy deception effort – since Pétain had not received orders to cover Paris, and since Haig's call to London was probably invented post hoc, one is forced to wonder how Haig could forget so quickly the vital help that he had received from French troops during the German offensive. Wounded pride provides one reason, but does not explain the historiography. The British official history reproduces Haig's version of events. Hence, on 21 March, Pétain was 'completely convinced' that the attack would come in Champagne, 'therefore delayed sending to the British the assistance which had been arranged'.[17] The French official history does little to counteract this false impression. The volume covering this period is slim, especially when compared to the space devoted to the 1914 Battle of the Marne. It was published very late (1932), because Foch and Pétain kept amending the various drafts, which as a result were consigned to a cupboard until after Foch's death. Even more surprisingly, Guy Pedroncini's study of Pétain's command accepts the Haig version of the events of March 1918. Accordingly, Haig's appeal to London meant that the British acceptance of unified command could be presented as a *political* decision, thereby covering up the *military* defeat that the BEF had suffered.[18]

A second and less well-known example of forgetting is provided by the capture of Mont Kemmel on 25–26 April 1918 during the second German offensive, Operation GEORGETTE, against the British lines in Flanders. To the south of Ypres and protecting the Channel ports lies a chain of low hills, dignified by the name *mont* because the surrounding land is so flat. The highest, most easterly of these hills is Mont Kemmel which was strongly fortified and whose summit provided an excellent vantage point. It had been in Allied hands since 1914 and in April 1918 was defended by General Henry Plumer's Second Army. The same heavy artillery barrage and storm troop tactics that had nearly separated the French and British armies in Picardy in March were repeated in Flanders when GEORGETTE began on 9 April. Once again, the British lines were driven back uncovering the important rail junction of Hazebrouck. Haig issued his famous order of the day on 11 April – 'With our backs to the wall and believing in the justice of our cause, each one of us must fight to the end' – and demanded that more French troops be moved to Flanders. Foch complied in part by moving two French armies to the northern bank of the river Somme, but refused to crowd more troops into the narrow belt between the frontline and the Flanders coast. By this time, the French had only 18 divisions left in line between the Somme and the Oise (more or less the sector that the British had taken over in January and abandoned in March), with a further 46 divisions holding the rest of the front from the Oise to Switzerland.[19]

Haig's nerves were clearly 'stretched' by this second German offensive[20] and by Plumer's withdrawal from the Passchendaele salient that had been won at such enormous cost the previous year. So Haig's 'raging . . . like a schoolboy'[21] because Foch would not send more French troops is understandable – despite the fact that a French army detachment had been created to administer the nine infantry and three cavalry divisions that Pétain had already sent to the north.[22] Pétain was also unhappy at the loss of his reserves to the British. Forty-seven French divisions had been sent to support the BEF at one time or other during the two offensives, and he wrote an angry letter to Foch demanding that 'the British Army and Empire, like the French Army and France' should make up their minds to 'make the *maximum effort*'.[23] One of those French divisions, 28 Division d'Infanterie, took over the defensive lines on Mont Kemmel on 18 April. Although the Flanders offensive had more or less died down, the Germans made a final attack to break through to the coast and attacked the Mont Kemmel lines on 25 April. After a brief but very heavy bombardment using gas, flamethrowers and high explosive shells (worse than before Verdun in 1916, some French declared), the élite Bavarian Alpine Corps assaulted the French lines and overran 28 DI in short order. Seventy minutes later, units of the Alpine Corps were in position on the summit of Mont Kemmel.[24] The hill remained in German hands until the general retirement in the last weeks of the war.

The British reaction was almost of pleasure. Lord Esher (unofficial liaison officer between London and Paris) noted the French loss of Kemmel. 'This will make them less critical of our gallant troops', he wrote, for 'the gossip in Paris has been on the usual lines of depreciation & criticism'. On the other hand, at the British headquarters it was believed that the French had simply run away. Haig was scathing: 'The French have lost Kemmel – a position of extraordinary strength. How they managed it I don't know'.[25] Although a degree of *Schadenfreude* and relief that the disasters were, finally, not all British is understandable, yet Haig's comment in his post-war statement is grotesque: 'between 21st March and 15th April, the French did practically nothing and took no part in the fighting'; and when, finally, French troops took over the Kemmel sector, 'these French troops lost one of the strongest positions on our front and practically made no effort to re-take it'.[26] Haig responded to Foch's three messages on 26 April, offering to come to British headquarters, by stating that there was no reply.[27] Once again, the British official history supports Haig's version of events.

Yet the evidence is clear that the German artillery barrages before launching the Kemmel attack were stupendous. They prevented the re-supply of the defenders with munitions.[28] And, for the French, it was another case of having to fill a gap in the line caused by a British retreat. Captain Henri Desagneaux arrived in the north with his unit on 14 April. The French inhabitants were pleased to see French troops arriving as they had lost confidence in the British. Relations between British and French troops were tense, Desagneaux claimed: roads were lined with enormous British camps, but the men were doing nothing except polish horse brasses and spruce up harnesses.[29] When extracts from the French translation of Haig's diary and papers were published in 1964, some readers were outraged. The British had run away at Kemmel 'like rabbits', one writer claimed.[30]

Despite Haig's scorn, the fighting for Kemmel hill had been fierce. The French memorial on the hill is an ossuary with the remains of 5,294 men, of whom only 57 are identified by name. The casualties for 28 DI who had defended the hill were 4,183 men and 106 officers for 25 April alone, bringing the total casualties for that day plus the preceding 9 days to 5,248 men and 131 officers. As their commanding general reported, the men were extremely tired, but there had been no signs of large numbers having abandoned the battlefield. The division now consisted of no more than 10 companies of men.[31] German casualties too were great (Fourth Army's battalions were reduced to 200–300 men, instead of 750–800),[32] and the enemy was unable to make any further progress. The Germans had planned to push the Allies back as far as the Ypres–Poperinghe line in the initial onslaught, supported by a huge artillery barrage which included guns as large as 42-cm calibre.[33] Yet, if the French had lost Mont Kemmel, it did not mean that the road to the coast was open to the enemy. Ludendorff closed GEORGETTE down on 1 May.

So Haig's resentment at the French loss of Kemmel hill, only weeks after the French saved his bacon in Picardy and only days after his 'backs to the wall' order of the day, reveals how easy it is to forget help offered in an emergency. (Obviously, rescue by troops whom he had qualified as 'a decadent race' the previous year was difficult to accept.) To acknowledge that help had been needed at all constituted a blow to British pride. Indeed, by 9 May when the position had stabilized, the French Military Mission at the British headquarters reported that the British high command was beginning to reflect on events and to regret having given away its independence to a French generalissimo.[34]

Allied counteroffensives

The last months of the war when first Bulgaria and Turkey, then Austria-Hungary and Germany were driven to request an armistice also gave rise to conflicting versions of events. Haig was perfectly sure that the BEF had won the war. There is a widespread British perception that the French Army was too exhausted to do any real fighting in the last offensives that pushed the German troops back through their last defensive lines (the *Hindenburgstellung*) to the Rhine. The fact that the last campaign of the war (coordinated very effectively by a French generalissimo) is frequently called the 'Hundred Days' reveals this point of view. Apart from its Napoleonic overtones recalling Britain and Prussia standing together at Waterloo – and Haig grumbled that Foch thought himself another Napoleon – such an appellation ignores the fact that the victorious final campaign began, not with the Battle of Amiens on 8 August (in itself, this leaves out the Montdidier portion of the battle and the contribution of France's First Army), but on 18 July.

It was on 18 July that the tide turned, a fact that the enemy recognized: the German Army's defence expert, General Fritz von Lossberg, called Foch's counterstroke of that date 'the sharp turning point in the conduct of the war'.[35] The inspiration for the Second Battle of the Marne, the Allied riposte to the final German offensive that had begun 3 days earlier, was French. Foch knew that the moment had come to make a move and he overrode Pétain's caution in suspending preparations for that move. Michael Neiberg has stressed the importance of this decision: it 'made possible something few on the Allied side had even dared to dream in early July: the end of the war in 1918'.[36] Yet this most 'allied' of battles is little remembered. Foch deployed American, British, French and Italian troops during the Second Battle of the Marne, but it is perhaps the battle's very international nature that means that no national army can claim the credit. It does not fit easily into any purely national account of the war.

The final German offensive had begun against French lines east of Paris on 15 July 1918. Building on the gains made during their earlier offensive against the Chemin des Dames in May, the Germans had created a huge salient in the Allied lines, bulging as far south as the river Marne. Between 15 and 18 July, despite desperate fighting to halt their expansion of that salient, the Germans managed to get a foothold on the river's south bank. The Italian II Corps suffered such great casualties that the British XXII Corps was ordered to relieve them. Nonetheless Foch refused to delay his counteroffensive. It was spearheaded by General Charles Mangin's Tenth Army, containing US troops and two further British divisions as well as the French. On the west side of the salient, Tenth Army debouched from the thick forest of Villers-Cotterêts, with Allied aircraft swarming overhead and French Renault tanks buzzing all around. General Berthelot's Fifth Army on the eastern side attempted to force the Germans back across the Marne by capturing the neck of the salient, thereby cutting the few German supply lines. Château Thierry was liberated in just 2 days, and the Germans were pushed right back to where they had started their attacks against the French lines in May. It was a stunning Allied success after the disasters of the earlier German offensives.

It had been a short successful campaign, an all-arms battle using tanks and aircraft. Yet it is the fighting to counter the desperate danger posed by the German salient across the Marne that is remembered, not what should be regarded as the classic international, all-arms success. Haig's post-war notes on the operations of 1918 contain the simple comment that the British 'became involved' on 20 July in the fighting begun by French and American troops 2 days earlier, and the fighting 'lasted until the end of the month'.[37] That it was successful is not mentioned. A British veteran of the campaign, Hubert Essame, remembered only the chaos of the approach to the frontline and the lack of familiarity with the terrain, with French equipment, French methods and the French language. For example, the French 'signal lights designed to indicate the position of the infantry to the artillery unfortunately could not be fixed to the British rifle'. Essame's incredulity might stand as an epitaph for the whole war: 'The virtually complete ignorance, after 4 years of war, of the British and French of each other's language, mentality, organisation and methods, now glaringly apparent, almost surpasses belief'.[38] Moreover, another British officer recalled the 'usual disappointing experiences' because the 'French rank and file were imbued with the idea that we [the British] had let them down when the great German attack of March 1918 broke through. Serious trouble in an estaminet was narrowly averted because of this'.[39]

Foch's role as generalissimo is often forgotten too. He himself downplayed supreme command, and he has left no body of battle plans for later historians and military to study. His style of command relied on personal communication, not the issuance of orders. He understood that he could command only by persuasion. It is, therefore, very easy to underestimate his understated style and to fail to accord the importance it deserves to this battle. Consequently, no scholarly monograph on one of World War I's most important battles appeared before Michael Neiberg's in 2008.

As for earlier historians, Marc Bloch, the great historian who served in the French army throughout the war, was shocked when he read H.G. Wells's *Outline of History*, published in 1920. Wells was no historian, but was influential as a popular writer. Bloch criticized Wells for writing as if there were no French soldiers in France in 1918. Bloch was the intelligence officer for his unit, 72 Régiment d'Infanterie; he was sent to the Amiens area in May 1918 after the German assaults against the British and he was in Villers-Cotterêts between June and July when Foch's counterstroke was prepared. He spent October in the Argonne and early November in Lorraine where the Franco-American offensives took place. In 1922, he wrote of Wells' book:

> I imagine that no-one in France would quibble over the contribution of each of our allies to the common victory . . . all the same, what to feel about an account of a campaign in which the last German offensive . . . and the victorious march that followed three days later are summed up thus: 'The battle of Château-Thierry (July 18th) proved the quality of new *American* armies. In August the *British* opened a great and successful thrust . . . Early in November, *British* troops were in Valenciennes and *Americans* in Sedan'? In truth, if one had not been there oneself, one would doubt whether there had been any French soldiers in that tragic summer and autumn fighting on our soil.[40]

The logistics of supply

Finally, it was not only the fighting that led to forgetfulness and reinterpretation. The two German offensives against the British lines had been resisted at enormous cost and with considerable French assistance, much as Haig preferred not to acknowledge the debt. The costs included a huge casualty bill, which forced Britain to tighten conscription, and a pronounced skewing of French reserves northwards – and British acceptance of a French generalissimo. These costs led to further strains in the coalition: what was the best use of the only major source of fresh manpower, America? And what were the implications of the costs of transporting that manpower across the Atlantic and providing weapons and equipment, at the possible expense of steel and raw material imports for munitions production, not to mention food imports?

The differing British and French manpower policies led to prime ministerial squabbling between Georges Clemenceau and David Lloyd

George. A French expert crossed the Channel to investigate the War Office's procedures, concluding that the British did not conscript enough men (compared with the French) and did not use efficiently those men that they did conscript. Lloyd George retorted that British sailors were being killed while ensuring that food and raw materials were delivered to France and that British ships were transporting American soldiers to France who were then serving in French sectors.[41]

American manpower depended on shipping. The German resumption of unrestricted submarine warfare in February 1917 was one of the factors that forced President Woodrow Wilson's hand in his decision for war, and the submarine nearly brought the Entente Allies to their knees, as Germany intended. The German aim was to destroy 600,000 gross tons of shipping per month, a rate exceeded in the first 4 months of the campaign. April 1917 was the worst month. During the two worst weeks, one in four ocean-going ships leaving British ports did not return.[42] Such losses forced cooperation, and an Inter-Allied Maritime Transport Council was created with programme committees and mechanisms for allocating priorities.

The main role in the war against the submarine fell to the British. France's navy had already fallen behind those of Britain and Germany by 1914, and France's main naval effort consisted of convoying troops, labourers and supplies from North Africa and Indo-China. Naval dockyards were converted to produce munitions for the army, so shipping losses to submarines in the Mediterranean could not be replaced.

Because French energies were concentrated on the land war on their own national territory, they were able to forget the naval effort that Britain was making. In British eyes, the French simply did not appreciate the difficulties in convoying American troop transports across the Atlantic. As Lord Esher remarked: 'They never have and never will appreciate or understand the meaning of the sea . . . These politicians and soldiers omit from their calculations all questions of freight and the submarine menace'.[43] Henry Wilson proclaimed that the French believed that sea was a smooth, flat and safe surface along which divisions and their supplies could be moved like draughts across a draughtboard.[44]

There had been no glorious Trafalgar in this war, only the inconclusive 1916 Battle of Jutland. The fact that thereafter the *Hochseeflotte* never ventured forth was for the Royal Navy a negative victory that had no propaganda potential to be exploited. Deliveries of coal for French railways and factories (e.g. Britain shipped 13.3 m tons to France in the 10 months of April 1918 to January 1919)[45] or of Canadian wheat for French bakeries were equally lacking in propaganda appeal. Indeed, the vital contribution of shipping to the Allied war effort was never fully recognized. Enemy action sank or damaged almost 5,000 British merchant vessels and 1,069 Royal Navy warships and auxiliaries, not counting neutral tonnage.[46]

Perhaps only one French minister – Commerce Minister Etienne Clémentel – fully recognized that 'la guerre, c'est le shipping'. He helped to create the vast logistics bureaucracy to manage supplies of wheat, sugar, coal and a multitude of other foodstuffs and metals. One can only speculate as to why this has left little trace on French memory of the war. One reason may be that French hopes for continuing economic cooperation after the war were dashed, and this perhaps made it easy to forget the vital financial, commercial and transportation help that Britain had provided during the war years.

Already in July 1918, while the last German offensive and first Allied counteroffensive were taking place in France, Clémentel and his commerce ministry officials began elaborating a wide-ranging plan to reorganize world trade and establish a new economic world order – much as President Wilson wished to do in the political and diplomatic sphere. An Allied economic union would be formed to counteract the German-dominated *Mitteleuropa* that existed following Germany's repressive treaty with Russia signed in March 1918 in Brest-Litovsk. Such a union would have at its core Allied control of raw materials with preferential tariffs, thereby protecting French industry from a post-war invasion (or dumping) of German finished goods. This economic union fitted Clémentel's hopes for the League of Nations concept. He urged that 'the complete reconstruction of Northern France and Belgium' was essentially 'everyone's business, the primordial task of the economic league of free peoples'.[47] Despite the support of Clemenceau and despite much energy expended during October by Clémentel and Jean Monnet, the minister's delegate in London, the war came to an end before the committee to control raw materials could be established.

Nor could it be revived during the treaty negotiations. The British Treasury representative, J.M. Keynes, sniffed that it was wrong to have an Allied body 'sit in judgment on the international distribution of British Empire supplies of wool or jute or tin or rubber. The French, on the other hand, mainly with an eye, in our opinion, on postbellum developments have made strong efforts to establish Inter-Allied Executives in just such cases'.[48] And Herbert Hoover, the American Food Administrator, refused to accept 'any programme that even looks like inter-Allied control of our economic resources after peace'.[49] France was similarly denied support from former allies in enforcing the reparation schedules that had been drawn up after much discussion and frequent modifications. Thus the 'new economic order' went the same way as the military guarantee that the US Senate failed to ratify and that Lloyd George (by deliberate sleight of hand?) withdrew from in consequence.

It is ironic that the same Jean Monnet who had tried so hard to create Allied post-war control of raw materials should have been the prime mover in events in the 1950s after a second world war. Instead of Britain, France and the United States, the 1950s' alignment saw Germany within the system and Britain without, an alignment confirmed by de Gaulle's veto of Harold Macmillan's application to join the European Economic Community in January 1963 – which only increases the irony.

Conclusion

Perhaps the rapid advance of forgetfulness, sped by the acrimony of the peace negotiations, is the most surprising aftermath of the Entente alliance's 1918 push to victory. Yet perhaps too the difficulty of continuing such an alliance reflects simply human emotions, given the price paid in blood and treasure. Just as marriages often fail after a tragedy such as the loss of a child, so too the nations that had managed to secure victory in 1918 found it too difficult to maintain the relationship after that victory had been sealed by a peace treaty. A Quai d'Orsay official used the marriage analogy when writing to a Foreign Office colleague in 1921: Britain and France were 'an old married couple going through a crisis'. His correspondent agreed that the two countries resembled a married couple, but rather they formed a 'young couple' who were 'incompatible', but who had to stay together for the sake of the children.[50]

Yet continuance of a Franco-British alliance would have constituted the world's strongest military force and the dominant power in Europe. Britain's Foreign Secretary stated in December 1921 that 'a combination of Great Britain and France would be so strong that no other likely combination could successfully resist it'.[51] The supreme Allied commander himself understood this. The British military attaché in Paris reported in January 1922 that Foch was 'anxious about the future – if only England & France hold together all will be well, if not the deluge'.[52] Foch himself never forgot. His statue in London's Grosvenor Square, near Victoria Station, is engraved with his words: 'I am conscious of having served England as I served my own country'.

By the mid-1930s, however, it became politic to remember the 1914–18 alliance, yet the popular and remarkably tenacious (mis)conceptions of a flighty France and a selfish Britain remained. In London in 1935, Marshal Pétain spoke at a banquet held by the Associations Unies France–Grande-Bretagne, recalling those days:

> The hill was hard to climb, and because we climbed it together, side by side we climbed to the top . . . Then peace came. You returned to the sea, leaving 800,000 dead on our soil. Victorious we parted, but we had got to know each other: the Briton persuaded that French flightiness [légèreté] could become tenacity; the Frenchman henceforth convinced that Britain knew how to take its share of sacrifices.[53]

Even allowing for the venue and the audience, which meant that compliments were in order, nonetheless Pétain evoked the separation in victory. It is a shame that the truly international and all-arms success of the 18 July 1918 counterstroke on the Marne enforced by a French generalissimo, intelligent enough to deal successfully with his allies, has not become the lodestone of remembrance, but rather either the near catastrophes of the German offensives or else the British (and the Australians and Canadians) at Amiens – not even Amiens-Montdidier.

It is an even greater shame that the huge, essentially bureaucratic success of the international logistic solutions found for transport and supply in 1918 has been almost entirely forgotten. The French head of logistics during the war, General Payot, remembered that although the Allies had been willing to share the fighting, they were not willing to share their wealth. In the report on the Allied logistics effort of the war, Payot used the family analogy again: if, as happens among members of the same family, the Allies did not hesitate to shed their blood together, he said, nevertheless 'they showed less eagerness to divide their resources'.[54] Yet the French had the opportunity to realize how much British coal, for example, meant to the war effort when Germany defaulted on its coal deliveries. In 1919 France was warned that supplies would be insufficient for French homes and industry right through to 1921.[55]

The mutual lack of comprehension stemmed from geography. Haig's official biographer, A. Duff Cooper, had omitted references to Haig's dislike and mistrust of the French, because in the 1930s such references might harm Franco-British relations.[56] Such feelings derived from the sense of superiority provided by the (English) Channel. The British Empire protected by its navy was helping the 'decadent' French to expel the invader. Haig's predecessor, Sir John French, had already expressed similar condescension in his memoir of 1914, published in 1919. He wondered whether Napoleon would 'not have rejoiced at this friendly invasion of France by England's "good yeomen," who were now offering their lives to save France from possible destruction as a Power of the first class'.[57] As a counterpoint to such sentiments, the words of the wife of the French doctor and writer, Georges Duhamel, might be cited. Blanche Duhamel watched British soldiers singing on their way to the battlefields of the Somme in 1916 and pondered why she was impressed but not moved: 'Is it really because they were not our troops? \ I have wept over so many departures already! But there I was merely curious. Why?'[58]

In 1918 the facts of invasion and occupation affected only the French. In 1942 another French writer, Georges Bernanos who had been a volunteer during World War I, published an open letter to the British which makes this point elegantly.

> I would not allow myself to speak of our former Victory, dear British, if I believed, despite having won it together, that it was truly a common victory, but I have never believed that. No doubt we paid the same price in blood and tears. But I wonder whether it ever had the same conscious meaning. Today you know what it is, a war for hearth and home. This war is your war. We pretended to share the other one with you . . . yet deep down we were convinced that it was ours alone . . . With your

well-to-do uniforms, your sparkling harnesses . . . [we French] took you for the sons of lords of the manor who come down to give a hand, out of the kindness of their hearts, on the day of the harvest.[59]

The fact of fighting on French soil, the fact of invasion and enemy occupation perhaps made it inevitable that French soldiers should consider the maritime nation and long-time enemy as partly detached and somewhat condescending. And British pride in having created a continental army and having defeated the enemy perhaps made it equally inevitable that from Haig down the British should have forgotten that the French bore the burden of the fighting for 2 years before that army was ready to join the fray.

Notes

1 'Pertes des armées françaises', cited in P. Guinard, J.-C. Devos and J. Nicot, *Inventaire sommaire des archives de la guerre Série N 1871–1919* (Troyes: Imprimerie de la Renaissance, 1975), t. 1 *Introduction*, p. 213.

2 Guinard, Devos and Nicot, *Inventaire sommaire des archives*, t. 1, p. 201. This figure includes, of course, many who were wounded more than once or who returned to the front and were killed there.

3 Lloyd Griscom, lecture on 'Liaison' delivered to Army War College, Washington, DC, 30 April 1940, p. 3, File # WP–1940–H5, US Army War College Curricular Archives, US Army Military History Institute, Carlisle Barracks.

4 Elizabeth Greenhalgh, *Victory Through Coalition: Britain and France during the First World War* (Cambridge: Cambridge University Press, 2005), p. 267.

5 Ibid, p. 269.

6 'Extension du front anglais', 20 December 1917, Clemenceau papers, 6N 166, [d]5, Service Historique de la Défense, Armée de Terre, Vincennes [SHD/T]; 'Extension du front anglais', 1 December 1917, ibid.

7 Cabinet Committee on Man-Power, Draft Report, December 1917, fo. 31, CAB 27/14, The National Archives, Kew [TNA].

8 John J. Pershing, *My Experiences in the World War*, 2 vols (New York: Frederick A. Stokes Company, 1931), 1: 365.

9 Ibid., 373.

10 E.L. Spears, *Prelude to Victory* (London: Jonathan Cape, 1939), p. 63.

11 Yves-Henri Nouailhat, 'L'Opinion publique à l'égard des Américains à Saint-Nazaire en 1917', *Revue d'Histoire Moderne et Contemporaine* 15, 1 (1968), 97–102, at 100.

12 Haig diary, 24 April 1915, 20 February 1916, WO 256/4 and 256/8, TNA.

13 Diary, Reverend George S. Duncan, 29 April 1917, in Alan J. Guy, R.N.W. Thomas and Gerard J. DeGroot (eds), *Military Miscellany* (Stroud: Sutton Publishing/Army Records Society, 1997), vol. I, p. 349.

14 Haig diary, 3 and 18 May 1917, WO 256/18, TNA.

15 Major a.D. Otto Fehr, *Die Märzoffensiv 1918 an der Westfront Strategie oder Taktik? Eine Studie auf Grund amtlichen Materials* (Leipzig: Kohler, 1921), pp. 25–6.

16 See Elizabeth Greenhalgh, 'Myth and Memory: Sir Douglas Haig and the Imposition of Allied Unified Command in March 1918', *Journal of Military History* 68 (2004), 771–820.

17 Brigadier-General Sir James E. Edmonds, *Military Operations France and Belgium, 1918*, 5 vols (London/Nashville, TN: Imperial War Museum/Battery Press, 1993–95), vol. II, p. 461.

18 Guy Pedroncini, *Pétain Général en Chef (1917–1918)* (Paris: PUF, 1974), pp. 332–5.

19 Greenhalgh, *Victory Through Coalition*, p. 204.

20 J.P. Harris, *Douglas Haig and the First World War* (Cambridge: Cambridge University Press, 2008), p. 470.

21 Spears diary, 14 April 1918, Spears papers, SPRS 5/17, Churchill Archives Centre, Cambridge [CAC].

22 Elizabeth Greenhalgh, *Foch in Command: The Forging of a First World War General* (Cambridge: Cambridge University Press, 2011), p. 316.

23 *Les Armées Françaises dans la Grande Guerre*, 103 vols (Paris: Imprimerie Nationale, 1932–38), tome 6, vol. 1 [AFGG 6/1], annex 1906, original emphasis.

24 Edmonds, *Military Operations 1918*, vol. II, pp. 410–13.

25 Esher diary, 27 April 1918, ESHR2/21, CAC; letter, Haig to Lady Haig, 25 April 1918, Haig mss, acc. 3155, no. 150, National Library of Scotland [NLS].

26 'Notes on the Operations on Western Front after Sir D. Haig became Commander in Chief 1915', 30 January 1920, Haig mss, acc. 3155, no. 213a, fo. 63, NLS.

27 Foch's three messages in AFGG 6/1, annexes 1984, 1986, 1988.

28 AFGG 6/1, 498.

29 Henri Desagneaux, *Journal de guerre 14–18* (Paris: Denoël, 1971), pp. 194, 196.

30 *Le Nouvel Candide*, 26–27 February 1964.

31 General Madelin to commander II Cavalry Corps, 26 April 1918, AFGG 6/1, annex 2018.

32 Fourth Army war diary, 28 April 1918, in René Tournès and Henry Berthemet, *La Bataille des Flandres d'après le journal de marche et les archives de la IVe Armée Allemande* (Paris: Charles Lavauzelle, 1925), p. 355.

33 Fritz von Lossberg, *Meine Tätigkeit im Weltkriege* (Berlin: Mittler, 1939), p. 339.

34 Report # 7077, 9 May 1918, 17N 348, SHD/T.

35 Lossberg, *Meine Tätigkeit*, p. 351.

36 Michael S. Neiberg, *The Second Battle of the Marne* (Bloomington/Indianapolis: Indiana University Press, 2008), p. 181. See also Robert A. Doughty, *Pyrrhic Victory: French Strategy and Operations in the Great War* (Cambridge, MA: The Belknap Press of Harvard University Press, 2005), pp. 467–73.

37 'Notes on the Operations on Western Front after Sir D. Haig became Commander in Chief 1915', 30 January 1920, Haig mss, acc. 3155, no. 213a, fo. 68, NLS.

38 H. Essame, *The Battle for Europe 1918* (London: B.T. Batsford, 1972), p. 97.

39 G.B. Daubeny to official historian, 19 June 1933, CAB 45/131, TNA.

40 Marc Bloch, 'Une nouvelle histoire universelle: H.G. Wells historien', *Revue de Paris*, 15 August 1922, 860–74, at p. 872. Bloch's emphasis.

41 See Elizabeth Greenhalgh, 'David Lloyd George, Georges Clemenceau, and the 1918 Manpower Crisis', *Historical Journal*, 50, 2 (2007), 397–421.

42 See Greenhalgh, *Victory Through Coalition*, 120–1. See also David Stevenson's recent study which emphasizes the crucial importance of logistics, *With our Backs to the Wall: Victory and Defeat in 1918* (London: Allen Lane, 2011), especially ch. 3.

43 Letter to wife, 23 April 1917, in M. and O. Brett (eds), *Journals and Letters of Reginald Viscount Esher*, 4 vols (London: Ivor Nicholson & Watson Ltd, 1934–38), vol. IV, p. 108.

44 Peter Wright, *At the Supreme War Council* (London: Eveleigh Nash & Grayson, 1921), p. 40.

45 Arthur S. Salter, *Allied Shipping Control: An Experiment in International Administration* (Oxford: Clarendon Press, 1921), p. 360, table 7.

46 Tables A–C, 'Merchant Shipping (Losses), 1914–18', and 'Summary of Losses—Warships', and 'Summary of Losses of Auxiliary Vessels', in *British Vessels Lost at Sea 1914–18 and 1939–45* (Wellingborough: Patrick Stephens, 1988, reprint of HMSO 1919 publication), pp. 162–4, 7, 28.

47 Marc Trachtenberg, *Reparation in World Politics: France and European Economic Diplomacy 1916–1923* (New York: Columbia University Press, 1980), pp. 10–20.

48 Elizabeth Johnson (ed.), *The Collected Writings of John Maynard Keynes 1883–1946*, 29 vols (London/New York: Macmillan/St. Martin's Press, for the Royal Economic Society, 1971–83), vol. XVI, pp. 289–90.

49 Trachtenberg, *Reparation*, 23.

50 Jacques Seydoux to Sydney Waterlow, 30 November 1921, and Waterlow to Seydoux, 6 December 1921, cited in Sally Marks, 'Mésentente Cordiale: The Anglo-French Relationship, 1921–1922', in Marta Petricioli (ed.), *Une Occasion Manquée? 1922: La Reconstruction de l'Europe* (Bern: Peter Lang, 1995), pp. 33–45, at pp. 36–7. Marks uses the marriage metaphor throughout the article.

51 Lord Curzon, cited in Alan Sharp and Keith Jeffery, '"Après la guerre finit, Soldat anglais partit . . . ": Anglo-French relations, 1918–25', in Erik Goldstein and B.J.C. McKercher (eds), *Power and Stability: British Foreign Policy, 1865–1965* (London/Portland, OR: Frank Cass, 2003), pp. 119–38, at p. 120.

52 Sackville-West [military attaché, Paris] to Henry Wilson, 2 January 1922, in Keith Jeffery (ed.), *The Military Correspondence of Field Marshal Sir Henry Wilson 1918–1922* (London: The Bodley Head/Army Records Society, 1985), pp. 219, 330.

53 Printed brochure of Pétain's speech in Spears papers, SPRS 1/266, CAC.

54 Military Board of Allied Supply, *The Allied Armies under Marshal Foch in the Franco-Belgian Theater of Operations*, 2 vols (Washington, DC: Government Printing Office, 1924–25), vol. I, p. 263.

55 Minister for Reconstruction Louis Loucheur to Chamber of Deputies, 18 October 1919, cited in Benjamin F. Martin, *France and the Après Guerre, 1918–1924: Illusions and Disillusionment* (Baton Rouge: Louisiana State University Press, 1999), p. 30.

56 John Charmley, *Duff Cooper: The Authorized Biography* (London: Weidenfeld and Nicolson, 1986), pp. 73–4.

57 Field-Marshal Viscount French of Ypres, K.P., O.M., etc, *1914* (London: Constable, 1919), 32.

58 Letter, 4 September 1916, in Georges et Blanche Duhamel, *Correspondance de guerre 1914–1919*, 2 vols (Paris: Honoré Champion, 2007), vol. I, p. 1198.

59 Georges Bernanos, *Lettre aux Anglais* (Paris: Gallimard, 1946 [3rd French edition]) p. 44.

PART TWO

The Second World War

Introduction

Akhila Yechury and Emile Chabal

The Second World War was a global conflict. Not only were the theatres of war spread from the deserts of North Africa to the islands of the South Pacific, but the war also touched a vast number of people all over the world. This was very largely because the war coincided with the apogee of European imperialism.[1] In retrospect, we can clearly discern the roots of decolonization in the interwar period but, at the time, there was little doubt that empire would be crucial to military success. This was something that the two key Axis powers clearly understood: Japanese expansion in East Asia and the Nazi occupation of Europe were integral to the ideology and strategy of both states. They wanted to have access to the natural resources, territorial security and manpower that were seen to be the greatest assets of empire. Mussolini, too, realized that empire was a precondition for great power status. The conquest of Ethiopia in 1935–36 – and the diplomatic crisis it caused – signalled Italy's rapprochement with Nazi Germany and was a reminder of the significance of empire for national pride, as well as the strategic role it might play in a future war effort.[2]

Of course, the Axis powers were merely trying to emulate the two greatest imperial powers of the age: France and Britain. Even if there is a vibrant historiographical debate about the extent to which the British and French people knew or cared about their empires, there can be no doubt that, in the two centuries preceding World War II, Franco-British relations were thoroughly 'globalized'. Indeed, by the twentieth century, confrontations outside Europe were as significant as those inside Europe: while France's greatest military humiliation at the hands of the British in the early nineteenth century was against Wellington at Waterloo in Flanders, the most vivid clash between the two powers at the end of the century was in 1898 at Fashoda, deep in the heart of central Africa.[3] The importance of empire had not diminished by the 1930s. Tens of thousands of colonial soldiers had fought (and died) in the trenches during World War I, and the changing geopolitics of the interwar years saw the French and British cling tightly to their empires as a sign of their military might and independence from the United States.[4] It was inevitable, then, that the two empires would be immediately drawn into World War II – and that some of the most acute Franco-British disagreements would take place, not in Paris or London, but in North Africa, Madagascar or Syria.

The inextricable relationship between colony and metropole meant that many of the processes, events and reactions that are discussed in the following three chapters were reflected in confrontations across the imperial world. The sense of French betrayal after Dunkirk, so vividly described by Martin Alexander, had its counterpart in the reaction to the sinking of the French fleet at Mers-el-Kébir, which had a decisive impact on France's African colonies. Sébastien Albertelli's chapter on the Special Operations Executive (SOE) highlights the 'highly unbalanced relationship' between the British and the Free French but, again, this had its echoes across the empires. As Martin Thomas puts it, '. . . the British were paymasters, arms providers, shippers and couriers to the Free French for much of the war'.[5] The British contributions to the invasions of the Levant and Madagascar, as well as British assistance with intelligence operations in Asia, were only the most obvious examples of the subservience of the Free French. Finally, the selective politics of memory described by Olivier Wieviorka in his chapter on the liberation of France is paralleled in the ways in which the British and French manipulated their empires to suit their (diminishing) post-war roles. In all three cases, processes that appear to belong to a European narrative of the war were reflected in events outside Europe. Thus, far from being marginal incidents in a larger ideological struggle for the future of Europe, events in the colonies have the potential to shed new light on the more familiar story of Franco-British conflict and cooperation in World War II.

Imperial entanglements: Suspicion, hostility and dependence

'C'est une tradition: la France fait des colonies pour que John Bull les lui prenne . . . '

Victor Bérard (1900)[6]

The fall of France in June 1940 left the French empire in an awkward position. It was no longer clear what it meant to be 'loyal' to France and there were now two claimants to the imperial throne: Pétain's Vichy government and de Gaulle's Free France. As a number of historians have argued, Vichy needed an empire in order to demonstrate its nominal independence from Nazi influence and restore a sense of national grandeur.[7] Pétain and his advisers knew that France's imperial possessions were one of the few bargaining chips they could use against the Germans and Italians. Securing the empire was, therefore, a major priority. The problem was that, as soon as de Gaulle launched his *appel* on 18 June, Free France also put the empire at the heart of its foreign policy. For an exiled government, an imperial Free France was one of the few plausible signs of legitimacy and manpower. In the absence of any authority inside metropolitan France, it became vital for de Gaulle to secure as many imperial possessions as possible in order to negotiate effectively with the British. For those stationed in the colonies, this question of double allegiance was a logistical and political headache. While a number of French colonial officials may not have liked the idea of the armistice, it was signed by a legitimate government given its powers by the elected National Assembly. As a result, in the weeks following the armistice, there was generalized confusion about who was in charge – a confusion that, until the end of the war, reflected both the changing fortunes of Vichy France and the vagaries of the Franco-British relationship.

One factor which went a long way in determining colonial allegiance to de Gaulle or Pétain was Anglophobia and the fear that the British were intent on undermining or taking over the French empire, just as they had stolen Québec and Mauritius earlier.[8] This abstract concern was made very real by the sinking of the French fleet stationed at Mers-el-Kébir on 3 July 1940, an event which became something of an 'imperial Dunkirk' and a compelling propaganda coup for the Vichy government.[9] The immediate sense of bitterness and betrayal – coming so soon after the Dunkirk retreat and the fall of France – was to be the first major catalyst for a realignment of imperial allegiances across the French Empire. In Madagascar and Afrique Occidentale Française (AOF), Mers-el-Kébir proved to be the turning point in the affirmation of support for Vichy instead of de Gaulle.[10] In French Indochina, too, the attack had a negative effect on both colonial authorities and settlers who, after a period of notional resistance to the Vichy regime, finally fell in line in July 1940.[11]

This growing sense of Anglophobia was given further credence after the botched British and Free French attack on Dakar on 23–25 September 1940. De Gaulle had persuaded the British that the principal city of AOF could be easily captured and that the authority of Free France would be widely accepted. In the event, the operation was a military failure which confirmed the willingness of local French forces to defend Vichy's colonial control and widespread sympathy for Pétain among the settler community.[12] The only meagre success for de Gaulle in the months following the armistice was in Afrique Équatoriale Française (AEF), where a small Free French delegation persuaded the Governor-Generals in Cameroon and Congo to change sides. But even here, in a pattern that would be repeated throughout the war years, the British were necessary partners and alibis for the Free French: the rallying of AEF was very largely because the British agreed to secure local banks against a sterling reserve and purchase local produce.

If relations between the British and the Vichy government were openly hostile – there was a deluge of anti-British propaganda in the wake of Mers-el-Kébir and the British embargo of Vichy overseas territories – the interaction with de Gaulle was almost as fraught, especially when it came to imperial policy. This was immediately apparent in the British and Free French invasion of the Levant in June 1941. The British had identified Vichy-controlled Syria and Lebanon as a major strategic threat; it was feared that they would provide access points for Axis forces into the Middle East. De Gaulle, meanwhile, came to see the Levant as a major 'prize' for the Free French and a potential base from which to launch the Resistance. This divergence of opinion was laid bare in a conversation with the British General Spears: "You think I am interested in England winning the war? I am not', [said de Gaulle], 'I am only interested in France's victory'. 'They are the same', I retorted. 'Not at all', he answered, 'not at all in my view'."[13] Ultimately, the joint invasion was a success and a Free French administration was installed. But, as Gaunson has argued, the profound disagreements surrounding the invasion marked the beginning of the acrimonious rift between de Gaulle and Churchill that would define wartime relations between the two allies.[14] At the same time, the invasion was a particularly poignant example of the complex allegiances on the ground, with many Algerian troops and *tirailleurs sénégalais* used as the first line of defence for the Vichy forces, and several units of Indian soldiers fighting alongside the British.[15] For these colonial soldiers – and the local populations they conquered – the differences between Vichy, Free France and Britain were not nearly as clear-cut as they were in Europe, and yet they played a crucial role in the strategy of all three powers.

The growing suspicion and hostility between the British and the Free French was made plain in two other diplomatic incidents: the St Pierre and Miquelon affair and the invasion of Madagascar. The unilateral occupation by Free French forces of the tiny islands of St Pierre and Miquelon off the Canadian coast in December 1941 came shortly after the tensions over the occupation of the Levant. It, therefore, provoked a quarrel out of all proportion to the strategic importance of the islands since the British and Americans saw Free French actions as a potentially dangerous breach of diplomatic protocol. This in turn confirmed de Gaulle's belief that the Allies did not take the Free French seriously and could not be relied upon for support.[16] Already, memories were diverging: in Gaullist myth, the invasion became a moment of Free French self-determination, while the British and Americans saw only the French general's stubbornness and intransigence. These differences were to have a direct impact on British plans to reclaim control of Madagascar, which had rallied to Vichy in 1940. With the fall of Singapore in February 1942, the island took on a renewed strategic significance as a base for British operations in the Indian Ocean and East Asia. The British were aware that de Gaulle had been pushing for an invasion for some time and wanted to instal a Free French administration on the island, but because of their hostility towards him, they kept him almost entirely in the dark about their own plans. When the British finally invaded in May 1942, they did so without Free French knowledge. Even though a Free French administration was, in the end, set up under Legentilhomme, the whole episode merely provided further proof – to both Vichy and Free France – that the British could not be trusted.[17]

It is important to remember, however, that this suspicion was hardly a phenomenon specific to the unusual context of World War II: the empire had long been a privileged site of Franco-British conflict. As much as anything, it was the memory of past betrayals and perfidy that structured French and British perceptions of each other overseas. Thus, even projects of an explicitly cooperative nature were viewed with scepticism – if not hostility. The five *comptoirs* of French India are a telling case study of these long-standing differences. As very minor but potentially threatening enemy territories scattered across the British Raj, French India was heavily pressured by the British to back de Gaulle in September 1940. Subsequently, Gaullists made much of the fact that French India was one of the first colonies 'spontaneously' to declare its support for de Gaulle.[18] In reality, it was the extreme economic and strategic dependence of the French on the British that tipped the balance – just as it had in AEF.[19] Given the circumstances, British attempts to secure and protect the territories in 1941 by offering a customs union and military aid to the French were greeted with cautious optimism by the Governor General of French India, Louis Bonvin, but British reports nevertheless claimed that propaganda had emerged in Pondicherry that accused the British of wanting the 'débâcle de l'Empire française'.[20] Even in a situation of unequivocal dependence, it seemed that the French still intended to cling on to their battered imperial pride.

Of course, a closer relationship with the British government in India could have myriad advantages. One of these was economic, with the Government of India facilitating trade between India, Syria and Lebanon. In the absence of exact trade figures it is hard to estimate the flow of trade, but official correspondence suggests that, by 1942, India had become an important 'source of supply' for Syria and Lebanon.[21] The British also helped to organize Free French propaganda. In 1941, when the Publicity Office of the Ministry of External Affairs was established in Delhi, a French section was created within it. The responsibility of this section was to spread 'British propaganda in the French language' among 'French speaking communities and individuals' and to spread 'Free French propaganda'. In addition the Free French in India were allowed to make regular radio broadcasts from Bombay.[22] Whether there was a greater design behind helping the Free French in India is unclear. It is possible that the British wanted to use this propaganda to counter incoming Japanese pamphlets in India and in Indochina. Or it may have been simply an exercise to strengthen the war effort. Whatever the reason, in offering such comprehensive assistance, the Government of India ensured that the Free French in India developed external links with other parts of the French and British empires. Here, as elsewhere, Franco-British cooperation provided the Free French with a platform to which they simply could not aspire had they been working alone.

This pattern of dependence, mutual cooperation and resentment was reproduced in the relations between the Free French secret service and the Special Operations Executive (SOE) in Asia in 1943–45. The main focus of attention was Indochina but, again, de Gaulle's men were entirely dependent on British infrastructure. Their base was in New Delhi and they relied on British air drops to supply the limited clandestine operations they pursued both before and after the Japanese coup in March 1945. However, operations on the ground were hopelessly ineffective, especially because the Free French refused to work with local resistance movements, the largest of which was the Vietminh. Moreover, the Free French were subservient to the Americans, who considered them to be little better than an aging, ineffectual and morally objectionable imperial power. American clandestine support for Ho Chi Minh merely confirmed this view. In the face of such difficulties, it can be hard to understand the logic behind maintaining a specifically Free French secret service unit. We can only understand this if we realize that, as in the case of French India, the reasons were more symbolic than practical. The aim was to preserve French grandeur and stake a claim to a post-war imperial future in Indochina.[23] The disastrous return to French rule after 1946 confirmed that little thought had been given about how to manage the colony; it was needed, above all, to restore French territorial pride. In this respect at least, the difference between Vichy and post-war French administrations was slight.[24]

These varied examples of encounters between French and British soldiers, officials and colonial subjects across the globe remind us that the story of Franco-British relations during World War II must incorporate a global dimension. The myths, memories and conflicts that are the subject of the subsequent three chapters found echoes in locations as far apart as St Pierre et Miquelon and Pondicherry. In the same way that Dunkirk marked a point of sharply diverging memories between the two metropolitan powers, Mers-el-Kébir inaugurated a period in which the empire played a vital role in shaping the future of both nations. Over the next 4 years, complex triangular relationships between Vichy, Free France and Britain made the empire an unusually rich site of Franco-British confrontation and cooperation. These interactions were also crucial in defining Franco-British relations after the war. The empire may have been a distant, exotic space for those living in France and Britain at the end of the war, but it was to cast a long shadow over a devastated Europe.

Imperial pride and post-war decline

On 25 May 1945, Gaston Monnerville – a black député from French Guiana – proclaimed in the Provisional Assembly that 'sans l'Empire, la France ne serait qu'un pays libéré. Grâce à son Empire, la France est un pays vainqueur'. He was not alone. The entire French political class – from ardent Communists to committed Gaullists – praised the role of the empire and its vital importance for France. As one socialist put it, the empire was the only thing that stopped France from 'falling to the level of Portugal'.[25] In retrospect, we can see just how much the French underestimated the degree of opposition to colonial rule. The struggle to restore French imperial control in the decades following the war resulted in protracted and terrifying violence in Indochina and Algeria. But the roots of this French hubris and myopia can, at least in part, be explained by wartime experiences and interactions with the British.

In the case of de Gaulle, the empire was a vital bargaining tool: stranded in exile on British soil, an imagined imperial resistance was to be the beginning of a domestic resistance to Nazi occupation during the war and to Anglo-American hegemony after the war. This strong belief in the strategic value of empire is not surprising, given that the Catholic and conservative milieu in which de Gaulle was brought up was strongly marked by tales of British imperial deceit at Fashoda.[26] Many of those in France who feared (and admired) the power of the 'Anglo-Saxon world' during the Third Republic did so precisely because of Britain and America's imperial reach.[27] As Robert Frank points out in his contribution, this sense of threat was exacerbated by territorial losses and occupation during World War II. The empire was the only means to secure the post-war future: a Gaullist France had to be an imperial France. Of course, with de Gaulle's withdrawal from politics in 1946, it was left to his ill-fated Fourth Republic successors to pursue France's faltering imperial dreams.[28] Where the British succeeded in letting go of parts of their empire in the 1940s and 50s (although not without significant violence), the French held on in an attempt to guarantee geopolitical parity with their former wartime allies.

But the wartime Vichy and Free French policy of prioritizing empire primarily as a symbolic site of loyalty or resistance – and refusing to countenance nationalist demands in North Africa, the Levant or Indochina – left a legacy of bitter resentment. Moreover, as David Reynolds and Olivier Wieviorka remind us, the rise of the United States fundamentally altered the global balance of power. The Suez Crisis in 1956 demonstrated the extent to which France and Britain no longer had the same imperial reach as before. This was something de Gaulle realized when he returned to power in 1958: the main battle to be fought was now against America. The French empire was a costly and dangerous distraction. By the time the new French president signed the 1962 Evian accords that brought the Algerian War to an end, he was already in the process of 'inventing' decolonization and creating a myth of himself as the great decolonizer.[29] This had nothing to do with de Gaulle's (non-existent) anti-colonial credentials. Instead, it was a recognition that the two-century battle between France and Britain for control of the world stage was drawing to a close. For both powers, the scars of empire would take a long time to heal but, henceforth, their interactions and confrontations would be constrained to a smaller stage within Europe.

Notes

1   For a compelling synthesis of the role of imperialism in interwar European history, see Mark Mazower, *The Dark Continent: Europe's Twentieth Century* (London: Penguin, 1997).

2   Richard Davis, *Anglo-French Relations Before the Second World War: Appeasement and Crisis* (London: Palgrave, 2001).

3   For an overview, see Robert Tombs & Isabelle Tombs, *That Sweet Enemy: Britain and France, The History of a Love-Hate Relationship* (London: Pimlico, 2007).

4   On French colonial soldiers in World War I, see, for instance, Driss Maghraoui, 'Grande guerre sainte': Moroccan colonial troops and workers in The First World War', *The Journal of North African Studies*, 9, 1 (2004), 1–21.

5   Martin Thomas, *The French Empire at War, 1940–5* (Manchester: Manchester University Press, 1998), p. 236.

6   Victor Bérard, *L'Angleterre et l'imperialisme* (Paris: Armand Colin, 1900), p. 99.

7   Ruth Ginio, *French Colonialism Unmasked: The Vichy Years in French West Africa* (London: University of Nebraska Press, 2006); Eric T. Jennings, *Vichy in the Tropics: Pétain's National Revolution in Madagascar, Guadeloupe, and Indochina, 1940–1944* (Stanford, CA: Stanford University Press, 2001).

8   Jennings, *Vichy in the Tropics*, p. 11.

9   Martin Thomas, 'After Mers-el-Kébir: The Armed Neutrality of the Vichy French Navy, 1940–43', *The English Historical Review*, 112, 447 (1997), 643–70.

10 Jennings, *Vichy in the Tropics*, p. 37; Thomas, *French Empire at War*, pp. 49–52.

11 Thomas, *French Empire at War*, pp. 46–9.

12 Thomas, *French Empire at War*, pp. 75–80.

13 Quoted in A.B. Gaunson, 'Churchill, de Gaulle, Spears and the Levant Affair, 1941', *The Historical Journal*, 27, 3 (1984), 698.

14 Gaunson, *Churchill, de Gaulle, Spears and the Levant Affair*, p. 713.

15 N.E. Bou-Nacklie, 'The 1941 invasion of Syria and Lebanon: The role of the local paramilitary', *Middle Eastern Studies*, 30, 3 (1994), 512–29.

16 Martin Thomas, 'Deferring to Vichy in the Western Hemisphere: The St Pierre and Miquelon Affair of 1941', *The International History Review*, 19, 4, (1997), 809–35.

17 Martin Thomas, 'Imperial backwater or strategic outpost? The British takeover of Vichy Madagascar, 1942', *The Historical Journal*, 39, 4 (1996), 1049–74.

18 P. Vuillaume, 'Les Indes françaises et leur ralliement à la France Libre en 1940', in *Revue de la France Libre* (No. 3b, October to November 1946).

19 Akhila Yechury, *Empire, Nation and the French Settlements in India, c. 1930–1954* (unpublished PhD thesis, Cambridge University, 2011), pp. 98–112.

20 Schomberg to Bonvin, 6 November 1940, National Archives of India, EA, 382(8)-X (Secret), 1940. See also Yechury, *Empire, Nation and the French Settlements in India*, p. 108.

21 Telegram 4277 from the Secretary of State, London, to the Governor General, New Delhi, 8 March 1942, National Archives of India, External Affairs, 240-X (Secret).

22 Unknown author, 'Le mouvement de la France Combattante aux Inde', in *L'Inde française dans la guerre* (Pondichéry: Imprimerie de la Mission, c. 1942).

23 Martin Thomas, 'Free France, the British Government and the Future of French Indo-china, 1940–45', *Journal of Southeast Asian Studies*, 28, 1 (1997), 137–60; Martin Thomas, 'Silent Partners: SOE's French Indo-China Section, 1943–45', *Modern Asian Studies*, 34, 4 (2000), 943–76.

24 Thomas, *French Empire at War*, pp. 244–8.

25 Charles-Robert Agéron, 'La survivance d'un mythe. La puissance par l'empire colonial (1944–1947)', in René Girault and Robert Frank (eds), *La puissance française en question (1945–1949)* (Paris: Publications de la Sorbonne, 1988), pp. 31, 46.

26 Tombs & Tombs, *That Sweet Enemy*, p. 569.

27 Emile Chabal, 'The rise of the Anglo-Saxon: French perceptions of the Anglo-American world in the long twentieth-century', *French Politics, Culture and Society*, 31, 1 (2013); Alan Pitt, 'A Changing Anglo-Saxon Myth: Its Development and Function in French Political Thought, 1860–1914', *French History*, 14, 2 (2000), 150–73.

28 For various perspectives, see Robert Gildea, *France Since 1945* (Oxford: Oxford University Press, 2002); Serge Berstein and Pierre Milza, *Histoire du XXè siècle, Tome 2: 1945–1973* (Paris: Hatier, 1995); Raymond Betts, *France and Decolonisation, 1900–1960* (London: Palgrave, 1991); and Jacques Marseille, *Empire colonial et capitalisme français: histoire d'un divorce* (Paris: Albin Michel, 1986).

29 The 'invention of decolonisation' is an idea discussed in Todd Shepard, *The Invention of Decolonization: The Algerian War and the Remaking of France* (London: Cornell University Press, 2006). On the 'Gaullist myth', see Sudhir Hazareesingh, *In the shadow of the General: Modern France and the Myth of de Gaulle* (Oxford: Oxford University Press, 2012).

CHAPTER FOUR

Dunkirk in Military Operations, Myths and Memories[1]

Martin S. Alexander

*If you ask anybody what they remember most clearly about
the retreat to Dunkirk they will all mention two things – shame
and exhaustion.[2]*

Sir Brian Horrocks

*29 May 1940. For about five miles we had to walk in single
file through the solid block of British and French vehicles. We
passed through one village which had been completely flattened
by bombing and was littered with charred corpses. . . . French
troops were much in evidence as they were defending Dunkirk
on the west . . . later came our turn: we . . . set off up the 300
yards of the mole at the double, with shells falling . . . and leapt
aboard the destroyer flotilla leader HMS Codrington. It sailed at
2130 with a thousand aboard . . . . We arrived in Dover harbour at
0130 on 31 May.[3]*

Christopher Seton-Watson

*1 June 1940. We continued towards Malo-les-Bains, . . . explo-
sions continually lighting up the scene for a second or two on
every side of us. . . . We were now in the region of the dunes, . . .
dotted with the still-blacker shapes of abandoned vehicles, half
sunk in the sand, fantastic twisted shapes of burned-out*

skeletons, and crazy-looking wreckage . . . silhouetted against the angry red glare in the sky, which reflected down on us the agony of burning Dunkirk.[4]

John Charles Austin

It was not supposed to end on a harbour wall or shoulder-high in the waves, tormented by enemy shellfire, bombs and strafing. As much as Dunkirk was about deliverance from the Germans and their PoW camps – for 215,500 British, 123,000 French and perhaps 8,000 Belgians – Dunkirk was also about deliverance from the Grim Reaper, who harvested greedily among the packed Royal Navy and French warships and requisitioned ferries. A high number of Allied troops and seamen died literally in the last ditch, drowning in the Channel as the Luftwaffe nailed ship after ship running the gauntlet to Kent.[5]

The British army could not have crossed that same water, en route to France, in a more different or safer order. Its deployment in September 1939 had been perhaps the smoothest move British troops had ever conducted overseas. Exploiting lessons filed in War Office drawers from the dispatch of Field Marshal Sir John French's British Expeditionary Force (BEF) in August 1914, the move of Field Marshal Lord Gort's BEF in the autumn of 1939 had been a well-oiled operation.[6] Military staff had met their French counterparts from mid-December 1935 to discuss imperial and East African defence coordination when Italy invaded Ethiopia; meetings reprised after Germany remilitarized the Rhineland on 7 March 1936.[7] Talks took place in London in April 1936, with an exchange of documents through Britain's military attaché in Paris the next month.[8] In late 1938, logistics officers led by Major General L.A. Hawes resumed work to put a British army into France if a war occurred. French ports from St. Nazaire to Le Havre were earmarked for British use, along with railway lines to transport a BEF to a concentration area behind the frontier with Belgium and supply it there 'for the duration'.[9]

This vital work progressed from the spring of 1939 through a series of wider-ranging Anglo-French staff talks. The first stretched from 29 March to 5 April 1939, followed by a second stage at the end of April and beginning of May. The third and last of the formal rounds occurred from 28 to 31 August 1939. These final meetings had, however, been prepared informally by the visit of General Maurice Gamelin, French chief of national defence staff and army commander-in-chief designate, to the summer exercises at Tidworth Camp in June 1939. That visit had been reciprocated by the attendance of Gort at the Bastille Day parade of 14 July 1939, the pomp and circumstance providing an ideal cover story for 'top brass' in Paris. Behind the scenes, nuts-and-bolts planning continued at Les Invalides, where Gamelin's staff had their offices. By September 1939, the BEF deployment to France was assured, 4 divisions expanding to 10 by 10 May 1940.[10]

The quality of the British troops and commanders broadly reassured the French that their ally meant business. And even more so, the army and defences of France inspired confidence among Britons. Morale and mutual respect ran high, and compliments were routinely exchanged before battle began and the Entente's stitching tore apart.[11] Yet, according to Brigadier George Davy, right from the start the French 'of all ranks' evinced 'a superiority complex' towards the British troops. They regarded Gort, his officers and men 'as learners in the military arts'.[12] This point is corroborated by what Lieutenant Colonel Ewan Butler and Major J. Selby Bradford, also serving in France in 1940, observed:

> Many of us were acutely conscious of the smallness of our force, when compared with the numerous divisions of our French allies, not to mention those of the enemy. Moreover, it had been dinned into the officers, at least, that in military matters we were the amateurs, the French the professionals.'[13]

This deference was amplified by robust faith in the Maginot Line and belief in French military skill among Britons. As late as April 1940 the view was expounded in a hastily published English edition of André Maginot's biography that his eponymous Line would be 'the greatest single contribution to the assured victory of the Allies'. The London *Evening Standard* reporter Harry Greenwall found the French populace content that behind the fortifications, 'nothing could happen to them'.[14]

A large British land force was not thought urgent to insure against Allied defeat. There were practical constraints anyway. Britain's peacetime army was small. In March 1939, Leslie Hore-Belisha, the Secretary of State for War, had announced a doubling of the Territorial Army and set a total force target by December 1940 of 32 divisions. After the Military Training Act of 27 April 1939, the objective became an eventual 55 division army.[15] 'Thank God we've [now] got conscription or we wouldn't be able to look these people in the face', muttered Winston Churchill as he headed to Paris for the July 1939 Bastille Day parade.[16] However, Field Marshal Sir Edmund Ironside, the chief of the imperial general staff (CIGS) and professional head of the army till 27 May 1940, knew that troops could be trained faster than weapons, vehicles and munitions manufactured. As he mused in late October: 'What is the use looking for astronomical numbers like 55 divisions? . . . We['ll] have to withstand an attack in the spring with what we have got'.[17]

All the same, Britain's inability to expand its forces made some French suspicious even before the German offensive. Was France shouldering an unfair burden, bearing an undue share of risk? Late in 1938 Henry Bérenger, the chairman of the French Senate foreign affairs commission, had spoken ominously of a French fear of the Entente waging war with 'sweat and treasure in comparative safety on the one side, and sweat and blood in constant danger on the other'.[18] Once one looks for it, one finds evidence that an alibi for defeat in 1940 was being prepared by some French before a shot was ever fired in the Battle of France. Constructing the Maginot Line had cost huge sums, said a book that hit the British market in April 1940. Echoing Bérenger, it warned: 'After the sacrifice of money comes the sacrifice of blood. The people who love liberty, including those of the New World, will owe a heavy debt to France'. Some eyebrows may have been raised among readers in London.[19]

The British departure from the Continent in 1940 had, then, been pre-figured – or at least imagined. With good faith fast evaporating, and just days before the Dunkirk evacuations began, the British hid from their French ally that withdrawal was being prepared by the Royal Navy's Admiral Bertram Ramsey, Captain W.G. Tennant and a small team at Dover Castle.[20] Over in France and Belgium, axes of retreat to the coast were identified by Lieutenant General Sir Ronald Forbes Adam, now commanding BEF III Corps, and Lieutenant Colonel the Viscount Bridgeman, one of Gort's GSO1s (heads of staff branches). With secret orders from Gort, these officers hastened to Dunkirk on 26 May and set about organizing a bridgehead and evacuation.[21]

Calais, meanwhile, was already encircled by the Wehrmacht. Defending the port from 22 to 27 May was Brigadier Claude Nicholson's 30 Brigade (King's Royal Rifle Corps, the Rifle Brigade, Queen's Victoria Rifles and other units). Though in a German throttle-grip, the town withstood everything thrown at it. 'The enemy', noted the war diary of General Ferdinand Schaal's besieging 10th Panzer Division, 'fights with a hitherto unheard of obstinacy. They are English [sic], extremely brave, and tenacious'.[22] Twice Nicholson rejected calls to surrender. Though Calais was known to be untenable, its resistance won three crucial days in which a strong defensive perimeter was constructed at Dunkirk. Only 30 riflemen from the Calais defence could be rescued by the Royal Navy. A further 'handful' rowed home.[23] The plight of Gort's main BEF, along with French units fighting by their side, was now desperate. Everything depended on Operation Dynamo and winning time had become imperative.

Roads to Dunkirk

French forces played an enormous part in shielding not just their own retreat to the Channel but that of neighbouring BEF formations. Those arranging the evacuation needed breathing space to improvise a cross-Channel rescue. Hence the last week of May saw not only the heroic defence of Calais but also doughty resistance by French and BEF rearguards.[24] Some of the firmest French resolve was seen at Lille. There, on 23 May, the 5th North African Division of General Augustin Agliany fought like furies, after being deployed between British troops and General Jean-Baptiste Molinié's French

25th Motorised Division.[25] Meanwhile, battling alongside British elements in Lille's shattered suburbs, was General Pierre Dame's 2nd North African Division and the 5th Motorised Division. Both were well equipped and disciplined – the commander of 5th Motorised, General Alphonse Juin, later leading the Free French corps in Italy in 1944–45 – and delayed the German advance by several days.[26]

Captain Daniel Barlone of 2nd North African was among those holding the Wehrmacht noose open for most of the BEF to get away, along with 123,000 French soldiers extracted from Dunkirk.[27] His diary illustrates the key contribution of Frenchmen in enabling the escape. Two French divisions near the frontier, reinforced by tanks and artillery from other formations falling back, defended the port's perimeter, led by General Marie-Bertrand Fagalde, the French XVIth Corps commander. They had already 'fought their way inch by inch for 20 miles until they reached the outskirts of the town, burning supplies, destroying tanks and guns'.[28] With German spearheads seizing the canal bridges and cutting roads to the coast, about 40,000 men of the BEF (along with a similar number of French) could not reach the port. For them the Dunkirk pocket was a *cul-de-sac*. Via railway stations and temporary camps, they were not transported to freedom but to an incarceration that for many lasted 5 years.[29]

Roger Ikor, meanwhile, was a corporal in the 106th Infantry Regiment, part of General Guillaume Janssen's 12th Motorised Division. The formation, among the French army's best, deliberately sacrificed itself to hold the approaches to Dunkirk. Janssen himself was killed by enemy fire at his temporary command post at Leffrinckoucke on the town's outskirts on 2 June. According to Ikor, the 106th Infantry resisted so staunchly that 'the Germans only rarely mounted frontal attacks when our units were properly formed; they paid dearly when they did, and with no great results'.[30] Ensconced in the frontier defences, the soldiers of 12th Division, in the words of Gregory Blaxland, 'showed themselves tough fighters'. They and their comrades of the French 32nd Division resisted 'with a spirit worthy of the Army's brightest glory'.[31] Another officer who distinguished himself was General Jules Prioux. He had assumed command of the French First Army on 22 May, after leading the two light armoured divisions of the French mechanized cavalry corps. The latter were among the finest formations on either side. They had, recognizes the German historian Karl-Heinz Frieser, 'already created enormous problems' for the Wehrmacht.[32] However, further retreat steadily dislocated Prioux's force. Their resupply became sporadic, and the troops got little food or rest. 'On the Lys', recorded Prioux on 29 May, 'there was now only a thin covering line; everything it had been possible to send back to Dunkirk having gone; during the morning I had directed some IVth Corps artillery whose ammunition boxes had been emptied in the night to make for the coast. They filed past me on the main street of Steenwerck at 10h00 in magnificent order'.[33]

To the west, the French IVth Corps, in contact with the BEF, was holding a frontage from Merville to Hazebrouck. Prioux took his own decision to halt on the River Lys and deploy detachments to cover the east- and west-facing flanks of the First Army. During the previous morning, 28 May, Gort had reached Prioux by wireless with an invitation to confer with the BEF commander-in-chief at La Panne on the coast. 'I'd always admired', wrote Prioux, 'how he cut such a fine figure as a soldier, one speaking to his loyalty and candour'.[34] Gort, who had won a VC leading 1st Battalion, the Grenadier Guards, in September 1918, was made of stern stuff. And the French general was also a 'great-hearted leader', in the words of a captain on the army staff, the renowned medievalist Marc Bloch.[35] Not all Franco-British relations in the crisis ended in bitter shouting matches. Even so, the fact remains that regrettably few British knew then, or know now, that 92,000 French officers, NCOs and soldiers along with 13 French generals died in 1940. French soldiers under Juin, Janssen, Fagalde and Fornel de la Laurencie (IIIrd Corps) took vital roles in screening the retirement to Dunkirk of British and French units. But not even the most energetic and able commanders could get a grip on the worsening mess around them. Wehrmacht spearheads found many gaps in the Allied lines. At midday on 29 May, Prioux himself was taken prisoner when his command post was overrun.[36] In the end, it was left to a French general, Maurice Beaufrère, with the remnants of his 68th Division, largely infantry reservists, to surrender Dunkirk on 4 June.[37]

Recriminations

Many Britons liked to imagine, as the historian Angus Calder noted, 'that the gutless collapse of the French had left no alternative to evacuation'. But French troops around Lille fought so valiantly that the Germans allowed the survivors to keep their weapons for the ceremonial surrender parade.[38] Other First Army soldiers, adds Marc Bloch, so feared being accused of cowardice that they fought on regardless of instructions to withdraw to the coast. Still, defeats tend to demand scapegoats and they always breed recriminations. It is unsurprising that dark sentiments and divergent memories ensued when one recalls how it was not until 29 May that the chief of the Dunkirk port authority, the French Admiral Jean-Marie Abrial, was told the BEF was homeward-bound. By then, 72,000 of its men had already departed. An agreement was admittedly reached to lift off equal numbers thenceforth and French troops evacuated from 1 June till the end (4 June) outnumbered British.[39] Yet it remained chiefly 'the French [who] went on defending the port's perimeter'. John Colville straightaway discerned the tangled skein of guilt, remorse and 'shame' in the making. 'It is accepted here', he wrote in his diary on 1 July 1940, that 'the general Anglophobia, spreading over the country [France], is a natural reaction to events. It has an element of justification in that we did not provide many divisions, but . . . now inadequate British assistance is the thin excuse used to explain the total collapse of France'.[40] Perhaps the most poignant and easily forgotten dimension of Dunkirk is that escape to England for most evacuated French troops was not a deliverance from the horrors of war but just a rapid deliverance by the Southern and Great Western railways to ports in Hampshire, Dorset and Devon and thence back to France – to endeavour to sustain the battle. If there is little awareness of the great numbers of French extracted from Dunkirk, there is even less that most were back in their own country in under a week. For them not only had the Battle of Britain not begun, but the Battle of France was not even over.[41]

Soon it would be, however, as a defenceless Paris was proclaimed an 'open city'. It was entered by the Wehrmacht on 14 June 1940.[42] For the Dunkirk evacuees wearing French uniforms, the fate of Lieutenant Paul Mousset exemplifies this sorry epilogue. After reaching Britain, Mousset was returned through Weymouth to Cherbourg. The voyage, however, proved easier than the search for his comrades. Within days Mousset was caught up in another chaotic retreat, this time south-westwards. Still a member of the military, Mousset had in reality become just a military member of the 'Exodus' – one more migrant among the 7 or 8 million French who could not escape to Britain but who nevertheless sought to escape from the Germans.[43]

To the British public, eager for news, Operation Dynamo was soon depicted as a miracle – albeit of 9 days' duration, not 3. Still, most soldiers realized that they had been very lucky. They also knew that the salvation of so many via the conduit of Dunkirk was in reality wrought by hard work. But it became an apotheosis of British ability to muddle through a crisis, no matter how big. As Captain Sir Basil Bartlett, a Field Security Officer with Major General Dudley Johnson's BEF 4th Division, put it in his diary: 'There's something almost miraculous in the British powers of improvisation'.[44] Huge good fortune also aided the Allies in the shape of the German *Haltbefehl*, the halt order of 24 May 1940. This instruction crucially froze the panzer spearheads on the canal lines west of Dunkirk. The Germans remained immobile just long enough for the BEF and men of the French First Army to constitute a perimeter defence around what was, by 27 May, the last northern Channel port in Allied hands.[45] This 'nonsensical order to stop the Panzer formations south of Dunkirk' allowed most of Gort's troops to pick up their bedrolls, blankets and walk across the sands – or along the harbour mole – and take ship back to Britain.[46]

But even if it generated a strong sense of deliverance, evacuation still meant abandonment of the BEF's vehicles, munitions and heavy equipment.[47] The escape was not by itself going to bring an immediate resurrection of the British Army.[48] And so alongside the relief and gratitude for the troops who had escaped, the evacuation stirred a swelling chorus of condemnation of France. The British felt their army had been deployed to assist allies – Belgians as well as French – in good faith. Soon British people, from high officials to ordinary public, were trading accusations that the BEF had been betrayed by poor strategic planning, an inept French high command and sheer spinelessness. Despite the gallantry of French rearguards in front of Dunkirk, the tissues coming together into the British myth were already acquiring another layer. Rumours of brave British troops being betrayed into mortal danger by feckless foreign allies, said a Home Intelligence report on 29 May 1940, gained 'authenticity by the reported conversation of soldiers lately returned from France, to whom various alarming stories are attributed'. The fabric of a version of events in which the French had shown no stomach for battle, not even to defend their own hearths and homes, was thickening.[49] On 1 June, in Kent, the writer Katharine Moore recorded how 'troops on their way back from France [were] coming through the town in charabancs and lorries past our house' all day long, 'the street lined with cheering people'. The soldiers 'looked very tired but were singing loudly. It is a miracle that they are here'.[50] This belief that the plight of the British Tommies was the fault of the French – and Belgians – gained force from key opinion-formers. Many British reporters had witnessed the retreats and the refugee columns, the stragglers and the surrenders.[51] Jimmy Drysdale, a *Sunday Chronicle* war correspondent, was among the last to escape through the Biscay ports in mid-June. On 3 July 1940, the day the Royal Navy shelled the French fleet at Mers-el-Kébir in Algeria and killed over 1,200 French *matelots*, James Drawbell, the *Sunday Chronicle* editor, noted: 'Long talk with Drysdale, back from France. Said French were a different race from last war – all fighting spirit dead. Running away. German soldiers laughing'.[52]

Within a defiant British discourse, the steadiness and bulldog character of the BEF, RAF and Royal Navy was now constructed as something totemic of an indomitable Albion. What Katharine Moore called the 'incredible stories of courage and daring, especially of the small craft', contrasted with shocking ones about French passivity, even blind panic.[53] Yet reports on British civilian morale showed there was a broad solidarity with the French and an appreciation that their troops had borne most of the brunt of the German attack. By contrast, the surrender on 28 May of the Belgian monarch Leopold III – who was not only the King but also the army commander-in-chief – sparked cries of treachery and cowardice. 'Bitter comments on Belgium's capitulation' were reported the next day from Edinburgh, while in London there was an outcry against Belgium 'even to the extent of saying the Belgian refugees should be sent back'. It all put the French, still battling on at this time, in a better light. From Newcastle a report on 29 May said criticism of France had now 'disappeared'.[54] What did greatest damage to Franco-British relations was not the supposed 'flight-not-fight' syndrome among French soldiers but learning on 17 June that Marshal Pétain's new government intended to quit the war. Britons immediately interpreted this as a scandalous betrayal of the 28 March 1940 agreement that neither London nor Paris would make a separate peace.[55] Thus the subjugation of France and the survival of Britain 'not only worked to confirm Britain's sense of innate national superiority' but also, as the historian Malcolm Smith remarks, 'a more general distrust of European entanglements for generations'.[56]

Of course myths, like comedy, only work if they contain grains of truth. There really were French soldiers – and indeed civilians – reluctant to see the phoney war of 1939–40, a cold war in more ways than one, turn hot. But lest this lack of any zest for a 'hot war' be thought a French trait alone, it should be recorded that British morale also ebbed in late 1939. The BEF chief of staff, Lieutenant General Pownall, found Gort 'a bit depressed about the Corps Commanders, especially Brooke [II Corps] who has got a very defeatist frame of mind'. Ominously, added the diarist, 'defeatism is very apt to spread downwards'. Across the Channel, Muriel Green in Norfolk was taking notes for the Mass Observation (MO) social survey organization founded in 1937 by Tom Harrisson, Charles Madge and Humphrey Jennings. On 5 May 1940, barely a week before the war ceased to be phoney, she experienced a 'sort of "don't care if we win or lose" feeling' and wondered 'is it any good fighting?' Reflecting in December 1940 on a 'grim and anxious year', she confessed she had 'thought the war was practically done, with us vanquished when France went under. For a little while I even felt glad that the war was going to be over sooner than we hoped'.[57] In Monmouthshire another young woman wrote for MO on 27 May (unaware this was the first full day of troop-lift from Dunkirk): 'If we have got to give in to Germany, I almost think it would be better to do it now, although I hate the thought of defeat as much as anyone. But I think that I hate the thought of mass slaughter even more.' She noted in mid-June the effect on civilians around her as news broke out that France was surrendering: 'In the afternoon people were feeling that we had better give in.'[58]

A more upbeat note was sounded by some sooner than others. Katharine Moore, close to the danger in Kent, observed on 1 June that 'since the evacuation . . . I feel that for the first time Hitler has not had it all his own way'.[59] On 26 June she wrote that the future 'looks immensely black', but added that 'I have recovered from the shock of the French capitulation and keep cheerful, making jam, gardening and doing odd jobs.' This was the quintessential 'Keep Calm and Carry On' stiff upper lip. For Muriel Green, on the other hand, 6 months would pass before she would feel, as she noted in her MO diary in December 1940, that 'we have turned the corner and we can really win'.[60] Among French people – save for de Gaulle in London, and others still in France with the first Resistance groups – few could have shared such optimism. Britain's abandonment of Europe was incomprehensible. The Dunkirk evacuation, along with the escape of the 'second BEF' from Brittany in late June, was not viewed as an unavoidable means to 'retreat to victory'. Rather, the withdrawal exposed afresh the selfishness of 'les Anglo-Saxons' when life's chips fell badly.[61] To some French it was worse than that: Dunkirk was an unforgiveable act of perfidy. Against so toxic a backdrop, the French inevitably sought scapegoats as they plunged into four black years of occupation, crippling economic exploitation and simmering Franco-French civil war.[62]

The disintegration of Franco-British military relations, superficially cordial in the phoney war, came frighteningly fast. In a longer perspective, however, Dunkirk cast little shadow upon subsequent French national controversies arising from World War II. The American historian and political scientist Stanley Hoffmann went so far as to claim that France underwent no '1940 Syndrome'.[63] But, as Robert Frank notes in a subsequent chapter, Dunkirk had a weightier legacy in respect of French foreign and defence policy.[64] Especially from de Gaulle's return to power in the early 1960s, successive French leaders insisted that national defence strategy and weapons (including nuclear ones) should be 'made in France'. Never again would Marianne trust Anglo-American allies who in the 1940 crisis had either deserted France – or not even entered the war to help.[65] At any rate, the French in the main sank their teeth in the post-war era into matters their historians found more pressing: the public policies of Vichy, the compromised private conduct of individuals, the extensiveness and actions of the Resistance and the extent to which collaborators ought to be purged.[66]

Representations

With such a legacy, it is not surprising that Dunkirk has not greatly interested French scholars since 1945 – not even the in-house professionals of the armed forces' historical branches (now amalgamated into the SHD, the *Service Historique de la Défense*). Major Pierre Lyet of the French army history department, in his 1947 book on the Battle of France, did argue that the evacuation was not just 'an undeniable German victory but "Dunkirk" was equally, in a certain measure, *an Allied victory*'. More ambiguously, the historian Jean-Pierre Azéma claimed that Dunkirk was a 'success [that] was at the very most no more than a retreat' – one that left Europe 'now abandoned by the British'.[67]

Dunkirk registers even more faintly on French film screens, in literature and art. 'The defeat of 1940 has never been central in French collective memory', writes Patrick Finney in a masterful survey of the state of the historiography on France at the outset of the 1939–45 war, 'since it has been serially obscured by the great dramas of the occupation and latterly by postcolonial traumas'. Irène Némirovsky's semi-autobiographical novel of the French people's exodus in 1940, *Suite française*, published posthumously and after the turn of the 70th anniversary, makes the point because it is such a rarity.[68] In French films about the country's experiences in 1939–45, it is Resistance, Collaboration and the Holocaust in 'the Hexagon' that have won dominance. This was so from immediately after the war, exemplified by the directors René Clément (*La Bataille du Rail*, 1946) and Jean-Pierre Melville (*L'Armée des ombres*, 1969, an adaptation of Joseph Kessel's eponymous book of 1943). These concerns remained central in the 1980s and 1990s, decades when Vichy and collaboration seemed 'an ever-present past'.[69] Cinema held up its own mirror to a near obsession with the Occupation including Jean Marboeuf's *Pétain* (1993), Marcel Ophuls' *Hôtel Terminus* (1988), Louis Malle's *Lacombe Lucien* (1974) and *Au revoir les Enfants* (1987), along with *Uranus* (dir. Claude Berri, 1990).

If not in feature films, what about Dunkirk in documentaries? The selective amnesia practised by the French – encouraged by a Gaullist quest to occlude the deep divisions of wartime behind a narrative of national unity centred on resistance, redemption and self-liberation – did not survive the celebrated 1969 exhumation of wartime ambiguities in *Le Chagrin et la Pitié* by Marcel Ophuls and André Harris. Yet even this documentary paid but fleeting attention to Franco-British relations. When *Le Chagrin* did focus on the cross-currents between the 'troubled neighbours' it was not to re-evaluate the controversies of Dunkirk. Rather, it was to examine how far Britain supported French resistance by teams of secret agents such as Denis Rake under Colonel Maurice Buckmaster, chief of F (French) Section of Special Operations Executive (SOE), which was established under Churchill's July 1940 order to 'Set Europe Ablaze'.[70]

In Britain, meanwhile, Dunkirk has usually been presented in one of two ways. First, it has appeared in a trope of escape from the jaws of disaster (jaws into which the BEF had been placed by feckless French allies), as is implicit in the 'France Falls' episode of Thames Television's documentary series *The World at War* (1973). Alternatively, what happened in Flanders has been subsumed in broader accounts of Western Europe's Nazi subjugation. Yet in that variant, too, the central explanations are incompetence from top to bottom in the French military and fractures in French society.[71] It would be another 30 years before a documentary entitled *The Other Side of Dunkirk* (even then, one produced for a minority-audience BBC channel) at last put French and German historians among the 'authorities' interviewed and positioned French and German viewpoints centrally within Dunkirk as history, not folklore.[72]

That folklore had already assumed potency in 1940 even as bedraggled Tommies exchanged their sea-soaked boots and tattered tunics for clean battledress. Straightaway the cinema newsreels from Gaumont-British, Pathé and Movietone began the construction of a narrative of rescue and rebirth.[73] In their turn, feature films made during Britain's flag-waving nostalgia for 1939–45 retained iconic themes and tones: plucky, outnumbered underdogs, surpassing themselves in appalling conditions far from home – and yet triumphing over the odds and despite unworthy allies. These themes appeared across the 'We Can Take It' British war films in the 1950s and 1960s. The struggle the British preferred to replay on celluloid found packed and none-too-critical audiences.[74] However, *Dunkirk* (dir. Leslie Norman, 1958), starring screen stalwarts John Mills, Richard Attenborough and Bernard Lee, conveyed more complex messages. The film encouraged cinema-goers –

many too young to remember where they had been during the real Dunkirk – to reflect on more nuanced meanings of the war's first great dramas by focusing not on the officer-class but on ordinary Britons at their best in the war's darkest days. As the 20th anniversary of Dunkirk came deep into the 13 years of Conservative government from 1951 to 1964, the film strove to consolidate a consensual remembrance of Dunkirk.[75]

Penny Summerfield has recently written instructively of the popular memory of 1939–45 as something fluid and requiring negotiation among Britons since the war ended. There were fissures, she shows, along class and gender lines in the reception of the film *Dunkirk*. Moreover, Operation Dynamo as 'real lived experience' for troops, sailors and civilians who encountered the returning men remains problematic even if, from the range of evidence and responses to the event, it is clear that the 'popular memory of Dunkirk in Britain mattered'.[76] The most dominant, albeit not unchallenged memory, rests within a constructed discourse of national regeneration – a discourse that articulates World War II's shocking early setbacks for Britain as deliverance, not disaster. To fabricate and transmit such a view back in the summer of 1940, some silken language, sonorous voices and technological access to the populace were essential. These elements came together through the wireless. Crucial in the creation of the Dunkirk myth was the Bradford-born writer J. B. Priestley. The BBC 'Postscripts' he broadcast after the main evening news emphasized the evacuation's civilian participants. His Yorkshire tones connoted a voice of the people. He raised to centrality the civilian boat crews and those who supplied hot tea, food and dry blankets to weary, bedraggled soldiers disembarking in Kent. Of course the other sonorous voice of 1940 belonged to the aristocratic Old Harrovian, Winston Churchill.[77] The prime minister 'has the power', as Katharine Moore put it after listening on her radio to his speech of 18 June 1940, 'to coin unforgettable phrases that light up something inside one'.[78] Hence by way of a mixture of positive messages, deliverance at Dunkirk was a narrative cemented in British psyches during the 1950s and 1960s – deliverance from the edge of utter disaster in May 1940 merging into later wartime evocations of the Battle of Britain and the success of 8th Army in North Africa in 1942–43 to constitute what Nicholas Harman has labelled Britain's 'necessary myth'.[79]

That myth, in truth a meta-narrative affirming Britain's indelible role in World War II, was necessary because the further the conflict receded into the past, the more Britons needed reassurance of their own key part in building Allied victory. The 1950s and 1960s delivered shocks to British self-esteem. By the mid-1960s Britain's centrality to the wartime Grand Alliance had given way to a far more fragile global standing – and a strategic relationship with the United States that retained 'specialness', but was now clearly that of a faded power.[80] Thus the constructed myth of Dunkirk, as part of a broader narrative of 'defeat into victory', fitted the post-war British temperament.[81] The salvation of the BEF, in Paul Addison's assessment, was treated in Britain as a kind of triumph 'and swiftly translated by the press and the BBC into a glorious episode which helped sustain morale at home and rally support in the United States'.[82] The myth had to be made – and was made – both inclusive and encompassing. The films that 15 to 25 years after 1940 retold a certain version of what had happened also helped the British shelter within a cultural cocoon. Celluloid was part of a broader nostalgia-tinted barrier against unwelcome challenges from a fast-changing world. For Britain in the prime ministership of Harold Macmillan – himself a government minister during the war and in dress and manners a self-consciously Edwardian anachronism – these stirring breezes soon became gale-force winds of disobliging change.[83]

Britain's celluloid industry, during this era of 'the surging success of the war film', turned out a stream of pictures populated by ubiquitous action-hero players.[84] They ranged from John Gregson in the Battle of Britain film *Angels One-Five* (dir. George More O'Ferrall, 1952), through Richard Todd (as Guy Gibson) in Michael Anderson's *The Dambusters* (1955) and Kenneth More (as Douglas Bader) in *Reach for the Sky* (dir. Lewis Gilbert, 1956), to Anthony Quayle and John Gregson (as Commodore Henry Harwood and Captain Frederick Bell) in Michael Powell and Emeric Pressburger's *Battle of the River Plate* (Royal Command Performance film for 1956). The genre even survived – or was rejuvenated by – an importation of American actors despite the stretch to historical plausibility, notably Cliff Robertson and George Chakiris in *633 Squadron* (dir. Walter Grauman, 1964). For these 'finest hour' films, the climax of the genre, like that of a firework display, also announced the end. This was the epic-scale *Battle of Britain* (dir. Guy Hamilton, 1969). Featuring the heavyweights of British thespianism since the 1940s, including Sir Ralph Richardson, Sir Laurence Olivier, Trevor Howard and Kenneth More – the cast appealed to a more youthful audience by assigning major roles as 1940 RAF fighter squadron commanders to Michael Caine, Christopher Plummer and Robert Shaw. The picture, released just before 1940's 30th anniversary, was arguably the finest hour of the British war film.[85]

In this cultural (re-en)acting of the war, the favourite trope of Britons triumphed every time: the little man from the lower classes against the odds – quintessentially, *Dunkirk*'s Corporal Binns. Extending from the early 1950s till at least the early 1970s these (re)constructions of 1939–45, and particularly of the war's first stages when Britain was in gravest peril, made a key cultural referent out of British 'character'. This was an ill-defined amalgam of pluck, good humour and hard work exemplified by 'digging for victory', and a capacity for unsystematic and successful improvisation ('muddling through').[86] All of this contributed to an idea which was born in early June 1940 and had no French equivalent: the 'Dunkirk spirit'. Connoting self-reliance and a 'stiff upper-lip', it grew to be regarded as a uniquely British trait. It was a source of pride in the British armed forces undone – but unbowed and essentially unbeaten – after going nobly to the aid of 'Johnny Foreigner'. Dunkirk mutated from a tale of chestnuts plucked from the fire into a comforting narrative of sacrifice stoically endured in 1940–41 by all of British society in a spirit of togetherness, comradeship, common cause and national unity. As the publisher's foreword to a book on 1939–40 by Anthony Gibbs, one of the press corps at BEF headquarters, expressed it: 'In June 1940, this country suffered one of the greatest disasters in its history, and yet, by some curious process of self delusion, the myth has grown up that it was one of the moments of which we have to be most proud.'[87]

The *Sunday Chronicle* editor, James Drawbell, was en route to London from Edinburgh on 24 June just hours before the Franco-German armistice came into force. His diary gives a glimpse of an emerging British legend that would retain emotive power and political traction for at least 70 further years:

> My train going back to London full of troops and officers. . . . Discussion on ability of our people 'to take it' when it comes. Everyone talks to everyone else now. The old British reserve is going. Reality is breaking in. Class values are going overboard. We're all in it together. So we get closer together for safety. Feeling . . . that this time we've got to face what comes all on our own.[88]

As Angus Calder has remarked of the trends Drawbell discerned, the war's trajectory in the autumn of 1940 and through the bombing of Britain's cities in 1941–42 ensured the account gathered forward momentum. Over time, Dunkirk-as-salvation and 'The Few' (the RAF pilots of Fighter Command), were dovetailed into the 'myth of the Blitz'. As a meta-narrative this became – to modify Churchill's phrase – not so much a finest hour as a finest year when Britain supposedly (re)defined its national character and 'alone' stood as Horatio on the bridge for all of civilization to beat the odds on defeat.[89]

This too is myth. For in no meaningful sense was Britain 'alone' from June 1940 to June 1941. 'If anything was alone', explains David Edgerton, 'it was the mighty British Empire' – an assemblage of countries, armed forces, manpower, raw materials and trading partners that stood 'in some respects, relative to other powers . . . at its strongest in this part of the war'.[90] Moreover, the Wehrmacht had suffered severely in defeating France (just as the French armies took heavy losses striving to defend it). The German high command looked aghast at the prospect of having to fight for Paris and take the city street by street. The German Luftwaffe had sustained such attrition that it would be too late in the year before it had refitted and could resume large-scale air operations, this time against southern England. The German logisticians had no plan with any prospect of success for a cross-Channel invasion.[91]

Plainly what was important after Britain's expulsion from the Continent was not the 'objective' calculus of material power. That was not the essence of the speeches by Churchill, newspaper articles and broadcasts about 'Britain alone' after Dunkirk. In the years and decades after 1945, it was, rather, 'the *belief* that Britain in this period had been alone, *and was weak*' that became the essence.[92] That is what still resonates with British people and has become 'central', as Edgerton puts it, 'to histories of Britain'.[93] Labour and the Conservatives alike have repeatedly exhorted Britons since 1945 to bear shortages (grumbling being permitted, but not riots), to 'make do and mend', and even accept a resumption of rationing (petrol during the Suez crisis of late 1956, electricity during the 3-day working week and power cuts when Edward Heath did battle with the trade unions in 1972–74).[94] Ten years on from the publication of Malcolm Smith's book on the popular memory of 1940 in Britain, the coalition government of Conservatives and Liberal Democrats, formed in May 2010, sought to win acceptance of public expenditure cuts by telling Britons: 'We're all in this together.' At every turn and no matter the stripe of the government, opportunistic appeals to the 'Dunkirk spirit' continue.[95]

Tangled memories

It was perhaps unavoidable that two divergent vectors of memory veered off into the future once German troops entered Paris and British ones returned to Dover. The immediate and longer-term aftermaths of military defeat in Belgium and Northern France were too painfully different for it to be otherwise. As Captain Bartlett, just disembarked at Dover, prophetically noted on 31 May 1940: 'I suppose that, in history, this campaign will count as a first-class military defeat. But it wasn't.'[96] Rescuing a third of a million soldiers to fight again meant Britons could still feel they were an indomitable island race. At the same time, the disastrous first 2 years of the 1939–45 war confirmed an underlying suspicion that they, with their Commonwealth and Empire, were well rid of near-catastrophic Continental entanglements. The American correspondent Eric Sevareid was in Bordeaux when Pétain pulled France out of the fight. 'I sensed a subtle change of relationship', he wrote, of the moment his fellow British journalists made for the last ship. 'They seemed almost happy; they were British and their course was clear. They were sticking together now'.[97] Likewise, King George VI, who had visited his British soldiers on the Franco-Belgian frontier in the Phoney War winter, famously remarked on 27 June 1940 that he felt 'happier now that we have no more allies to be polite to and pamper'.[98] Britain might now be playing a solo hand – but it need only count on itself.[99] Even the French-speaking Lieutenant General Sir Alan Brooke, once schooled in Pau, had by mid-June spent long enough in a land he had loved as his second home. On 16 June, at Redon near St. Nazaire to oversee the 'Second BEF' evacuations, he assured the commander of RAF forces in France, Air Marshal Sir Arthur Barratt, he was anxious 'not to remain in this country an hour longer than necessary'.[100]

Two days later, on a trawler bound for Plymouth, an exhausted Brooke stretched out on the deck in the sunshine, 'thanking God that we were safely out of France for the second time'.[101]

As for the French, they could (and did) nurture their sorrow and pity at being abandoned to German and Italian occupiers and to home-grown collaborators. The conduct of the British fed a French distaste for Albion – a persistent conviction, lingering still, that more should have been done to help, more army divisions raised and equipped, more RAF fighter planes sent over, more British blood shed on the soil of France. 'But the fact is that they let each other down', as Robert and Isabelle Tombs point out, 'and neither has entirely forgotten it'.[102] Indeed, the French view of British performance in 1940 is far from flattering – the 'final undignified scurry', in Michael Glover's words, tending to 'lend colour to the persistent French belief that, when the going gets tough, the British will always make for their boats'.[103]

There was some truth to this claim since, some 3 weeks after Dunkirk, the British and Commonwealth contingents still in France, amounting to some 200,000 troops and airmen, did indeed take ship. It remains insufficiently understood that as many British and Commonwealth troops as had evacuated from Dunkirk were yet to be extricated from western France as the government of Paul Reynaud (prime minister from 21 March 1940) gave way to that of Pétain on 16–17 June 1940. Replicating the 'miracle of Dunkirk', most of these British and Commonwealth personnel in western France managed to embark for Poole, Weymouth, Plymouth and Falmouth from the docksides of St. Nazaire, Lorient, Brest and Cherbourg.[104] Paradoxically, though, it was in this stage of Britain's retreat – not off Dunkirk but in the Bay of Biscay – that the most horrific episode in the evacuations came about. This was a real shipwreck, not a figurative one. On 17 June 1940, around 2,000 troops and civilians, including female nurses and some children, died off St. Nazaire when the Luftwaffe sank the S.S. *Lancastria*, a crowded ex-Cunard steamship working as a troop transport, tragically 'bombed like a sitting bird'.[105]

Alan Brooke on his trawler, sticky with 'beastly black fuel oil' after helping to rescue *Lancastria* survivors, realized that for Anglo-French relations the problem was going to be 'the impression that we were abandoning our ally in its hour of need'.[106] Going on to be Churchill's principal military counsellor from 1941 to 1945, Brooke was right to fear poisonous long-term legacies. Also at St. Nazaire, waiting to embark on the S.S. *Florestan*, was a detachment of the 6th Battalion, Royal Sussex, under Major M. L. Walkinton, who heard five or six children playing in a garden: 'One of the fathers came to me and asked: "Are you English deserting us and running away to England?" I tried to reassure him that it was a matter of "Reculer pour mieux sauter" and that we would be back one day . . . . I found my brief talk with this Frenchman most unpalatable.'[107] Yet, as the anglophile Lieutenant Roland de Margerie, a junior French diplomat in London before the war and reservist officer in 1939–40, would remark of the BEF's retreat to the sanctuary of the British Isles: 'Who could blame them for that, especially at a moment when the United Kingdom was utterly denuded of troops thanks to the way the French general staff had deployed the BEF in Flanders?'[108] This reminds us that the essence of understanding Dunkirk is probably captured by seeing it not as a miracle of deliverance but as 'a great relief'.[109] If Dunkirk was not 'the callous desertion that many Frenchmen felt', its relative success owed a very great deal 'to the unsung sacrifices of French soldiers'.[110]

Notes

1 Melvyn Bragg, *The Adventure of English – The Biography of a Language* (London: Hodder & Stoughton, 2003), p. 35, says Dunkirk has been 'subversively inspirational'; for directing me to certain sources and for comments on early drafts, I am grateful to Dr Jeremy A. Crang of Edinburgh University and to Prof A.J. Hinks. Translations from French are my own.

2 Lt.-Gen. Sir Brian Horrocks, *A Full Life* (London: Collins, 1960), pp. 81, 89 (emphasis in original), in 1940 the commanding officer of 2nd Middlesex.

3 Christopher Seton-Watson, *Dunkirk-Alamein-Bologna. Letters and Diaries of an Artilleryman, 1939–1945* (Dover: Buckland Press, 1995), pp. 37–9, then a 2nd Lieut. in the Royal Horse Artillery.

4 John Charles Austin, 'Dunkirk: The Beaches, 1 June 1940', in John Carey (ed.), *The Faber Book of Reportage* (London and Boston: Faber, 1987; pb. reissue, 1996), quotation from latter edn., pp. 529–30; cf. the rapidly written account by John Masefield (Poet Laureate, 1930–67), suppressed by the British government and finally published by William Heinemann in 1972, 5 years after the author's death. John Masefield, *The Twenty-Five Days, The Flanders Campaign and the rescue of the BEF from Dunkirk, 10 May – 3 June 1940*. Introduction by Jon Cooksey (Barnsley: Pen & Sword, 2004); cf. Joshua Levene, *Forgotten Voices of Dunkirk* (London: Ebury Press, 2011); also Ronald Atkin, *Pillar of Fire. Dunkirk 1940* (London: Sidgwick & Jackson, 1990; Edinburgh: Birlinn, 2000); Général Jules Armengaud, *Le Drame de Dunkerque, mai-juin 1940* (Paris: Plon, 1948); Jacques Mordal, *La Bataille de Dunkerque* (Paris: Self, 1948).

5 Many RN warships, and French ones such as the destroyer *Sirocco*, were sunk while evacuating troops (far more of whom journeyed to Britain on naval vessels and passenger ships taken up for war service than on the legendary 'little ships' crewed by volunteer civilians). See Angus Calder, *The Myth of the Blitz* (London: Jonathan Cape, 1991 & Pimlico pb. reprint, 1992), pp. 96–8 (subsequent refs. to this edn.).

6 Keith Jeffery, *Field Marshal Sir Henry Wilson. A political soldier* (Oxford: Oxford University Press, 2006), pp. 85–105, 128–37; Elizabeth Greenhalgh, *Foch in Command. The forging of a First World War general* (Cambridge: Cambridge University Press, 2011), pp. 9–12, 23–42, 81–5.

7   One had been then-Colonel (later General) Sir Ronald Forbes Adam, Bt. (correspondence and interviews with the present author, 1977–79); in a preview of the rifts between the French and British 'players' on the Allied military 'team' in May–June 1940, Adam told me he found the stop-start of the pre-war meetings 'like a football match with the referee continually whistling for offside'; also Michael L. Dockrill, *British Establishment Perspectives on France, 1936–40* (Basingstoke: Macmillan, 1999), pp. 38–9, 126–35; Jeremy A. Crang, 'Adam, Sir Ronald Forbes, second baronet (1885–1982)', in *Oxford Dictionary of National Biography* (Oxford University Press, 2004); online edn., January 2011, http://www.oxforddnb. com/view/article/57705 (accessed 6 May 2012).

8   J.T. Emmerson, *The Rhineland Crisis, 7 March 1936. A study in multilateral diplomacy* (London: Temple Smith, 1977), pp. 136–42, 189, 193–6, 217–8, outlines these staff talks; also Martin S. Alexander, *The Republic in danger. General Maurice Gamelin and the politics of French defence, 1933–1940* (Cambridge: Cambridge University Press, 1992), pp. 236–78.

9   Maj.-Gen. L.A. Hawes, 'The Story of the "W Plan": The move of our forces to France in 1939', *The Army Quarterly*, 101 (1970–1), pp. 445–56; Brian Bond (ed.), *Chief of Staff. The Diaries of Lieutenant-General Sir Henry Pownall* (London: Leo Cooper, 1972, 2 vols), Vol. I: *1933–1940*, pp. 149–50, 164–5, 171–2, 195–6, 204–13, 232–43; idem, *Britain, France and Belgium, 1939–1940* (London: Brassey's, 1990), pp. 5–34.

10 J.R. Colville, *Man of Valour. The Life of Field-Marshal The Viscount Gort, VC* (London: Collins, 1972), pp. 125–7, 129–30; Brian Bond 'Preparing the Field Force, February 1939–May 1940', in Brian Bond and Michael Taylor (eds), *The Battle of France and Flanders, 1940: Sixty Years On* (London: Leo Cooper/Pen & Sword, 2001), pp. 1–11; William Philpott and Martin S. Alexander, 'The French and the British Field Force: Moral Support or Material Contribution?', *Journal of Military History*, 71, 3 (July 2007), pp. 743–72.

11 Philip M.H. Bell, 'L'évolution de l'opinion publique anglaise à propos de la guerre et de l'alliance avec la France (septembre 1939-mai 1940)', in *Français et Britanniques dans la drôle de guerre. Actes du colloque franco-britannique tenu à Paris du 8 au 12 décembre 1975* (Paris: Editions du CNRS, 1979), pp. 123–51.

12 G.M.O. Davy, unpub. typescript memoirs (copy in present author's possession by courtesy of the late Brig. Davy), p. 1209

13 E. Butler and J. Selby Bradford, *Keep The Memory Green. The First of the Many. France 1939–40* (London: Hutchinson, n.d.), p. 17; cf. Penny Summerfield, 'Dunkirk and the Popular Memory of Britain at War, 1940–58', *Journal of Contemporary History*, 45, 4 (December 2010), pp. 788–811 (esp. pp. 797–8).

14 Pierre Belperron, *Maginot of the Line* (London: Williams and Norgate, 1940), p. 124; Harry J. Greenwall, *When France Fell* (London: Allan Wingate, 1958), p. 39; cf. Judith M. Hughes, *To the Maginot Line. The politics of French military preparation in the 1920s* (Cambridge, MA: Harvard University Press, 1971).

15 R.J. Minney, *The Private Papers of Hore-Belisha* (London: Collins, 1960), pp. 171–206.

16 Churchill from Pownall's diary, 10 July 1939 (Bond, *Chief of Staff*, I, p. 213); cf. Churchill's later comment on conscription that 'It was, however, a symbolic gesture of the utmost consequence to France'. Winston S. Churchill, *The Second World War. vol. I: The Gathering Storm* (London: Cassell, 1948), pp. 318–19.

17 Col. Roderick Macleod and Denis Kelly (eds), *The Ironside Diaries, 1937–40* (London: Constable, 1962), (24 October 1939), pp. 134–5; Bond (ed.), *Chief of Staff*, I, pp. 191, 201–2. For British munitions shortages in 1915, see Hew Strachan, *The First World War, vol. 1: To Arms* (Oxford: Oxford University Press, 2001), pp. 993–1005, 1065–89.

18 London (Kew): The National Archives (TNA) – Public Record Office (PRO): Foreign Office General Correspondence FO371, 21597, C15175/36/17, British Embassy (Paris) to Foreign Office (London), 7 December 1938; cf. Anthony P. Adamthwaite, *France and the Coming of the Second World War* (London: Frank Cass, 1977), p. 251. Phoney War cross-Channel distrust can be explored in Eleanor M. Gates, *End of the Affair. The Collapse of the Anglo-French Alliance, 1939–40* (London, Boston and Sydney: Allen & Unwin, 1981); P.M.H. Bell, *A Certain Eventuality. Britain and the Fall of France* (Farnborough: Saxon House, 1974), esp. chs. 1–4, 6; John C. Cairns, 'Great Britain and the Fall of France: a study in Allied disunity', *Journal of Modern History*, 27, 4 (December 1955), pp. 365–409; Joel Blatt (ed.), *The French Defeat of 1940: Reassessments* (Providence, RI and Oxford: Berghahn, 1998).

19 Belperron, *Maginot*, p. 92.

20 Robin Brodhurst, 'The Royal Navy's role in the campaign', in Bond and Taylor (eds), *The Battle of France*, pp. 129–38; W.J.R. Gardner (ed.), *The Evacuation from Dunkirk: Operation Dynamo, 26 May–4 June 1940* (London: Frank Cass, 2000).

21 Gregory Blaxland, *Destination Dunkirk. The Story of Gort's Army* (London: William Kimber, 1973), pp. 254–7, 307–11; interviews with Gen. Adam by the present author at Carylls Lea, Faygate, Sussex, and with Maj.-Gen. the Viscount Bridgeman, at Minsterley, Salop (both August 1978); Bridgeman, unpublished typescript memoirs (consulted by kind permission of their author, and now on deposit at the Liddell Hart Centre for Military Archives, King's College London); Christopher Page (ed.), *The Royal Navy in Home Waters and the Atlantic. vol. II: 9 April 1940 to 6 December 1941* (London: Frank Cass, 2004).

22 Quoted in Terry Coleman, '1940 Revisited. 26 May: Calais defence gives respite to Dunkirk', *The Independent* (26 May 1990), p. 6.

23 Coleman, 'Calais defence' (*supra*); cf. John Cooksey, *Calais. 30 Brigade's Defiant Defence, May 1940* (Barnsley: Leo Cooper, 1999); Michael Glover, *The Fight for the Channel Ports, Calais to Brest 1940: A Study of Confusion* (London: Leo Cooper, 1985); Airey Neave, *The Flames of Calais* (London: Hodder & Stoughton, 1972); Eric Linklater, *The Defence of Calais* (London: HMSO, 1941); Pierre Le Goyet and Jean Foussereau, *Calais, Mai 1940. La corde au cou* (Paris: Presses de la Cité, 1980).

24 Jeremy A. Crang, ' The Defence of the Dunkirk perimeter', in Bond and Taylor (eds), *The Battle of France*, pp. 72–85; Major L.F. Ellis, *The War in France and Flanders 1939–1940* (London: HMSO, 1953), pp. 174–98.

25 On Molinié, 'La Bataille de France' at http://batailles-1939-1940. historyboard.net/t657-le-general-molinie (accessed 23 April 2012); Blaxland, *Destination Dunkirk*, pp. 337–9.

26 See Anthony Clayton, *Three Marshals of France. Leadership after Trauma* (London and Oxford: Brassey's, 1992), pp. 10–22, 65–91, 165–97; Général Alphonse-Pierre Juin, *Mémoires*, vol. 1 (Paris: Fayard, 1959); and the diary of a 27-year-old French ranker captured at Lille: René Martin, *Journal de guerre de captivité (1939–1945)* (Bga Pernezel, 2007).

27 On the rescue of French troops in still-unappreciated numbers, I have drawn on Rhiannon Looseley, '"Le Paradis après l'Enfer". The French soldiers evacuated from Dunkirk in 1940', MA dissertation (History), University of Reading, 2005; even less exists on evacuation of Belgians (their army officially surrendering on 28 May), but see Jean Vanwelkenhuyzen, < *Miracle* > *à Dunkerque. La fin d'un mythe*, (Brussels: Racine, 1994); idem, *1940. Pleins feux sur un désastre* (Brussels: Racine, 1997); and Belgian campaign memoirs including those of the army chief of staff, Lieut.-Général Oscar Michiels, *18 Jours de guerre en Belgique* (Paris: Berger-Levrault, 1947), esp. pp. 208–49; also, Jacques Prieux, *Grandeur Nature. Carnet de Mobilisation et de Guerre* (Brussels: Nossent, 1947); Raymond Leblanc, *Dés pipés. Journal d'un Chasseur Ardennais* (Brussels: André Gilbert, 1942).

28 D. Barlone, *A French Officer's Diary (23 August 1939 to 1 October 1940)*, trans. L.V. Cass (Cambridge: Cambridge University Press, 1942), pp. 66–7; cf. Pierre Porthault, *L'Arrière-garde meurt mais ne se rend pas* (Paris: La France Européenne, 1970), esp. pp. 67–180.

29 Sean Longden, *Dunkirk: The Men They Left Behind* (London: Constable, 2009); Bob Moore and Kent Fedorowich (eds), *Prisoners of War and their Captors in World War II* (Oxford and Washington, DC: Berg, 1996); David Rolf, *Prisoners of the Reich. Germany's Captives, 1939–1945* (London: Leo Cooper, 1988). On French PoWs: Robert Guerlain, *Prisonnier de guerre* (London: Hachette, 1944); Yves Durand, *La Captivité. Histoire des prisonniers de guerre français 1939–1945* (Paris: Fédération nationale des combattants prisonniers de guerre – combattants d'Algérie, de Tunisie, du Maroc, 1980); Jacques Benoist-Méchin, *La Moisson de Quarante. Journal d'un prisonnier de guerre* (Paris: Albin Michel, 1941).

30 R. Ikor, *O soldats de Quarante!* . . . (Paris: Albin Michel, 1986), p. 140.

31 Blaxland, *Destination Dunkirk*, pp. 317, 341.

32 K.-H. Frieser (with John T. Greenwood), *The Blitzkrieg Legend. The 1940 Campaign in the West* (Annapolis, MD: US Naval Institute Press, 2005), pp. 281–2. Cf. Gen. Henri Aymes, *Gembloux: succès français. Le 4ᵉ corps d'armée dans la bataille de la 1ʳᵉ Armée en Belgique et en France 10 mai-3 juin 1940* (Paris: Berger-Levrault, 1948); Jeffery A. Gunsburg, 'The Battle of the Belgian Plain, 12–14 May 1940: The First Great Tank Battle', *Journal of Military History*, 56, 2 (April 1992), pp. 207–44; idem, 'The Battle of Gembloux,

14–15 May 1940: The "Blitzkrieg" Checked', *Journal of Military History*, 64, 1 (January 2000), pp. 97–140.

33 Général J. Prioux, *Souvenirs de guerre, 1939–1943* (Paris: Flammarion, 1947), p. 135; see also Marc Bloch *Strange Defeat. A Statement of Evidence Written in 1940*, trans. G. Hopkins (New York: W.W. Norton, 1968), pp. 13–18, recounting his retreat from 23 to 30 May 1940 through Steenwerck and Zuydschoote to Bray-les-Dunes.

34 Prioux, *Souvenirs*, pp. 129–30; cf. Miles Reid, *Last on the List* (London: Leo Cooper, 1974), pp. 29–58.

35 Bloch, *Strange Defeat*, p. 16.

36 Ibid.; Prioux, *Souvenirs*, pp. 134–7. Cf. account by a British lieutenant in the sector in Peter Hadley, *Third Class to Dunkirk. A worm's-eye view of the BEF, 1940* (London: Hollis and Carter, 1944), pp. 119–44.

37 Blaxland, *Destination Dunkirk*, pp. 345–6.

38 Calder, *Myth of the Blitz*, p. 94; Blaxland, *Destination Dunkirk*, pp. 337–9. The Belgian army felt cut adrift by 26 May by both the British and French; cf. sub-section: 'The Belgians abandoned', in their chief of staff's memoirs (Michiels, *18 Jours de guerre*, pp. 208–9); and Thomas J. Knight, 'Belgium Leaves the War, 1940', *Journal of Modern History*, 41, 1 (March 1969), pp. 46–67.

39 Philippe Masson, *La Marine française et la guerre 1939–1945* (Paris: Tallandier, 1991), pp. 50–7.

40 Sir John R. Colville, *The Fringes of Power. Downing Street Diaries, 1939–1955* (London: Hodder & Stoughton, 1985), p. 182.

41 Nicholas Atkin, *The Forgotten French. Exiles in the British Isles, 1940–1944* (Manchester: Manchester University Press, 2003), pp. 43–52, 93–8; Robert and Isabelle Tombs, *That Sweet Enemy. The French and the British from the Sun King to the Present* (London: Heinemann, 2006), pp. 554–5.

42 Herbert R. Lottman, *The Fall of Paris, June 1940* (London: Sinclair-Stevenson, 1992).

43 P. Mousset, *Quand le temps travaillait pour nous. Récit de guerre* (Paris: Grasset, 1941), pp. 232–97; Hanna Diamond, *Fleeing Hitler, France 1940* (Oxford: Oxford University Press, 2007); Pierre Miquel, *L'exode, 10 mai–20 juin 1940* (Paris: Plon, 2003). Cf. the similar saga of Bloch (*Strange Defeat*, pp. 20–4), also taken by train and ship from Dover to Plymouth, thence back to Cherbourg, finding himself in Brittany when the armistice came about.

44 Captain Sir Basil Bartlett, Bt., *My First War. An Army Officer's Journal for May 1940. Through Belgium to Dunkirk* (London: Chatto & Windus, 1940), p. 127.

45 See Frieser, *The Blitzkrieg Legend*, ch. 8 'The "Miracle of Dunkirk"', pp. 291–314; Vanwelkenhuyzen, *Miracle à Dunkerque*, pp. 42–74; Mungo Melvin, *Manstein. Hitler's Greatest General* (London: Weidenfeld & Nicolson, 2010), pp. 161–6; Matthew Cooper, *The German Army 1933–1945. Its Political and Military Failure* (London: Macdonald & Janes, 1978), pp. 224–37.

46 Quoted in Frieser, *The Blitzkrieg Legend*, p. 296. Walter Lord, *The Miracle of Dunkirk* (New York: Viking, 1982); Hugh Sebag-Montefiore, *Dunkirk. Fight*

to the Last Man (London: Viking, 2006); David Divine, *The Nine Days of Dunkirk* (London: Faber & Faber, 1959).

47 The discourse and imagery, conspicuously Biblical and evoking the Israelites' passage of the Red Sea in the Old Testament, supplied Churchill the title for the Dunkirk chapter in his memoirs, *The Second World War. II: Their Finest Hour* (London: Cassell, 1949), pp. 87–104; and titles for two books published for the 60th anniversary: Patrick Oddone, *Dunkirk 1940. French Ashes, British Deliverance – The Story of Operation Dynamo* (Stroud: Tempus, 2000); Patrick Wilson, *Dunkirk. From Disaster to Deliverance* (Barnsley: Leo Cooper, 1999).

48 Maj-Gen. Julian Thompson, *Dunkirk: Retreat to Victory* (London: Sidgwick & Jackson, 2008).

49 Paul Addison and Jeremy A. Crang (eds), *Listening to Britain Home Intelligence Reports on Britain's Finest Hour – May to September 1940* (London: The Bodley Head, 2010), p. 52; Martin S. Alexander, '"No taste for the fight?" French Combat Performance in 1940 and the Politics of the Fall of France', in Paul Addison and Angus Calder (eds), *Time to Kill. The Soldier's Experience of War in the West, 1939–1945* (London: Pimlico, 1997), pp. 161–76.

50 K. Moore, *A Family Life, 1939–45* (London: Allison & Busby/W.H. Allen, 1989), pp. 54–5.

51 For example, Alexander Werth, *The Last Days of Paris. A Journalist's Diary* (London: Hamish Hamilton, 1940); Greenwall, *When France Fell*; Gordon Waterfield, *What Happened to France* (London: John Murray, 1940); George Millar, *Road to Resistance. An Autobiography* (London: The Bodley Head, 1979); Geoffrey Cox, *Countdown to War. A Personal Memoir of Europe, 1938–1940* (London: William Kimber, 1988). There were Americans, too, several writing interesting accounts. Cf. Eric Sevareid , *Not So Wild a Dream* (New York: Alfred A. Knopf, 1946); Hamilton Fish Armstrong, *Chronology of Failure. The Last Days of the French Republic* (New York: Macmillan, 1941); A.J. Liebling, *The Road Back to Paris* (New York: Paragon House, 1988).

52 J.W. Drawbell, *The Long Year* (London: Allan Wingate, 1958), p. 186; cf. analysis in Stephen Badsey, 'British High Command and the reporting of the campaign', in Bond and Taylor (eds), *The Battle of France*, pp. 139–60.

53 Moore, *A Family Life*, p. 55.

54 Addison and Crang (eds.), *Listening to Britain*, pp. 50–2.

55 Colville, *The Fringes of Power*, pp. 158–70; David Dilks (ed.), *The Diaries of Sir Alexander Cadogan, 1938–1945* (London: Cassell, 1971), pp. 296–305; Paul de Villelume, *Journal d'une défaite, août 1939-juin 1940* (Paris: Fayard, 1976), pp. 245–55; P.M.H. Bell, *France and Britain, 1900–1940. Entente and Estrangement* (Harlow: Longman, 1996), pp. 240–9.

56 Malcolm Smith, *Britain and 1940. History, Myth and Popular Memory* (London: Routledge, 2000), p.40; cf. Bell, *France and Britain, 1900–1940*, pp. 251–4; Dockrill, *British Establishment Perspectives*, pp. 157–63.

57 Bond (ed.), *Chief of Staff*, I, p. 243 (12 October 1939); Muriel Green diary (6 May 1940), in Dorothy Sheridan (ed.), *Wartime Women. An Anthology*

of Women's Wartime Writing for Mass Observation, 1937–45 (London: Heinemann, 1990; Mandarin pb., 1991), p. 90.

58 MO diary excerpted in Calder, *Myth of the Blitz*, pp. 134–5; Addison and Crang (eds.), *Listening to Britain*, pp. 55–6, 60, 90–1, 98, 110–13, 117–8, 124, 132, 141.

59 Moore, *A Family Life*, pp. 55, 58.

60 Moore, *A Family Life*, p. 60; Sheridan (ed.), *Wartime Women*, pp. 91–2.

61 Bruce I. Gudmundsson, 'Dunkirk', *Military History Quarterly* (Winter 1997), pp. 63–70.

62 See John C. Cairns, 'The French view of Dunkirk', in Bond and Taylor (eds), *The Battle of France*, pp. 87–109; Maurice Rajfus, *Les Français de la débâcle. Juin-septembre 1940, un si bel été* (Paris: le cherche midi éditeur, 1997), pp. 111–27, where he notes (p. 115) that: 'For the majority of French, the "treacherous" attack [of 3 July 1940] on Mers-el-Kébir [the French Mediterranean fleet anchorage in Algeria] was an event flowing in a direct line from the Dunkirk evacuation a month before.'

63 S. Hoffmann, 'The Trauma of 1940. A Disaster and its Traces', in Blatt (ed.), *The French Defeat*, pp. 354–70.

64 See Chapter 8.

65 Jean Doise and Maurice Vaïsse, *Diplomatie et Outil militaire, 1871–1969* (Paris: Imprimerie Nationale, 1987), pp. 343–51, 426–32, 471–99.

66 See Herbert R. Lottman, *The People's Anger. Justice and Revenge in post-Liberation France* (London: Hutchinson, 1986); Martin S. Alexander, 'Repercussions – The Battle of France in History and Historiography: The French View', in Bond and Taylor, *The Battle of France*, pp. 181–205.

67 Commandant P. Lyet, *La Bataille de France (mai-juin 1940)* (Paris: Payot, 1947), p. 113; J.-P. Azéma, *From Munich to the Liberation, 1938–1944*, trans. Janet Lloyd (Cambridge: Cambridge University Press, 1984; original French edn. Paris: Seuil, 1979), p. 33. Tellingly, two fine French books of more recent vintage have numerous non-French contributors, viz. Maurice Vaïsse (ed.), *Mai-Juin 1940. Défaite française, victoire allemande, sous l'oeil des historiens étrangers* (Paris: Autrement, 2000); Christine Levisse-Touzé (ed.), *La Campagne de 1940. Actes du colloque: 16 au 18 novembre 2000* (Paris: Tallandier, 2001).

68 P. Finney, *Remembering the Road to World War Two. International history, national identity, collective memory* (London and New York: Routledge, 2011), p. 179; I. Némirovsky, *Suite française*, trans. Sandra Smith (London: Chatto & Windus, 2006; original French edn. Paris: Denoel, 2004).

69 Eric Conan and Henry Rousso, *Vichy, An Ever Present Past* (Hanover, NH: University Press of New England, 1998).

70 M. Ophuls and A. Harris, *The Sorrow and the Pity* (St. Albans: Paladin, 1975), pp. 100–108; M.R.D. Foot, *SOE in France. An Account of the Work of the British Special Operations Executive in France 1940–1944* (London: HMSO, 1966); Mark Seaman, 'Good thrillers but bad history: A review of published works on the Special Operations Executive's work in France

during the Second World War', in K.G. Robertson (ed.), *War, Resistance and Intelligence. Essays in Honour of M.R.D. Foot* (Barnsley: Leo Cooper, 1999), pp. 119–133.

71 *The World at War* (Series producer: Sir Jeremy Isaacs for Thames Television, 1973; Thames Video TV9924, TV9925 & TV9926), Episode 3: 'France Falls, May-June 1940' (writer and producer: Peter Batty); Episode 4: 'Britain Alone – Britain, May 1940 – June 1941' (writer: Laurence Thompson; producer & director: David Elstein); also, 'The Battle of France' in the video-documentary series *Battlefield. A Definitive History of the Decisive Battles of World War Two* (Lamancha Productions/Polygram Video, no. 634 030-3, 1994).

72 *The Other Side of Dunkirk*, (Producer: Alastair Laurence, BBCFour, 2004); the present author is also one of those interviewed.

73 Smith, *Britain and 1940*, esp. chs. 3 and 4; Philip Bell and Ralph White, *Our Great Ally France 1938–1940*, Archive series No. 4 (Prod: The Inter-University History Film Consortium, 1986), Flash Video, The British Universities Film & Video Council website, http://bufvc.ac.uk/ filmandsound?film_name = bell_white_ogaf_as4 (accessed 4 May 2012).

74 See Mark Connelly, *We Can Take It! Britain and the Memory of the Second World War* (Harlow: Pearson-Longman, 2004), pp. 54–94; Summerfield, 'Dunkirk and the Popular Memory', pp. 796–7, 803–4.

75 Leslie Norman (Dir.), 'Dunkirk' (1958), Optimum Classic Releasing Ltd. DVD, 2009; Summerfield, 'Dunkirk and the Popular Memory', pp. 809–10; S.P. Mackenzie, 'Victory from Defeat: The War Office and the making of *Dunkirk* (Ealing Films, 1958)', *War, Literature & the Arts*, 51, 1–2 (2003), pp. 241–57.

76 Conversation with Dunkirk veteran Capt. Matthews's son, Mr William T. Matthews of Tower Hill, Ormskirk (12 May 2012); quotation: Summerfield, 'Dunkirk and the Popular Memory', p. 790.

77 Summerfield, 'Dunkirk and the Popular Memory', pp. 790–2; Siân Nicholas, '"Sly Demagogues" and Wartime Radio: J.B. Priestley and the BBC', *Twentieth Century British History*, 6, 3 (1995), pp. 247–66.

78 Moore, *A Family Life*, p. 57; also Ian McLaine, *Ministry of Morale. Home Front Morale and the Ministry of Information in World War II* (London, Boston, and Sydney: Allen & Unwin, 1979).

79 N. Harman, *Dunkirk: The Necessary Myth* (London: Hodder & Stoughton, 1980).

80 Dominic Sandbrook, *Never Had It So Good. A History of Britain from Suez to the Beatles* (Boston: Little, Brown, 2005); Bernard Porter, *Britain, Europe and the World: Delusions of Grandeur, 1850–1982* (London: Unwin Hyman, 1983); David Reynolds, *Britannia Overruled. British Policy and World Power in the 20th Century* (Harlow: Longman, 1991); Donald Cameron Watt, *Succeeding John Bull: America in Britain's Place 1900–1975* (Cambridge: Cambridge University Press, 1984).

81 This phrase supplied the title of the memoirs of another British army 1939–45 colossus – Field Marshal Sir William Slim – who extricated the Commonwealth forces from disaster in Burma. See his *Defeat into Victory*.

The Memoirs of Field-Marshal The Viscount Slim (London: Cassell, 1956); and Ronald Lewin, *Slim: The Standardbearer. A Biography of Field-Marshal The Viscount Slim* (London: Leo Cooper, 1976).

82 Addison, review of Harman's *Dunkirk: The Necessary Myth*, available at http://www.historytoday.com/print/2707 (accessed 20 April 2012).

83 Summerfield, 'Dunkirk and the Popular Memory', pp. 803–4; Peter Hennessy, *Having it So Good. Britain in the Fifties* (London: Allen Lane, 2006).

84 Summerfield, 'Dunkirk and the Popular Memory', p. 799.

85 Calder, *Myth of the Blitz,* pp. 155–68, 244–56; a later spasm of war films had to be differently framed, in part to reduce production costs, for example, the more sentimentalized child's eyes view of *Hope and Glory* (dir. John Boorman, 1987). Cf. John Ramsden, 'Refocusing "The People's War": British War Films of the 1950s', *Journal of Contemporary History*, 33, 1 (January 1998), pp. 35–63.

86 It seems to be an ineffably British quality to treat this as a virtue, well demonstrated by the way the French equivalent – especially in a military context (Le Système-D, or 'se débrouiller') – is deplored in the land of systematic Cartesian rationality as signifying failure by the very absence of 'system'.

87 Peter Dawnay, 'Foreword', in Anthony Gibbs, *Gibbs and a Phoney War* (London: Peter Dawnay, 1967), page un-numbered; Gibbs' father, Sir Philip Gibbs, had been a distinguished war correspondent and press advisor to Field Marshal Sir Douglas Haig on the Western Front in 1915–18.

88 Drawbell, *The Long Year,* p. 183.

89 Churchill, *The Second World War,* II, pp. 87–104; Calder, *Myth of the Blitz,* pp. 1–3, 20–38, 46–52, 90–101; indicating the very different French geographical-cum-metaphysical perspective, Pierre Belperron's book published in London in April 1940 (*Maginot of the Line*, p. 124), had already identified the Maginot Line, not the Channel, as 'the last rampart of Western civilisation'.

90 David Edgerton, *Britain's War Machine. Weapons, Resources and Experts in the Second World War* (London: Penguin, 2012), p. 47.

91 Martin S. Alexander, 'After Dunkirk: the French Army's performance against "Case Red", 25 May to 25 June 1940', *War in History* 14, 2 (April 2007), pp. 219–64.

92 Edgerton, *Britain's War Machine,* p. 47 (emphasis added).

93 Edgerton, *Britain's War Machine,* p. 85.

94 Smith, *Britain and 1940,* pp. 111–129; Summerfield, 'Dunkirk and the Popular Memory', pp. 809–10.

95 Calder, *Myth of the Blitz,* pp. 269–72.

96 Bartlett, *My First War,* p. 127.

97 Sevareid, *Not So Wild a Dream,* p. 155.

98 Tombs, *That Sweet Enemy,* p. 570 (also pp. 558–69, 592–6); for the King's visit to the BEF see Alex Danchev and Dan Todman (eds), *War Diaries*

1939–1945. Field Marshal Lord Alanbrooke (London: Weidenfeld & Nicolson, 2001 – hereafter: *Alanbrooke War Diaries*), pp. 22–3; Bond (ed.), *Chief of Staff*, I, pp. 265–6; Colville, *Man of Valour*, pp. 157–61.

 99 Bell, *France and Britain 1900–1940*, pp. 249–54; idem, 'The Breakdown of the Alliance in 1940', in Neville Waites (ed.), *Troubled Neighbours. Franco-British Relations in the Twentieth Century* (London: Weidenfeld & Nicolson, 1971), pp. 200–27. For subsequent relations: Peter Mangold, *The Almost Impossible Ally. Harold Macmillan and Charles de Gaulle* (London: I. B. Tauris, 2006).

100 Danchev and Todman (eds), *Alanbrooke War Diaries*, pp. 84–5.

101 Quoted in Glover, *Fight for the Channel Ports*, p. 224; cf. Danchev and Todman (eds), *Alanbrooke War Diaries*, pp. 86–8; Blaxland, *Destination Dunkirk*, pp. 376–87.

102 Tombs, *That Sweet Enemy*, p. 598.

103 Glover, *Fight for the Channel Ports*, p. 229.

104 British forces in Normandy and Brittany were commanded from 23 May to 13 June by Lieutenant General Sir Henry Karslake, and from 13 to 17 June by Lieutenant General Sir Alan Brooke (whom the War Office ordered back into France to oversee their extrication); the chain-of-command was complicated, however, by the dispatch of another team on 29 May under Lieutenant General Sir James Marshall-Cornwall to the headquarters of General Robert Altmayer, French Tenth Army commander in Normandy. See Danchev and Todman (eds), *Alanbrooke War Diaries*, pp. 79–88; and J.H. Marshall-Cornwall, *Wars and Rumours of Wars. A Memoir* (London: Leo Cooper/Secker & Warburg, 1984), pp. 138–66; Glover, *Fight for the Channel Ports*, pp. 184–240; Basil Karslake, *1940, The Last Act. The Story of the British Forces in France after Dunkirk* (London: Leo Cooper, 1979).

105 Major A.G.W. Tonkin, 669 POW Wkg 46 Coy, Greenford, Middlesex, *The Pioneer Magazine* (March 1947), available at http://www.royalpioneercorps. co.uk/rpc/history_lancastria.htm (accessed 23 April 2012). An exact number is elusive because the ship was massively overloaded in a bid to leave as few personnel as possible behind in France. Cf. survivors' testimonies in John L. West, *The Loss of 'Lancastria'* (Rossendale: Millgate Publishing Ltd., 1988); Brian James Crabb, *The Forgotten Tragedy. The Story of the Sinking of HMT Lancastria* (Bristol: Paul Watkins Publishing, 2002); Jonathan Fenby, *The Sinking of the Lancastria. Britain's Greatest Maritime Disaster and Churchill's Cover-Up* (London: Simon & Schuster UK, 2005).

106 Danchev and Todman (eds), *Alanbrooke War Diaries*, p. 87.

107 M.L. Walkinton, *Twice in a Lifetime* (London: Samson Books, 1980), pp. 208–9.

108 Eric Roussel (ed.), *Roland de Margerie. Journal 1939–1940* (Paris: Grasset, 2010), p. 353.

109 Calder, *Myth of the Blitz*, pp. 94–5.

110 Tombs, *That Sweet Enemy*, p. 566.

CHAPTER FIVE

The British, the Free French and the Resistance

Sébastien Albertelli

In the history of Franco-British relations, both the saga of the Free French and British relations with the Resistance have provided each side with a rich and contradictory set of memories. Cooperation and competition were intertwined; so too were disagreements over common objectives and the defence of the national interest. Of course, neither the British nor the Free French nor the Resistance can be taken as unified entities. We must examine the tensions and divisions within each, as well as the balance of power between them and the evolution of their positions in a rapidly changing context. If there was one constant, however, it was the highly unbalanced relationship between the British and their Free French counterparts. The latter were always entirely dependent on British material and logistical assistance. French agents sent from the United Kingdom were trained in British centres, while the Free French used British planes, ships, communication lines, diplomatic outposts in neutral countries and money. Not to mention the large number of arms and weapons.[1] Without this help, neither the Free French nor the Resistance would have been able to function.

Multiple actors in a three-way relationship

There were many more actors in the relationship between the Free French, the British and the Resistance than were immediately apparent. Let us turn first to the Resistance. It would be more accurate to talk of 'resistances' in the plural since there was no unified opposition to Vichy and the German occupation until at least 1942, after which its growth was closely linked to the fortunes of Free France. *Résistants* were divided between pioneers and those who joined later; they were split between movements and parties; and there was an important distinction between those operating in the occupied zone and those in Vichy France. From 1941 onwards, the main leaders of the resistance movements – in particular, Emmanuel d'Astier de la Vigerie, the founder and leader of Libération-Sud, and Henri Frenay, his counterpart at *Combat* – sought assistance directly from the British rather than from the Free French, to whom they owed nothing. D'Astier made this position quite clear in the first report he addressed to London at the end of 1941.[2] When he first met de Gaulle in London in May 1942, he was 'a little disappointed' to find him so critical of the British. A few months later, Frenay expressed a point of view that he would continue to articulate throughout the war and that was shared by many of his fellow *résistants*. He maintained that it was important to keep good relations with the British to obtain their help and simultaneously argued that resistance movements, while preserving their independence, should rally to the Free French (France Combattante from July 1942).[3] This was because he believed the British would be more inclined to acknowledge the support of independent resistance movements than the support of groups subservient to the Free French. It is clear, then, that *résistants* were not willing to be simply the object of discussions between de Gaulle and the British; they also wanted to impose themselves as independent actors.

De Gaulle had a radically different interpretation of the situation. His aim was to undermine the legitimacy of the Vichy regime and raise Free France to the status of government-in-exile. He hoped that the Free French would ultimately be seen by the Allies as the guarantors of the French national interest and recognized as guardians of French sovereignty and sole central authority. The success of this project depended on the Allies. They alone could confer legitimacy on de Gaulle and give him the means with which to impose himself. But de Gaulle also needed the Resistance. It provided him with men and, because of the continued existence of the Vichy regime, was the only entity that might give the Free French some kind of 'democratic' base that could be used to persuade the Allies of French support for de Gaulle.

De Gaulle's attitude towards his allies hardly changed over the years. Far from being grateful to the British, his dependence only made him more intransigent in his defence of what he perceived to be France's national interest. He was equally uncompromising when it came to French participation in planning for the D-Day landings. For de Gaulle, the Free French were the only legitimate political authority: in his view, any activity that took place on French soil had to be under his supervision, at the risk of undermining France's national sovereignty.[4] He was outraged that, without his permission, the British spoke to whichever leader or movement they chose. Until 1944, he denounced the direct recruitment of French volunteers by the British and condemned the sections of MI6 and the SOE (Special Operations Executive) that operated in France independently of the Free French. But his protestations always fell on deaf ears. Nevertheless, de Gaulle's view of Britain was widely shared among the leaders of the Free French – such as André Diethelm and especially André Philip and Emmanuel d'Astier – and French military commanders – such as Colonel Billotte, General d'Astier and General Koenig. General Cochet, who was more favourably disposed towards the British, was rapidly marginalized from 1943 onwards.[5]

The special relationship that had been forged between de Gaulle and Winston Churchill in the summer of 1940 came apart as the war progressed. The Prime Minister soon began to emphasize the global aspects of the war and sought total victory at minimal human cost to Britain.[6] This logic was considerably strengthened by America's entrance into the war. From this point on, the British refused to tie themselves exclusively to de Gaulle; instead, they reserved the right to turn to any power that seemed capable of bringing victory. Hence the frequent contacts with potentially useful individuals and groups in the Vichy government. On a number of occasions, the British let it be known – through Anthony Eden – that they valued their collaboration with the Free French.[7] But they made it clear that they would maintain contact with any person in France whom they considered useful. It was out of the question that de Gaulle should be their only interlocutor. In any case, his actual power was frequently questioned and the British secret services were more than willing to support resistance groups that did not recognize de Gaulle's authority.

Differences among British leaders nevertheless became apparent as the war developed. If some generals – such as the Chief of the Imperial General Staff, Alan Brooke – were sceptical about de Gaulle and the potential role of the Resistance in the liberation of France, others in the cabinet were more sympathetic. The Foreign Secretary, Anthony Eden, argued that the Resistance would never follow Pétain and that it was in Britain's interest to support de Gaulle. Indeed, all the evidence suggested that the Free French leader was playing a pivotal role in unifying the Resistance and that he was the only person with the legitimacy to govern the territories liberated by the Allies, at least in the first instance.[8] As time went on, this view became more and more widespread in the War Cabinet, Parliament, the press and public opinion. The consensus was such that Churchill had to backtrack when he was seen too openly to be supporting Roosevelt's desire to break with de Gaulle.[9]

For both the Free French and the British, the secret services were critical in maintaining links with the Resistance. The role of de Gaulle's intelligence service run by 'Colonel Passy' (2ème Bureau, subsequently renamed SR and finally BCRA) was to limit the three-way contact between the Free French, the Resistance and the Allies to a bilateral relationship between the Free

French and the Allies on the one hand, and between the Free French and the Resistance on the other. It, therefore, worked hard to break any direct contact between the British secret services and the Resistance. At first, Passy's organization thought it would be possible to work closely alongside the British. But, very quickly, it reached the same conclusion as that of de Gaulle. It suspected the British of hijacking some of its secret agents and resented British support for non-Gaullist groups beyond their control. Predictably, Passy's organization found it hard to accept being placed under British tutelage when its aim was to develop genuine cooperation. Encouraged by de Gaulle, and frustrated in its attempts to control clandestine activity on French soil, the BCRA eventually adopted a policy of greater independence from the summer of 1942. It was to be a period marked by suspicion and hostility towards the British secret services.[10]

MI6 and the SOE each had at their disposal one service working with the Free French for operations on French soil (the Cohen Section at MI6 and RF Section at the SOE) and one service entirely independent of de Gaulle's administration (the Dunderdale Section at MI6 and F Section at the SOE). In accordance with British policy, their aim was to establish contact with *résistants* in France. This included those who accepted de Gaulle's authority and those who did not. In return for the help provided to the Free French secret services, they received a copy of all the telegrams and reports sent to London. Nevertheless, the British made little effort to allay the fears of their Free French counterparts. They recruited French agents for themselves, entered into direct contact with Gaullist agents in France and on numerous occasions suggested that the BCRA's security measures were inadequate – a rumour as damaging as it was unsubstantiated.[11]

In search of the Resistance: The Free French and the British in 1940–41

From the summer of 1940 onwards, the British and the Free French had the same goal, namely to make contact with those in the field who had decided to resist German occupation and/or the Vichy government. Cooperation between the Free French and the British began with the exchanging of information – the result of an agreement between de Gaulle's 2ème Bureau and MI6. Agents in France soon made it clear that some French citizens wanted to develop resistance activities. In 1941, these agents reported that the most determined actors in the field were organizing themselves into increasingly sophisticated resistance groups that would be able to take advantage of the growing hostility towards the German occupation.

On the British side, establishing contact with the Resistance was the responsibility of the SOE, created by Churchill in early July 1940 to develop clandestine activity in occupied territories. Despite opposition from MI6 – who saw the SOE as little more than a group of amateurs whose meddlesome tactics threatened the security of MI6 agents – the SOE approached the Free French at the end of 1940 with a view to recruiting parachutists willing to go to France. This partnership was strengthened by mutual assistance, in particular, the successful Josephine B operation on a transformer station at Pessac, near Bordeaux in June 1941. Several teams were subsequently sent to France with the responsibility of contacting known *résistants*.

Of course, SOE leaders also had their own agenda. They hoped that, by extending cooperation, they would more effectively be able to control the activities of the Free French. As one of them explained:

> The real difficulty for de Gaulle is that, even if he wants to lead certain operations of a subversive nature in France, he has no means with which to do so – such as planes, radios etc. I think therefore that if we provide the instrument, we will almost certainly be able to call the tune.[12]

Frank Nelson, Executive Director of SOE, whose strong personality dominated the service, never imagined an equal collaboration with the Free French:

> The ideal would be to let the Gestapo and de Gaulle's High Command think that we are 100% with the latter – whereas, in fact, even if I want you to have the most cordial daily relations with de Gaulle, I do not want you to reveal to him our most secret and confidential plans.[13]
> To put it bluntly, this should be one-way cooperation; in other words, I want our own F Section to know exactly what de Gaulle's men are doing, but I don't want de Gaulle to know anything at all about SOE.[14]

This independent stance was confirmed in 1941, when F and RF sections established their own contacts in France.[15] The SOE's direct recruitment of French agents was humiliating for de Gaulle's men but, at this early stage, the coexistence of two separate sections working in parallel in France did not pose any significant logistical difficulties.

The movement that now goes by the name of 'La Résistance' emerged between 1942 and the spring of 1943. It consisted of disparate groups that, over time, came together to resist German occupation and the Vichy government. In particular, the southern resistance movements (Libération, Combat and Franc-Tireur) had a strong sense of internal identity. With the active encouragement of the Free French, they agreed to form a Comité de Coordination under the direction of Jean Moulin and an Armée Secrète (AS) under the direction of General Delestraint, who had been appointed by de Gaulle in October 1942. Over the course of the first quarter of 1943, these attempts at unification spread to the Northern Zone, which ultimately led to the creation of a national AS and the National Council of the Resistance.

Yet, as the Resistance became stronger and more united, it turned into one of the principal sources of tension between the Free French and the British.

The arrival of Jean Moulin in London in October 1941 was the beginning of a series of incidents all of which hinged on one crucial question: since the Free French did not have sole control of operations in France, would they at least retain a monopoly on relations with resistance movements with whom they had made contact? Moulin's stay in London confirmed that the Gaullist administration had no intention of allowing the British to contact Free French *résistants*. As soon as Moulin told the SOE that he had joined the Free French, he refused to share any details of his 'movements' with the British. Once he had chosen Free France, he considered the latter as a necessary intermediary. This attitude – from a man who had initially claimed that his mission was primarily to 'come to an agreement with the British authorities' – infuriated the leader of F Section, Maurice Buckmaster. But, despite being noticeably more sympathetic than de Gaulle to the work of F Section in mobilizing French *résistants* who were 'anti-German without being pro-de Gaulle', Moulin was adamant that they would all end up rallying to Free France.[16] It is still unclear whether Moulin's attitude explains the delay on the part of the British in parachuting him back to France.

Since the publication of General de Gaulle's memoirs in 1954, it has generally been accepted that Moulin returned to France in early 1942 as de Gaulle's representative in the Unoccupied Zone. In fact, this could not have been the case. The reasons for this are too lengthy to be discussed here, but it seems clear that Moulin was not assigned this task by de Gaulle. Instead, he took it upon himself. He became the necessary mediator between the Free French and the Resistance. He succeeded in marginalizing rival projects – such as those of General La Laurencie – and convincing the main resistance leaders of the Unoccupied Zone to accept de Gaulle's authority. Over the course of the summer of 1942, the Free French administration and de Gaulle himself became aware of the success of this operation and made Moulin the *de facto* representative of Free France in the Unoccupied Zone, even if this kind of centralization went against all their previous policy. We can only understand the decision to accept a structure built around Moulin if we consider the importance of the Resistance to Free France in its relations with the British.

Over the course of 1942, the British continued to develop their contacts outside the Free French sphere of influence. They still argued that it was important to develop links with any French organization that could be used to combat the Germans.[17] The leaders of the SOE placed much of their hope in the Carte group.[18] This was led by André Girard, who was adept at speaking the language of the military and loudly proclaimed his aversion to politics. He claimed to have the support of top officers in the High Command of the French Army and laid out carefully prepared plans for a substantial secret army that could support the Allied landings in France. The agents of F Section wrote enthusiastically about the potential of Girard's organization and invited Carte's Chief of Staff, Henri Frager, to spend time in London in July and August 1942.[19] After this visit, the SOE was convinced that members of the Vichy Army's High Command were training reservists, hiding arms and preparing an offensive against the German Army. In short, that they were laying the foundations of a promising resistance movement and that it would be unwise to compromise this emerging force by allying too closely with the Gaullists.[20] The same was true of the hopes invested in General Giraud's plans in North Africa: these took priority over Free French agitation.

It is not surprising, then, that the British viewed Free French attempts to control and direct spontaneous resistance movements in France with some scepticism. They underlined how difficult it was to 'evaluate the usefulness and strength' of these 'newspaper movements' of the Unoccupied Zone. The British also highlighted the extent to which these movements were divided by internal squabbles and had, under the influence of de Gaulle, prioritized politics and propaganda over military preparation.[21] The heads of MI6 and the SOE were, at this time, a major influence on the way in which the British authorities assessed de Gaulle's influence in France. Thus, when Churchill asked his personal assistant, Desmond Morton, to produce a report on the extent of support for de Gaulle in France, the end result was a document that reflected above all the view of MI6 and the SOE. They were far less favourably disposed towards the Free French leader than the Foreign Office. The report acknowledged that a majority of the French recognized de Gaulle as a symbol of their desire to repel the German occupier. But few were willing to take risks for him. Under these circumstances, it was impossible to guarantee that disparate Gaullist resistance movements would be of significant (military) help. De Gaulle's future, it was argued, would depend largely on his relations with the generals of the French Army of the armistice who would control the political and military situation at the time of the Allied landings.[22]

This growing scepticism did not go unnoticed among the leaders of the Free French. It was from spring 1942 onwards that the BCRA began openly to criticize the SOE. The Free French resented British attempts to limit their sphere of influence by providing only very limited access to material and logistical assistance, exercising undue control over Free French agents, and making the most of their material advantage to interfere with relations between the Free French and the Resistance. For instance, MI6 and the SOE decided to block the exfiltration from France of members of the Resistance whose activities were judged to be more political than military.[23] The leaders of the Free French denounced such intolerable 'supervision' on the part of the British but were powerless to do anything about it.[24] In the end, it was not so much the erratic nature of communication or the inadequacy of air operations that riled the Free French. It was the degree to which they were kept away from communication exchanges and airfields from which they might have been able to get an overall view of operations in France.

Two events reinforced the sense among the Free French that the British were trying to hijack resistance movements that had already been contacted by the BCRA. The first was the departure from France, in April 1942, of Emmanuel d'Astier on board a British submarine. The SOE was accused of having engineered his escape without consulting the BCRA, despite the fact that d'Astier was already in contact with the Free French. De Gaulle was incensed and warned Alan Brooke that he would suspend any collaboration. The British were never able to convince their opposite number of their good intentions, even if these were very real. It seemed to the Free French that, come what may, the British had reserved the right to maintain independent relations with those organizations that had rallied to Free France.[25]

The second incident took place at the end of July 1942. In a telegram, Yvon Morandat, a Free French agent in the Unoccupied Zone, reported that British agents had been offering arms to the Combat and Franc-Tireur movements, on the condition that they follow British orders. For the first time, the question of material assistance to resistance movements became an important issue. The BCRA accused the SOE of cancelling their operations in order to deliver weapons to resistance movements themselves and, at the same time, divert them away from the Free French. The SOE denied the allegations but, once again, refused to condemn the initiatives of British agents in the field. The Free French then decided formally to ask the British authorities whether they recognized that the major resistance movements in the Unoccupied Zone had placed themselves spontaneously under de Gaulle's command. In reply, the SOE maintained that the situation was unclear. They argued that d'Astier and Frenay had rallied to the symbol of de Gaulle but had not necessarily placed themselves under his command. This being the case, the British should not be prevented from contacting members of the Resistance, whatever their affiliation.[26]

Over the course of the summer of 1942, the Free French devised numerous strategies in the hope that de Gaulle would be recognized as the legitimate commander of a French front (the opening of which seemed, at this stage, imminent). At the very least, they wanted him to play a key role in the elaboration of any operations on French territory after the Allied landings. But these efforts were greeted with little enthusiasm by Alan Brooke, who disliked de Gaulle and had always emphasized links with the Vichy High Command.[27]

Paradoxically, however, the result of Free French pressure was to reinforce the role of the SOE: a memo sent on 2 June made the SOE the only coordinating institution for all clandestine operations on French soil (except those of MI6) and the sole interlocutor with the Free French.[28]

By August 1942, it seemed as if there would be little or no coordination between the British and Free French secret services – and the controversy surrounding Morandat's telegram meant that suspicions were running high. It is no coincidence that this was the moment when the BCRA raised the issue of Moulin's role as chief coordinator in the field for the French National Committee (the official name for the Free French movement after September 1941). The BCRA pointed out that, if anyone was allowed to deliver arms to resistance movements without prior authorization from Moulin as the representative of Free France, it would create a good deal of confusion on the ground. The leaders of the Free French were aware that they were being held at arm's length by the SOE. They evidently thought that, by making all relations with the Resistance pass through Moulin, the latter would eventually become the focal point even for those movements that had hitherto been in direct contact with the British. The stern response to this proposal was proof that such a situation had not been envisaged in late 1941: the British made it clear that they had never intended Moulin to act as a coordinator of operations in France. This was to be the responsibility of the SOE alone.[29]

The British had placed great hopes in Giraud to circumvent Vichy's North African army at the time of the Allied landings in North Africa. The leaders of the SOE were, therefore, bitterly disappointed with the agreement signed with Darlan and Giraud's willing acceptance of Darlan's authority.[30] The early events of the North African campaign, therefore, unexpectedly contributed to a rapprochement between the SOE and their Free French counterparts. Influenced by reports from British agents and the presence of Frenay and d'Astier in London, the British considered that the very survival of the Resistance as a potential support for the Allied cause could be undermined by Darlan's nomination. They could see that, after the Allied landings in North Africa, support for de Gaulle had grown among the Resistance. They communicated this to the Foreign Office which in turn shared this information with all the members of the War Cabinet.[31] De Gaulle dined on several occasions with the head of the SOE, Lord Selborne, who was convinced that Darlan would disappear and that a new opportunity to unite resistance forces outside France would emerge. In the meantime, Lord Selborne instructed the SOE to provide the maximum support for Free France.[32]

Ultimately, however, political considerations came first. Since Churchill had declared himself Roosevelt's 'ardent and enterprising servant', he could not accept any criticism of the American president's policy in North Africa.[33] At the same time, the Foreign Office blocked the transmission in French North Africa (AFN) of a message of support from the Comité de Coordination to de Gaulle on 17 November.[34] Above all, Darlan's assassination made it possible for Giraud to reposition himself as the preeminent interlocutor with the British. Far from encouraging a rapid unification of resistance forces, this was the start of an intense battle for control between de Gaulle and Giraud. The establishment of Giraud's secret service branches in London and their desire to start working in France with the help of the British services put an end to the more cooperative relationship between the SOE and the BCRA that had begun with Operation Torch.

Preparing for D Day

The mutual distrust between the Free French and British secret services that had been held at bay by a common disapproval of the pact with Darlan returned with renewed force in the following months and continued until 1944. The leaders of the SOE had initially hoped to act as a 'bridge' between Gaullists and Giraudists. They soon realized, however, that a merger between the secret services based in London and Algiers would be much more difficult than they had anticipated. As a result, they opted to maintain the status quo in the hope of preserving good relations with Giraud and de Gaulle.[35] But the Free French soon suspected Churchill's motives. They feared that de Gaulle would be replaced by Giraud as the head of the Resistance on the grounds that the former was concerned primarily with political objectives. This was consistent with accusations that the BCRA was using British military assistance for political ends, an argument used by MI6 to block temporarily the departure of Colonel Passy's mission to Paris. In the end, this mission – which took place between January and April 1943 and was led by Passy, Pierre Brossolette and the British officer Forest Yeo-Thomas, deputy head of RF section – highlighted the hitherto unknown military potential available in the North Zone.

The increased awareness of the possibility of military activity in France made arms provision a key issue in 1943. The earliest requests for military assistance had been put forward in the autumn of 1942 in the presence of Frenay and d'Astier. At the time, the British had made promises they were not able to keep. Moulin and Delestraint's stay in London from 14 February to 19 March 1943 provided another opportunity to return to this sensitive issue. Since the autumn, the position of the SOE had evolved. The hopes invested in the Carte organization had evaporated. Moreover, the British secret services had been forced to acknowledge that, not only were there many resistance movements in France, but also that they might even have 'enormous potential value for an Allied landing'. Aware that they were in a position to implement a coordinated programme of sabotage, the SOE requested an increase in arms provision from the military authorities. The aim was to develop guerrilla activities and ensure that *résistants* remained motivated and willing to fight.[36]

In London, Delestraint was able personally to explain to Alan Brooke the objectives and requirements of the Armée Secrète. He made a good impression and the British services responsible for overseeing his request found it to be reasonable. Of course, the SOE was well aware that the RAF was unlikely to assign additional planes to provide arms to the Resistance at the expense of aerial bombing campaigns.[37] As early as January 1943, the British had unambiguously stated that the Free French could expect no rapid increase in air support for arms provision.[38] Despite the flood of alarming messages about French labour conscription (Service du travail obligatoire) on 16 February 1943, there was to be no change in British policy until 1944. On 22 March 1943, the military authorities confirmed that the SOE should not engage in a vast operation of arms distribution to the Resistance.[39] Churchill told de Gaulle that the objective remained to deploy Resistance forces only at the time of the Allied landings. It was, therefore, critical to prevent a 'premature rising of the French resistance' that would lead to its annihilation.[40] This placed de Gaulle and the Free French in an awkward position. On the one hand, they were being pressed by their own agents to provide arms; on the other, they shared British fears that a rapid increase in arms would result in a hasty – and suicidal – uprising that had to be avoided at all costs.

This dilemma notwithstanding, the question of arms provision remained the primary criterion used by the Gaullists to assess the extent of British support for the Resistance. The month of September 1943 was a disaster for aerial operations and this revived Free French fears that the British were reserving an ever greater number of air operations for F Section. Robin Brook – a high-ranking SOE leader – admitted that this was true and promised to rectify the imbalance in the coming months. But the terrible climatic conditions of the winter of 1943–44 meant that Brook could not keep his promise.[41] It was only in February 1944 that Churchill, under pressure from Emmanuel d'Astier among others, gave strong support to the provisioning of arms to the Resistance.[42] Between 1943 and 1944, deliveries of explosives multiplied by seven (from 74 to 518 tonnes), while deliveries of machine-guns multiplied by six (from 28,000 to 169,000). Of the containers delivered before D Day, 55 per cent were destined for groups controlled by the BCRA, but as time went on, this proportion steadily decreased (68 per cent in March, 51 per cent in May and less than 42 per cent in June–July). Not surprisingly, the Free French resented the change since they were convinced they had to arm much larger movements than the limited groups made up of Buckmaster's men.

Other than arms provision, the major sticking point in negotiations between the Free French and the British was the question of who would control the Resistance before and during the Allied landings. The Free French were never admitted to the inner circle of Allied military decision making. In 1944, neither General d'Astier nor General Koenig was allowed to attend meetings of the Supreme Headquarters of the Allied Expeditionary Force (SHAEF) under the authority of General Eisenhower. On a number of occasions, Eisenhower expressed an interest in the Resistance but each time referred the issue to the secret services.[43] On 5 June, the Free French were, therefore, confronted with a *fait accompli* when Eisenhower called upon them to support the landings by beginning immediately all the sabotage operations that had been prepared by the SOE and the BCRA, even though these were initially to be launched progressively. After the landings, Koenig became the head of a tripartite high command – but his success came late and made little difference.[44]

The unequal division of responsibilities meant that the British were the only ones who had an overall view of the situation in France. Despite serious misgivings, in 1942 they were all but forced to accept the centralization of the Resistance around Moulin and Delestraint. But their successive arrests in June 1943 led the Free French to fall in line with the British policy of promoting a decentralized Resistance. It was agreed that a Regional Military Delegate (DMR) would maintain contact with resistance movements in each of France's 12 regions. This was satisfactory to the British until it became clear that the Free French also wanted to send a National Military Delegate (DMN) and two Zonal Military Delegates (DMZ), thereby recreating a pyramidal hierarchy.[45] After a stormy exchange, the request for additional delegates was withdrawn, but the SOE suspected the Free French of wanting to dupe them.

Since 1941, the Free French had had a specific code for communicating with their agents. However, they lacked the necessary manpower to encipher and decipher messages. As a result, this code was hardly used and served more as a symbol of Free French sovereignty than as a practical tool. In any case, whenever they sent coded messages, they provided the British with a decoded copy. But in October 1943, the BCRA tried to send a coded message with details of the role of the DMZ that were absent from the decoded copy. The SOE found out and put an immediate stop to the use of the Free French code. Outraged, the Free French claimed that the British had violated the 1941 agreement by consulting a copy of the code provided by the French; the SOE responded that the code had simply been cracked by its agents.[46] The actual story is unclear but, whatever the reason, this move on the part of the SOE reinforced the sense that the British were interfering unduly in the relationship between Free France and the Resistance.[47]

These tensions were exacerbated by a growing concern among the British secret services about the perceived lack of security of their Free French counterparts. This key issue highlighted the difference between, on the one hand, London-based organizations responsible for military operations (such as the SOE and BCRA), and, on the other, political organizations (such as the Commissariat à l'Intérieur) and actors in the field. Whereas the former were genuinely preoccupied with problems of security in France, the latter felt such concern to be excessive. For the SOE, the disastrous arrest of Moulin and Delestraint in June 1943 was a clear indication that many Gaullist organizations had been infiltrated by the Germans. While accepting that a number of SOE groups had also been compromised, they maintained that the Gestapo had detailed knowledge of the Gaullist Resistance and was simply waiting for the right moment to close the net. In this context, a succession of messages from Yeo-Thomas in September and October 1943 had considerable impact. The SOE agent indicated that there had been a series of arrests and that the archives of the 'Délégation Générale en Zone Nord' had been captured. Along with Brossolette, he also deplored Claude Serreulles and Jacques Bingen's recklessness at the head of the 'Délégation

Générale' and demanded their recall to London. These reports strengthened the British conviction that the Resistance had been dangerously infiltrated and that it would now be necessary to bypass the existing organizational structure if they wanted a force capable of assisting the Allies after D Day.[48] As the SOE put it in a memorandum in October 1943, 'the only workable system would seem to be . . . to make contact with groups of resisters at the lowest echelon . . . and to see that no communications pass through the already tainted lines of the old structure in France'.[49] Worried that the BCRA would be sidelined from an event – the Allied landings – for which they had long been preparing, the BCRA was soon arguing along the same lines as the British were. They harassed agents to increase security and put in place a fully decentralized structure. Ironically, the BCRA's new-found zeal led to accusations from Emmanuel d'Astier that they had undermined French sovereignty.[50]

The issue of the *maquis* further heightened Free French fears that decentralization was simply another way for the British to exercise control over the Resistance. In September 1943, shortly after the departure of the first Franco-British mission to develop contacts with the *maquis* in the Alps (the Cantinier mission), the Free French were told about a meeting held at the SOE headquarters. Apparently, somebody said during that meeting that the Armée Secrète was little more than 'a joke', that the British could not count on 20 per cent of its members and that the SOE should take control of 'all the possibilities of the French Resistance'.[51] Since Churchill was, for the first time, arguing for the necessity of expanding the guerrilla movement in the Alps, the leaders of the Free French were quickly convinced that this was 'an attempt on the part of the Allies to seize control over one part of the Resistance'.[52] These worries were confirmed when, despite the opposition of the BCRA, the SOE ordered the British officer on the Cantinier mission to 'make many contacts' and establish 'direct connections with Switzerland'.[53] In the end, it was the American intelligence agency that played the deciding role. Just as the Office of Strategic Services had asked for the Free French to be associated with the Sussex and Jedburgh plans to decentralize the Resistance, they were instrumental in making sure that the Free French were involved in the *maquis* plan. The aim was to rebuild the *maquis* along decentralized lines, with each unit in direct contact with London and independent of other resistance movements.[54]

The combination of a Free French siege mentality and a British inability to cope with the upheavals in the organizational structure of the French secret services precipitated a major crisis by the end of 1943. The marginalization of General Giraud, the civilian control over military affairs in the CFLN, the nomination of Emmanuel d'Astier as head of the Commissariat à l'Intérieur and the nomination of Jacques Soustelle as the head of special services . . . All of these changes convinced the British that the Free French – and especially the 'feudal lords of the Resistance' – were no longer interested in military cooperation with the Allies; instead, they had their minds firmly set on

France's future political configuration.[55] The SOE believed that it was too late to accomplish the task of decentralizing paramilitary resistance groups and suggested concentrating only on those groups over which it had direct control. In addition, the SOE recommended giving the CFLN an ultimatum in order to pre-empt Free French claims that the British were refusing to help the Resistance. This would stipulate that arms deliveries would only be guaranteed if regional resistance leaders and heads of the *maquis* took orders directly from the Allies (through the SOE) at the time of the D-Day landings.[56] The evidence suggests that this proposal was met with some hostility in the Foreign Office, which eventually came to the conclusion that any such ultimatum would be detrimental to British interests, especially in matters of intelligence information.[57]

The SOE had failed to impose its own agenda. But this did not prevent it from exerting significant pressure on the BCRA. The SOE maintained that Eisenhower would refuse to provide more planes for arms deliveries if the Free French could not prove the effectiveness of their resistance operations.[58] Since 1943, the priority had been to elaborate various plans to destroy infrastructure and arms on D Day. These included the Green/Frog Plan (for railway lines) and Tortoise (for armoured divisions), both of which were completed in 1944. The British demanded regular reports not only on the progress of the operational planning, but also on sabotage operations that had already been completed. When these were not forthcoming, they threatened to reallocate arms deliveries to F Section.[59] The Free French were caught off balance by this sudden emphasis on current sabotage operations and, in turn, exerted considerable pressure on the Resistance to account for every operation and put in place numerous sabotage missions against industrial plant, canals and power lines.

Conclusion: Shared experiences, divergent narratives

We can draw two conclusions from this survey of relations between the British, the Free French and the Resistance. The first has to do with the military effectiveness of the Resistance and the second relates to the continued pre-eminence of 'national' readings of shared wartime experiences. We know that Allied High Command relied above all on aerial bombardments to hinder the arrival of German reinforcements around the bridgehead. They did not expect a significant contribution from the Resistance and thought of Free French assistance as a 'bonus'.[60] Moreover, they did not believe that the industrial sabotage that had taken place before D Day was of great strategic importance.[61] But opinions changed rapidly after the event. The Allies quickly recognized that the sabotage operations which had accompanied the landings were of great tactical benefit.[62] As early as 17 June, the SHAEF paid tribute to the French Forces of the Interior and their role in helping the Allies to achieve most of their first objectives.[63] Lord Selborne conveyed the same message to Churchill.[64] With additional hindsight, a British report from September 1944 concluded that the disruptive operations carried out by the Resistance had contributed decisively to the success of the Allied landings.[65]

However, this contemporary recognition of the Resistance on the part of the British did little to modify subsequent views of the event: these have remained resolutely anchored in their respective national narratives. A good example of this was the fate of M.R.D. Foot's book on SOE in France, first published in 1966.[66] It was conceived as an 'official' history and sought to correct the existing bias in the French literature that had overemphasized the role played by the Free French during the war. The book was entirely based on British archives and, as a result, shared the same vision of Franco-British relations as the leaders of the SOE. In this view, all Resistance agents that had benefited from British logistical support, including agents sent by the BCRA, were agents of the SOE.[67] Foot's book was immediately translated into French, but the publisher abandoned the project in the wake of Gaullist antagonism. 'M.R.D. Foot: do not unfairly attack Free France!' thundered Colonel Passy in the press, accusing the British historian of underestimating the role played by the Gaullists in the Resistance.[68] The Foreign Office was aware of the sense of national humiliation in France. It feared the book would 'provoke the irritation of de Gaulle, then at the very height of his powers, and would be condemned by former *résistants* for presenting an unduly Anglo-centric official history of British operations in France'. Ultimately, Foot's book was prohibited from being published in France until 2008.[69] It was a clear indication of the tensions, fractures and bitter recriminations that have, until recently, defined the memory of Franco-British engagements during the war.

Translated by Emile Chabal

Notes

1   It was hoped that the Americans, after their entry into the war, would be able to contribute, but assistance was limited, except with respect to American aircraft, large numbers of which were mobilized after 1944 to support the Resistance from London and Algiers.

2   'Rapport Bernard reçu par les Services britanniques le 23 décembre 1941', Archives Nationales [AN] 3AG2/378/d.2/7.

3   Wybot, 'Compte-rendu d'entretien avec Nef', 2 October 1942, AN 3AG2/410/d.1/5.

4   Dansey to Loxley, 21 December 1941, The National Archives [TNA] HS6/311.

5   Sébastien Albertelli & Johanna Barasz, 'Un résistant atypique: le général Cochet, entre vichysme et gaullisme', in *Histoire@Politique. Politique, culture, société* (No. 5, May–Aug 2008), http://www.histoire-politique.fr/index.php?numero=05&rub=autres-articles&item=39

6 Robert Frank, 'Résistance et résistants dans la stratégie des Britanniques et Américains', in L. Douzou et al. (eds.), *La Résistance et les Français: Villes, centres et logiques de décision* (Cachan: Supplément au Bulletin de l'IHTP n°61, 1996), pp. 471–83.

7 Eden to de Gaulle, 20 January 1942, TNA HS6/311.

8 On this, see Frank, 'Résistance et résistants'.

9 Frank Kersaudy, *De Gaulle et Churchill* (Paris: Perrin, 2001), p. 314. Jean-Louis Crémieux-Brilhac, *La France Libre* (Paris: Gallimard, 1996), pp. 681–4, 819–32.

10 Sébastien Albertelli, *Les services secrets du général de Gaulle: le BCRA, 1940–1944* (Paris: Perrin, 2009), pp. 209–40.

11 'Security at Fighting French Headquarters', 22 July 1942, TNA HS6/308.

12 Gubbins to Nelson, 8 February 1941, PRO/HS6/311.

13 Nelson to Humphreys, 11 October 1940, TNA HS6/311.

14 Nelson, 'S.O.2. and the de Gaulle Intelligence Organisations', 25 December 1940, TNA HS6/311.

15 M.R.D. Foot has examined these contacts in some detail in his book *SOE in France. An account of the Work of the British Special Operations Executive in France, 1940–1944* (London: HMSO, 1966).

16 Sporborg to Buckmaster, 3 November 1941. Buckmaster to Sporborg, 3 November 1941, TNA HS6/602.

17 [SOE], France and Fighting France, 12 August 1942, TNA HS6/312.

18 On this, see Thomas Rabino, *Le réseau Carte* (Paris: Perrin, 2008).

19 Foot, *SOE in France*, pp. 181–7; Cremieux-Brilhac, *La France Libre*, pp. 408–9.

20 [SOE], France and Fighting France, 12 August 1942. Keswick, Relations with Fighting French, 12 September 1942, TNA HS6/595.

21 [SOE], France and Fighting France, 12 August 1942. Keswick, Relations with Fighting French, 12 September 1942, TNA HS6/595.

22 Morton, French support for General de Gaulle, draft, n.d., TNA HS6/316.

23 A. Dewavrin (Colonel Passy), *Souvenirs. 10 Duke Street Londres* (Paris: Raoul Solar, 1947), pp. 161–3.

24 Philip to Eden, 4 August 1942, AN3AG2/15/4.

25 Piquet-Wicks to Gubbins, 6 May 1942. Gubbins to D/CD, 1 May 1942, TNA HS6/311.

26 De Gaulle to Eden, 5 August 1942. Keswick to Gubbins, 8 August 1942. Keswick to Hambro, 5 September 1942, PRO/HS6/312; Passy, 'Note au sujet du dîner tenu le 2 septembre 1942', AN 3AG2/15/13.

27 Alan Brooke, *War diaries, 1939–1945* (London: Weidenfeld & Nicolson, 2001). 'Plan to give support to the French Army in Unoccupied Territory. Memorandum by the Chief of The Imperial General Staff', 12 May 1942, TNA HS6/311.

28 A. F. Brooke, Memorandum, 2 June 1942, TNA HS6/313.

29 Keswick to Gubbins, 8 August 1942. Keswick to Hambro, 5 September 1942, PRO/HS6/312.

30 Bingen, Compte-rendu d'entretien avec Sporborg, 17 November 1942, AN 3AG2/175/d.3/5.

31 Gubbins to Lord Selborne, 'French Affairs', 18 November 1942, TNA HS6/321. Selborne to Eden, 20 November 1942. Sporborg to Selborne, 21 November 1942, TNA HS6/595.

32 AD/S to CD, 1 December 1942, TNA HS6/595.

33 Frank Kersaudy, *De Gaulle et Roosevelt. Le duel au sommet* (Paris: Perrin, 2004), pp. 175–6.

34 CD to SO, 22 November 1942, TNA HS6/595.

35 Gubbins to CD, 1 January 1943, TNA HS6/595.

36 'The function of resistance groups in France–Memorandum by SOE', 15 March 1943, TNA HS6/963.

37 'Precis of note by General del'Estran[sic] on the equipping and arming of the secret army in France', 13 March 1943; TNA HS6/963.

38 PLANS/380/633, 14 January1943, TNA HS6/332.

39 D.M.O. to CIGS, 22 March 1943, TNA HS6/963.

40 Churchill to deGaulle, draft letter, n.d., TNA HS6/313.

41 Passy to Brook, 30 September 1943, AN 3AG2/17/28.

42 See the transcriptions of these interviews in Henri Noguères, *Histoire de la Résistance, tome 4* (Paris: R.Laffont, 1976), pp. 299–309.

43 Eisenhower to d'Astier, 18 March 1944, SHD237K/2. Cluset à d'Astier, 25 March 1944, AN3AG2/414/189.

44 Foot, *SOE in France*, p. 33; M.R.D. Foot, 'De Gaulle et les services secrets pendant la guerre' *in Espoir* (No. 71, June 1990), pp. 46–52.

45 Gubbins to Cochet, 10 October 1943, AN3AG2/17/7, 29.

46 Leo Marks, *Between Silk and Cyanide: A Codemaker's War, 1941–1945* (New York, NY: FreePress, 1998), p. 387.

47 Cochet to Gubbins, 19 October 1943, AN 72AJ440.

48 'Memorandum de RF/C pour DR', 16 October 1943, TNA HS6/376. 'The present value and tempo of Resistance, Memorandum by S.O.E.', October 1943, National Archives (College Park, Washington, DC)[NA] RG226-190-329-16.

49 [SOE], Memorandum No. 1,23 October 1943, TNA HS6/376.

50 D'Astier to de Gaulle, 31 March 1944, ANF1a3713.

51 Manuel to Passy, 6 October 1943, AN 3AG2/15/11.

52 Telegram to P. Viénot, 29 September 1943, AN 72AJ439.

53 Telegram from Passy to Pélabon for Gaulle, 9 October 1943, AN 72AJ440.

54 Forestier to Frenay, 3 November 1943, IHT PARC078.

55 AMR to CD, 15 November 1943. AD/E to V/CD,D/RetAMR, 20 November 1943, TNA HS6/313.

56 AD/E to V/CV, D/Ret AMR, 20 November 1943 TNA HS6/313.

57 AD/E to V/CD, 25 November 1943. Speaight to Sporborg, 13 December 1943, TNA HS6/313.

58 Suggested letter from the brigadier to commandant Manuel, n.d.[December 1943], TNA HS6/330.

59 DTSS, 'Compte-rendu de la conférence du 5 janvier 1944', 5 January 1944, AN 3AG2/175/d.3/8. D'Astier to Gubbins, 20 January 1944, AN 3AG2/237.

60 Foot, *SOE in France*, p. 340.

61 Foot, *SOE in France*, pp. 381–5.

62 Foot, *SOE in France*, pp. 386–7.

63 Vander Stricht, *Resistance in France, June 5–19, Its Accomplishments and Its Potential*, NARG226-190-441-1004.

64 Selborne to Churchill, 20 June 1944, NARG226-190-329-16.

65 'Delays to the German build-up in the Northern battle area from 6 June 1944', 7 September 1944, TNA HS8/423.

66 See Foot, *SOE in France*.

67 Jean-Louis Crémieux-Brilhac, 'Avant-propos', in *Des Anglais dans la Résistance. Le Service Secret Britannique d'Action (SOE) en France 1940–1944* (Paris: Tallandier, 2008).

68 Colonel Passy, 'Unknown article' in *Figaro Littéraire*, 16 June 1966.

69 See Crémieux-Brilhac, 'Avant propos'.

CHAPTER SIX

The British and the Liberation of France

Olivier Wieviorka

To contemporary historians, it is self-evident that the British made an important contribution to the liberation of France. They participated equally in Operation Overlord, with British troops fighting valiantly in Normandy. And, from mid-August, they began to push up towards Belgium and Holland, which meant that Picardie and the Nord-Pas-de-Calais were liberated remarkably quickly. It is true that they spent many long weeks in the 'lodgement area' before the breakthrough by General Omar Bradley towards Avranches. But, after the encircling of the Falaise pocket, they moved quickly. The small town of Houlgate in Normandy had to wait until 19 August 1944 to celebrate the departure of the hated occupier, but Amiens was taken on 31 August 1944 and France's two northern most *départements* came under Allied control between 1 and 5 September. In a stark reversal of fortunes, Commonwealth forces advanced more rapidly in the summer of 1944 than the German army had in the summer of 1940. It seemed as if the Allies had finally made amends for the humiliation of the retreat at Dunkirk.

Whether in the realm of history or memory, these facts should not, however, hide the very real disagreements that lay behind the triumphal onward march of the Allied forces. In fact, the British faced vigorous criticism from all sides. The Americans deplored Montgomery's failure to take Caen rapidly and his inability to close the pocket of resistance near Falaise. The French, too, argued that the Royal Air Force's bombing campaigns over

Caen and Le Havre were needlessly destructive. Worse still, the subsequent memory of World War II has marginalized the British, casting them as little more than a 'junior partner' of Uncle Sam.

This sidelining of the British was in large part the consequence of actions on the ground: the 2nd British Army under the command of General Miles Dempsey only covered a small part of France when compared with the Americans, whose intervention was crucial not only in Normandy but also, from 15 August 1944 onwards, in Provence. From a symbolic point of view, it was important that the most significant towns and regions were all reclaimed by the Americans. This included Paris, Strasbourg and Alsace, as well as less emotionally charged areas such as Brittany, Provence and the Rhône Valley. By contrast, Amiens, Arras and Lille did not carry the same emblematic status. Moreover, a selective memory of the war has contributed to the minimization of the British involvement in the liberation of France. For example, the American film *The Longest Day* (1962) studiously placed all the Allies on an equal footing, to the extent that the meagre ranks of French troops were made to play a ridiculously disproportionate role in Operation Overlord. This question of balance was less of an issue in *Saving Private Ryan* (1998), which simply reduced the D-Day landings to an entirely American affair. What was true in film was also true of French commemorative practices: while the memorial ceremonies of 1984, 1994 and 2004 all acknowledged the British presence, in 2009 Sarkozy downplayed their contribution. The President preferred to meet with the newly elected Barack Obama, while Prince Charles, who received a tardy invitation, was little more than a bit player in the ceremony. Finally, local and municipal governments have been sparing in their celebrations. Of the ten *départements* the British passed through, seven honour Winston Churchill, but Montgomery is remembered only in Caen and Dempsey is entirely forgotten.[1] The evidence is unambiguous: the memory of the D-Day landings has gradually been Americanized at the expense of the British, a process that cannot simply be attributed to the criticisms of military strategy during the war itself. It is now up to the historian to piece together the true extent of the British contribution.

Beginnings

A firmly romantic reading would suggest that, in the eyes of Winston Churchill, the liberation of France was an urgent imperative. As a Francophile of the first order – and having supported de Gaulle during the dark years of the early 1940s – the British Prime Minister would seem to be a natural advocate of the French cause. This idealized vision does not, however, reflect reality. In the first instance, relations between Churchill and de Gaulle were far from idyllic.[2] Churchill was profoundly shaken by the defeat of France – a defeat that had almost dragged Britain down with it. This trauma led him to cultivate the 'special relationship' between London and Washington that had been all but non-existent before 1939. Churchill was also disappointed with the contribution of the Free French to the war effort. Despite his obvious charisma, de Gaulle had failed to turn the Empire to the Allied side (a belief confirmed by the pitiful Dakar Expedition of 1940) and relatively few Frenchman were lining up outside his headquarters at Carlton Gardens. As the historian Jean-François Muracciole puts it:

> For the British, who until late 1942, were fighting tooth and nail against Nazi Germany, support was measured first and foremost in the number of divisions engaged in combat. How, then, could [de Gaulle] claim to embody France when he was incapable of rallying French West Africa to the Allied cause or gathering together more than 200 French soldiers each month, when millions were dying on the Eastern Front? Despite their heroism the Forces Armées de la France Libre could offer only 186 pilots; in comparison, the Czechs offered 546 and the Poles more than 1,800.[3]

Given the limited contribution of the Free French, it is not hard to understand British scepticism. This was compounded by the fact that France was an inconvenient ally: in Syria, North Africa and Madagascar, de Gaulle had defended with intransigence the national interest. But no *entente cordiale* was important enough to risk undermining Churchill's relationship with Roosevelt. The British Prime Minister made this abundantly clear to de Gaulle shortly before the D-Day landings: 'Know this! Whenever we have to choose between Europe and the open sea, we will always choose the open sea. Whenever I have to choose between you and Roosevelt, I will always choose Roosevelt.'[4]

Strategic preoccupations added to these diplomatic considerations. With limited forces, and relying heavily on the Navy and the RAF rather than on ground forces, Churchill preferred a war of attrition rather than a direct confrontation.[5] Before launching his troops on Fortress Europe and administering the final blow, he intended to bleed Germany dry. He stressed actions in the Mediterranean, convincing Roosevelt to land first in North Africa, Sicily and, finally, Italy. It was only at conferences in Washington (12–25 May 1943), Quebec (14–24 August 1943) and, above all, Tehran (28 November to 1 December 1943) that the decision to land in north-western Europe was taken and Operation Overlord became an 'overriding priority'. Nevertheless, Churchill defended his position to the end. In his memoirs, he maintained that

> I was willing to do everything in the power of His Majesty's Government to begin 'Overlord' at the earliest possible moment, but I did not consider that the very great possibilities in the Mediterranean should be ruthlessly sacrificed and cast aside as if there were of no value, merely to save a month or so in the launching of 'Overlord'. There was a large British

army in the Mediterranean, and I could not agree that it should stand idle for nearly six months.[6]

This rearguard action remained a dead letter, but it did not stop the British Prime Minister from fighting on. Even if he (reluctantly) accepted the principle of Operation Overlord, he tried to stop the landings in Provence, which Eisenhower considered essential. The American general wanted to engage German troops far from Normandy, protect the southern flank and capture Marseille – a port city of great strategic importance. Churchill, on the other hand, hoped that those troops involved in Operation Anvil in the south of France would ultimately end up in Italy. He, therefore, did his utmost to prevent the operation. On 12 April 1944, he requested that the highest priority be accorded to the operations aimed at uniting the Allied forces fighting in Italy and those that had landed at Anzio. On 12 July, the British Chief of Staff reminded his American counterparts that Anvil was 'not the correct strategy for the Allies'.[7] On 19 July, Churchill suggested to the American envoy Harry Hopkins that Anvil be cancelled, highlighting the dangers of Soviet penetration in Eastern Europe. However, Eisenhower held firm. He agreed to separate the two landings, but, to Churchill's annoyance, argued for the need to continue Operation Anvil. The British Chief of Staff capitulated on 10 August 1944 and Churchill gained only a modest consolation, namely the right to baptize the operation 'Dragoon', so named because he had emerged from the negotiations thoroughly downtrodden.

Churchill, then, was not at the forefront of Operation Overlord. As the guarantor of British interests, he preferred a war of attrition rather than risking a frontal assault that would bring back sinister memories of the bloodbath at Passchendaele in 1917. Thus, if France was to be liberated in 1944, it was not thanks to the British Premier but against his wishes. Nevertheless, on the morning of 6 June 1944, British troops were fully involved in the landings on Normandy's beaches.

Disappointment in the East

Conceived by General Montgomery, who was in command of ground operations, Operation Overlord was made up of three elements. During the first 20 days, troops would have to secure the 'lodgement area' in order to prepare the ground for the movement of men and material across France. The British objective was to capture Caen, while the Americans would advance up the Cotentin coast and aim for Cherbourg, whose deep-sea port was of primary strategic importance. In the second stage, the US Army would begin a circular action with a view to liberating Brittany. After 35 days, the Allied troops would align themselves on a line stretching from Deauville to the area just north of Le Mans. After 90 days, the Allies would reach the Seine, after which the Anglo-American forces would have to destroy the German lines, preferably west of the Rhine, before penetrating into the Saarland and the Ruhr where 'much of Germany's warmaking power' lay.[8] The aim, therefore, was not to march on Berlin – considered too far to the east to be a viable target – but to destroy the bulk of Germany's industrial potential.

The pessimistic predictions of strategists, who had expected carnage on the beaches of Normandy within a few hours of landing, turned out to be unfounded. In fact, Allied losses were relatively light, in particular, in the three Anglo-Canadian sectors. The 50th Infantry Division on Gold Beach lost only 413 men (1.7 per cent of those who landed); on Juno Beach, the death toll was slightly higher at 805 (3.35 per cent); and on Sword Beach, it was 630 (2.2 per cent). These were all regarded as reasonable, given the strength of German defences and the complexity of the operation.[9] There were a number of reasons for this success, which contrasted sharply with the near disaster on Omaha Beach. First, the British decided to launch their amphibious vehicles less than 12 km from the shore, whereas the Americans opted for 15 km. This meant that they benefited from strong support from armoured vehicles (96 tanks on Gold, 88 on Juno and 47 on Sword; by contrast, of the 32 tanks destined for Omaha Beach, 27 sank). The British also used specially adapted vehicles (Flail and Crocodile tanks) that the Americans had chosen not to deploy. It seemed as if the situation had begun under the best possible conditions for the British. However, it was not long before things started to deteriorate.

The British were able to take control of an undamaged Bayeux on 7 June; and, by 8 June, the troops who had landed formed a continuous front, thereby closing the worrying gaps between the five beaches. But the Allies failed to take Caen – a city considered of central strategic significance. The *préfecture* of Calvados was the centre of a star-shaped communication network and opened out on to a plain that was ideal for air installations and armoured vehicles. Not surprisingly, therefore, both Tedder and Eisenhower were keen that Montgomery should capture the city. But the Germans blocked access to the area on 6–7 June. Montgomery was forced to change his tactics and he tried to take the city in a pincer movement. The Allies were once again thwarted. Finally, the British commander decided to launch a full-scale offensive, the name of which (Epsom) indicated that he wanted rapid results. The plan was to attack Caen from the west with a view to encircling the city from the south. A total of 60,000 men, 550 tanks and 300 guns were to be used in the battle. Yet, despite a few early successes, the Germans launched a counter-attack on 29–30 June, which forced the British to stop their assault.

With support from the Canadians, troops began the operation again in early July, but even with the help of an intense bombing campaign, they only managed to capture Carpiquet airport on 4 July and the left bank of Caen on 9 July. In the face of these repeated failures, Montgomery immediately prepared a second plan, code-named Goodwood. It began with repeated aerial and artillery bombardments, followed by a ground attack involving three armoured divisions. It was the task of General O'Connor's VIII Corps to take the plain around Caen before moving on to the town of Falaise. The results were mixed. From the moment it started on 18 July, the operation encountered stiff German resistance and, on the 21st, Montgomery suspended the attack because of the growing number of casualties. Between 18 and 21 July, General Dempsey had lost 6,168 men and 36 per cent of his tanks for a territorial gain of little more than 55 km.[10]

Disappointed with this inability to complete an important strategic move, the Americans took over control of operations around Caen. Realizing that Montgomery was able neither to take Caen (which finally fell on 19 July) nor break down the German defences, General Bradley suggested that the focus of attention shift to the Cotentin coast. On 25 July, after a series of bombing raids, he moved American forces on to the Saint-Lô-Périers-Lessay road. Three infantry divisions opened a gap in German lines, through which seven divisions and 10,000 vehicles subsequently passed after the fall of Avranches. Only too aware of their defeat, there was little the Germans could do but organize an orderly retreat.

The reasons for British failure

The failure of the offensive near Caen provides an excellent opportunity for the historian to examine the weaknesses of the British forces. As we have seen, the master plan drawn up by Montgomery clearly stated that Caen should be taken within the first day, an objective the British singularly failed to achieve. In his memoirs, Montgomery turned this failure into success by arguing that his aim was to draw the bulk of German forces towards the west, thereby giving the Americans room to manoeuvre in the east: 'I was convinced that strong and persistent offensive action in the Caen sector would achieve our object of drawing the enemy reserves on to our eastern flank: this was my basic conception. From the beginning it formed the basis of all our planning.'[11] But this *post hoc* explanation is not convincing. As the British military historian Liddell Hart puts it: 'It was "Monty's way" to talk as if any operation that he had conducted had always proceeded exactly as he intended, with the certainty of a machine – or of divine providence. That characteristic has often obscured his adaptability to circumstances, and thus, ironically, deprived him of the credit due to him for his combination of flexibility with determination in generalship.'[12] It is certainly true that the British strategy forced a considerable number of German troops to move into Normandy: in July, the 2nd British Army was facing two infantry divisions and more than seven armoured divisions, which represented two-thirds of the enemy's tanks. By contrast, the Americans were faced with only seven less well-armed divisions. Even so, it is not possible to ignore the basic fact that the objective assigned to the British – namely, to capture Caen and open up Normandy – was not achieved.

In part, this failure was due to the strategy that was adopted. British generals put too much faith in aerial bombardments, which were something of a blunt instrument and frequently lacked precision. Even if, between 7 and 9 July, 1,598 aircraft flew over Caen and dropped no less than 2,750 tonnes of bombs, much of this was in vain since the Germans had positioned their defences outside the city. Moreover, the craters and ruins proved to be an impediment to the Anglo-Canadian advance.[13] The British also relied too heavily on their armoured vehicles. Montgomery knew full well that it was impossible to gain territory without engaging his infantry, but he was equally aware of the limited number of soldiers available. We should not forget that, compared with Germany or the United States, Britain had relatively few resources on which it could draw: its population was a mere 47.7 million, little more than a third of the US population of 135 million. Worse still, infantry casualties in the Normandy campaign had been unusually high, even by the pessimistic standards of Allied strategists. The War Office estimated that 48 per cent of deaths were from infantry units, 15 per cent from armoured units and 14 per cent from artillery units; among Canadian troops, the figures were even higher at 76 per cent, 7 per cent and 8 per cent, respectively.[14] British generals immediately factored these calculations into their planning. They knew that these heavy losses would not be offset by reinforcements and they, therefore, decided to engage as few infantry divisions as possible, choosing instead to rely on air and armoured offensives that ultimately contributed to their strategic failure. The British made a number of tactical errors as well. The pace of operations was, in many cases, excessively slow. The 27th Armoured Brigade should have begun its assault on Caen from 6 June, but two-thirds of its tanks were stranded on the beaches or already active in the interior. The gap between the aerial raids and ground offensive was so large that, by the time Operation Goodwood began, the Germans had had ample time in which to reorganize their defence. Finally, British tactics proved overly timid: Dempsey ordered his three armoured divisions to halt their offensive on the evening of D-Day, even though Caen and Carpiquet were within sight.

The obvious responsibility of the British generals should not obscure the fact that they were deploying unmotivated troops. For the most part, Her Majesty's soldiers did not believe they were engaged in an ideological battle, a matter of some concern to their superiors: 'The longer the war goes on, the more do the conditions of life of his family and dependents, things which in the first flush of enthusiasm in the early stages of the war are relegated well to the background, matter.'[15] Indeed, they seemed mostly concerned with what would happen after the war: 'the ordinary soldier is not pre-occupied with political theory, but he is intensely interested in "post-war planning" insofar is it affects his home, his job, and the prospects of his family'.[16] In addition, the legacy of interwar pacifism cast a long shadow: in 1944, Montgomery admitted to General Brooke that 'the problem with our British lads is that they are not killers by nature'.[17] It is of course necessary to avoid essentialist assumptions, such as supposing that certain peoples are, by nature or culture, more bellicose than others. Nevertheless, it is notable that the German army on average inflicted losses 50 per cent higher on British and American infantry than it suffered.[18]

These weaknesses became all too apparent during the Normandy campaign. British troops seemed to be more adept at staying put than at advancing, a fact that was not helped by preparation which had emphasized the 'landings' at the expense of a subsequent ground offensive. This left soldiers inadequately prepared for the difficulties of a deadly and bloody war. On the evening of 6 June, the British were so convinced that this was the 'end' of the operation that 'the tendency was to stop to brew up a tea and congratulate themselves on having accomplished their objective – getting ashore'.[19] Some armoured and infantry units had also been fighting for more than 3 years; by this stage, they were quite legitimately unwilling to take excessive risks.[20] This feeling was summarized by the New Zealand General James Hargest who maintained that 'our tanks are badly led and fought . . . They bunch up – they are the reverse of aggressive – they are not possessed of the will to attack the enemy'.[21]

Strategic blunders, poorly motivated troops and firm German resistance (whose best units were fighting the British) all help explain why Montgomery was not able to secure his sector. His failure to do so, however, caused a major crisis in the High Command and exacerbated existing tensions between the Allies. A number of British and American commanders condemned Montgomery's failings. The Commander-in-Chief of the Allied Expeditionary Air Force, Air Marshal Leigh-Mallory, confessed 'to being very much disappointed by the Army. I don't say that another Anzio is probable but it is certainly possible. They cannot expect the Air to do everything for them, and on dead days like this when the weather is bad it is up to them to push forward'.[22] Above all, Montgomery's failure came at a time when the balance of power within the High Command was shifting in favour of the United States. On 6 June, the two countries had deployed comparable numbers of troops but, as time went on, the Americans sent more reinforcements. By 25 July, there were 867,662 American soldiers in the field, compared to only 640,000 of their British counterparts.[23] The implication was clear: as General Alan Brooke wrote in his diary on 30 June 1944, 'the situation is full of difficulties. The Americans now begin to own the major strength on land, in the air and on the sea. They therefore consider that they are entitled to decide how their forces are to be employed'.[24] Indeed, the Americans were already contemplating taking command of the operation and the failed Goodwood offensive gave them the perfect opportunity to do so.

Eisenhower, upon learning of this setback, was furious: 'Tedder called Ike and said Monty had, in effect, stopped his armour from going farther. Ike was mad . . . With 7,000 tons of bombs dropped in the most elaborate bombing of enemy front-line positions ever accomplished, only seven miles were gained – can we afford a thousand tons of bombs per mile? The air people are completely disgusted with the lack of progress'.[25] Moreover, General Richardson revealed on 7 July 1944 that, in the British sector, 8 divisions controlled 70 km², whereas, in the American sector, 9 divisions controlled 100 km². Between 21 July and 20 August, the Anglo-Canadian 21st Army Group had occupied 3,800 square miles, but the American 12th Army Group under General Bradley had succeeded in reclaiming 21,500 square miles.[26] As far as the Americans were concerned, the British were leaving them with the primary responsibility for combat, while simultaneously trying to cut their losses. The available statistics seemed to confirm this conclusion. Between 6 June and 1 September, the British, Canadians and Poles had 83,825 casualties, of whom 21,139 were killed, while, during the same period, the Americans had 125,847 casualties, with 20,838 deaths.[27]

It was clearly time for the Americans to impose themselves. On 19 July, Bradley asked that a new 12th Army Group be formed – a proposition accepted by Montgomery. However, this change was more important than it seemed at first, for it elevated Bradley to the same level as that of Montgomery. In so doing, it undermined the carefully crafted hierarchical structure of Allied High Command. Although Eisenhower had been named Supreme Commander, it was initially understood that his immediate subordinates would be British. This was a shrewd tactical move on the part of the British as it allowed them to retain control of actions in Italy, while leaving the Americans to deal with delicate diplomatic matters such as managing de Gaulle's intransigence and sorting out the Algerian question. As General Alan Brooke put it in his diary: 'we were pushing Eisenhower up into the stratosphere and rarefied atmosphere of a Supreme Commander, where he would be free to devote his time to the political and inter-allied problems, whilst we inserted under him one of our own commanders to deal with the military situations and to restore the necessary drive and co-ordination which had been so seriously lacking of late.'[28]

Seen from a British perspective, Bradley's promotion was not a good omen. Nor was Eisenhower's decision on 21 July to take control of ground forces from 1 September onwards. This was a planned takeover, but it felt to Montgomery like a stinging critique of his achievements. Even his promotion on 1 September to Field Marshal could not hide the fact that control of the Normandy operations was now firmly in American hands. Montgomery understood this only too well; in his Memoirs, he confided that 'just when final victory was in sight, whispers went round the British forces that the Supreme Commander had complained that we were not doing our fair share of the fighting. I do not think that great and good man, now one of my greatest friends, had any idea of the trouble he was starting. From that time onwards there were always "feelings" between the British and American forces till the war ended'.[29]

Needless to say, the consequences of the change of command after 25 July suggested that Eisenhower had been right. The Supreme Commander wanted the Anglo-Canadian troops to lead the offensive towards Avranches.

On 25 July, the 2nd Canadian Corps launched an attack in the direction of Falaise (Operation Spring), while Dempsey took charge of an offensive in the direction of Vire (Operation Bluecoat). Both operations were failures – and this despite the fact that Montgomery had fired both Generals Erskine (commander of 7th Armoured Division) and Bucknall (commander of XXX Corps). Mediocre equipment and damaged terrain had benefited the Germans. After American success in Operation Cobra, it was not surprising that Eisenhower elected to modify his strategy by moving his forces further to the east and asking the Anglo-Canadian troops to move in on Falaise in order to trap the German army. On 7 July, the Canadians began their assault on Falaise, while one part of the 3rd Army began to march along the Le Mans-Alençon-Argentan route. But the Canadians moved too slowly to close the net around the enemy forces. In the end, the pocket of Falaise was only closed on 19 August. The Germans had lost 5–6,000 men, 30–40,000 prisoners and most of their equipment, but anywhere between 45-100,000 men had escaped. In total, more than two-thirds of German troops had been able to make an orderly retreat. In the words of the American historian Martin Blumenson: 'What was, in fact, a great Allied victory in Normandy was, in long-range terms, inconclusive. Substantial remnants of the Germans defeated at Argentan and Falaise and harassed at the Seine River would reappear and again face the Allied armies.'[30]

As we have seen, the Germans put up strong resistance against those who had landed on D Day. Well aware of the dangers of Operation Cobra, they tried to mount a counteroffensive, the aim of which was to separate the 1st and 3rd American armies by reaching the Cotentin Coast. Their strategy was unsuccessful. As early as 2 August, the Ultra interception system had decoded German plans, giving ample time for the Americans to prepare their defence. When the Germans did attack Mortain on 6 August, they were immediately blocked. This tactical reversal of fortunes was compounded by a strategic one: on 15 August, Allied forces landed in Provence and began moving rapidly up the Rhône Valley. This prompted Hitler's decision to retreat *en masse* from western France, with the exception of a few garrisons stationed in the Atlantic ports. Henceforth, it would become much easier for the Allies to progress through northern France as they encountered little or no resistance, except in the Vosges and Alsace at the end of the year. Aside from a few regions that held out until the final capitulation, by February 1945, Allied dominance in France was assured. However, with victory fast approaching, one question became increasingly urgent: to whom would the Allies transfer power?

The Liberation and after

We already know that Churchill did not unconditionally support de Gaulle. Even if the Comité français de la libération nationale (CFLN) was partially recognized in August 1943, it was not seen to be the legitimate government of post-liberation France. Despite the fact that, as early as November 1943, the CFLN had asked for the opening of negotiations, the Allies preferred to leave things vague. Roosevelt ignored the CFLN's pleas and Churchill fell in line with the American president: 'We ought not to quarrel with the President for fear of offending de Gaulle. De Gaulle, for all his magnitude, is the sole obstacle to harmonious relations between Great Britain and America on one hand, and the skeleton and ghost of France on the other . . . He will be the bitterest foe we and the United States have ever had in France.'[31] There seemed to be no reason for London and Washington to pursue a strategy that had few negative repercussions, especially considering that they expected little from the French Resistance. The latter would be no more than a 'bonus' according to Brigadier Morgan and, in any case, supporting the CFLN would limit British and American room for manoeuvre. They, therefore, remained as non-committal as possible. In March 1944, Roosevelt gave General Eisenhower the responsibility for choosing French civil authorities without any obligation to negotiate with the Gaullist Gouvernement provisoire de la République française (GPRF). This did not mean – as some Gaullists claimed – that the Americans wanted to impose some kind of Allied Military Government of Occupied Territory (AMGOT). There was no plan to appoint American administrators to manage France and the Allies considered France as a friendly country to be liberated, not as an enemy country to be occupied. Nevertheless, the Americans did intend to choose leaders of whom they approved.

But, if it was possible to cultivate ambiguity up until May 1944, this position was untenable by the time of the D-Day landings. The Allies now had three major problems. Would the GPRF assist Allied troops? To whom would power be transferred in the liberated regions? And who, finally, would impose and guarantee the new French currency? To try and answer some of these questions, Churchill invited de Gaulle to Portsmouth on 4 June. The meeting was tempestuous. De Gaulle was incensed when the British Prime Minister asked him to begin the discussion: 'What! On more than one occasion I have tried to initiate discussions. I have been making proposals since last September. You have never replied . . . . Why do you seem to think that I need to submit my candidacy for [exercising] authority in France to Roosevelt? The French government exists. I have nothing to ask of the United States in this respect, nor of Great-Britain.'[32] De Gaulle likewise refused to read on the radio the text Eisenhower had prepared exhorting the French population to 'carry out his orders'. Instead, the leader of the GPRF spoke on his own terms, demanding that the 'recommendations given by the French government, and those French leaders chosen by this same government, be followed exactly'.[33]

For all the sabre-rattling, however, this exchange did not get to the heart of the problem. For a start, de Gaulle refused to recognize the francs that the Allies were preparing to issue, calling them 'false money'. This was more than just an idle threat: without clarifying who would issue the new currency, the Anglo-Americans would find themselves responsible for all of their expenses, a prospect that concerned Churchill. 'Under the mutual aid arrangements which we are making with the other European Allies, they will bear the cost of civil administration and of supplies and services to our troops in their countries. But if we should become responsible of the military notes issued in France, the French would contribute no mutual aid to the American and British Armies of Liberation.'[34] Ultimately, the Allies decided not to issue their own francs and signed a global agreement on 25 August. The GPRF alone would be authorized to issue money and would provide funds to the Anglo-American authorities in exchange for dollars; France would also benefit from British mutual aid and the Lend Lease programme.[35]

Rather than imposing his authority from above, de Gaulle succeeded above all in imposing it from below. He landed in Normandy on 14 June 1944 for a 1-day visit and proceeded to name François Coulet as *commissaire de la République* and Pierre de Chevigné as military attaché. The Allied generals seemed unconcerned with this move: Montgomery cabled Churchill to tell him that 'he has left behind in Bayeux one civilian administrative officer and three colonels but I have no idea what is their function'.[36] The officers of the Civil Affairs department, on the other hand, were more astute; they realized that these were the foundations of a new civilian government. 'Lacking instructions from London, the Senior Civil Affairs Officer (SCAO) decided that his best policy was to accept Gen. de Gaulle's representatives as the *de facto* civil authority for the region of Rouen, since they appeared to be acceptable to the French themselves, and had already dismissed M. Rochat from the Sous-prefecture of Bayeux'.[37] General Lewis of the 21st Army Group summarized the situation thus: 'The next days will show whether Coulet and Triboulet can establish themselves and win the people's confidence as the de facto government. Meanwhile we are treating them as such; the high question of "recognition" has now left the stratosphere of diplomatic exchange and is being decided on the ground.'[38]

Fortunately, the men de Gaulle had appointed were fully equal to the task: 'it would appear that if we accept the administration now functioning in France, and furnish them a reasonable degree of assistance, both administrative and in a material sense, there is no need to particularly worry about ability or desire of the people to do a good job.'[39] The Gaullist authorities improved their image still further by preserving the peace in Normandy. In this relatively conservative region, Communist agitation was a negligible threat and, in contrast to other liberated areas, there were few revenge attacks, all of which did much to reassure the Anglo-American authorities. The Gaullist success in Normandy had become a triumph by the time de Gaulle reached the Champs-Elysées on 26 August 1944, where a crowd of two million came out to greet him. At this point, it was impossible for London and Washington to ignore the evidence: the head of the Resistance was, in the eyes of the French, the country's legitimate leader, not least because his new government included members of every political persuasion, from the Communists to the conservative right. Yet even at this late stage, the British and Americans were reluctant to hand over control. The GPRF was only officially recognized on 23 October – a decision taken unilaterally by Roosevelt without Churchill's knowledge.

Britain: A junior partner?

In the end, the influence of Britain had waned considerably. On the eve of the D-Day landings, they had a number of trump cards. The master plan had been elaborated by Montgomery on the basis of a plan devised by another British officer – Brigadier Frederick Morgan. Although they were not Supreme Commanders, they had a leading role in the daily running of military operations: Air Marshal Sir Trafford Leigh-Mallory was in charge of the Allied Air Force, Admiral Sir Bertram Ramsay was in command of the naval forces and General Montgomery was in command of the ground forces. It is also worth remembering that, on 6 June 1944, the British were numerically comparable to their American counterparts, providing as many men (but rather less equipment). All of these factors meant that the British could quite legitimately imagine that the war would be conducted according to their priorities. Does this mean that the Allies did not agree on their goals? Such a conclusion would be excessive: both Churchill and Roosevelt wanted to defeat the Third Reich and build a new world order. However, they did not necessarily see eye to eye on everything, particularly when it came to handling the Soviets. If, like Clausewitz, we argue that war is a military means of achieving political goals, then we can see how control of military operations could be of great significance.

Unfortunately, the dismal performance of British forces on the battlefield gave the Americans the ideal opportunity to retake control. British troops were unable to secure Caen – widely considered to be a vital strategic goal – and they were slow to encircle the Germans in the pocket of Falaise. The lack of motivation, the timidity of the generals, the unwillingness to deploy infantry, the sluggish pace of the British offensive and stubborn resistance on the part of enemy troops tarnished the image of the British army. The Americans promptly took advantage of these setbacks by changing the chain of command and reducing the British to the role of junior partners. London always seemed to be following Washington, as the latter imposed first its military objectives and subsequently its diplomatic priorities. This was perfectly exemplified in 1944, when the British were not even informed that the GPRF had been recognized as France's official government.

This is not to take away from the fact that the liberation of France would have been impossible without the efforts and sacrifices of the British. The Americans would not have had the human or material resources to launch such a complex operation alone. Moreover, the retreat of the Wehrmacht made rapid progress in August and September that much easier. Still, it is hard to avoid the conclusion that it was the Americans who were in control: they were able to change the hierarchy at will and divide the Allied forces, a decision that came as a bitter blow to Montgomery. Of course, this situation was simply a reflection of the changing global balance of power. The British – who had previously been the world's greatest power – could no longer compete with the Americans, whose military, demographic and economic advantages were plain to see. A new world was being born, one that would be dominated by the bipolarity of the Cold War. In this altered landscape, Britain and France could only claim to be medium-sized powers. As we have seen, memory often provides an imperfect representation of the past. Over time, the French have forgotten British involvement in the liberation. This has been for objective reasons (the British only liberated a small part of French territory) and for cultural reasons (the Americanization of the memory of the D-Day landings). But, on this occasion, France's distorted memory reflects a wider truth. Exhausted after 4 years of war, the British could no longer impose their political strategy. Their limited success during the second French campaign ultimately anticipated their relative decline in the second half of the twentieth century.

Translated by Emile Chabal

Notes

1   The ten *départements* were Calvados, Orne, Eure, Eure-et-Loir, Seine-Maritime, Oise, Somme, Aisne, Pas-de-Calais and Nord.

2   On this, see Jean-Louis Crémieux-Brilhac, *La France libre. De l'appel du 18 juin à la libération de Paris* (Paris: Gallimard, 1996) and François Kersaudy, *De Gaulle et Churchill. La mésentente cordiale* (Paris: Perrin, 1982).

3   Jean-François Muracciole, *Les Français libres : l'autre Résistance* (Paris: Tallandier, 2009), p. 143.

4   Charles de Gaulle, *Mémoires de guerre, tome II, L'unité* (Paris: Presse-Pocket, 1980 [1956]), p. 266.

5   Trumbull Higgins, *Winston Churchill and the Second Front. 1940–1943* (New York, NY: Oxford University Press, 1957).

6   Winston Churchill, *Closing the Ring* (London: Penguin, 2005), p. 370.

7   Forrest C. Pogue, *The Supreme Command* (Washington, DC: Office of Military History, Department of the Army, 1954), p. 224.

8   General Dwight Eisenhower, *Crusade in Europe* (London: Johns Hopkins University Press, 1997), p. 285.

9   I. Evans, Comparison of British and American Areas in Normandy, 24 August 1945, (British) National Archives [TNA], War Office [WO] 291/270.

10 Terry Copp, *Fields of Fire. The Canadians in Normandy* (Toronto: Toronto University Press, 2003), p. 153.

11 Bernard Law Montgomery, *The Memoirs of Field-Marshal the Viscount Montgomery of Alamein* (London: Collins, 1958), p. 228.

12 Basil H. Liddell Hart, *History of the Second World War* (London: Cassel, 1970), p. 546.

13 Air Commodore E.J. Kingston-McGloughry and Prof S. Zuckerman, 'Observation on RAF Bomber command's Attack on Caen July 7, 1944', TNA, Royal Air force 37/61.

14 Carlo d'Este, *Decision in Normandy: the Unwritten Story of Montgomery and the Allied Campaign* (London: Collins, 1994 [1983]), p. 255.

15 War Office Council and Army Records, Morale Committee, Moral Report, May to July 1943, TNA WO 163/161.

16 War Office Council and Army Records, Morale Committee, Moral Report, November 1943-January 1944, TNA WO 163/162.

17 Quoted by Stephen Ambrose, *D-Day, June 6, 1944: The Climatic Battle of World War II* (New York, NY: Simon and Schuster, 1994), p. 50.

18 Olivier Wieviorka, *Normandy. The landings to the liberation of Paris* (Cambridge, MA: The Belknap Press of Harvard, 2008), pp. 156–7.

19 Wieviorka, *Normandy*, p. 525.

20 Max Hastings, *Overlord: D-Day and the Battle for Normandy* (London: Michael Joseph, 1984), p. 135.

21 Notes on the Normandy Campaign by Brigadier James Hargest, 6 June to 10 July 1944, TNA CAB 106/1060, quoted by Carlo d'Este, *Decision in Normandy*, p. 260.

22 Air Marshall Leigh-Mallory, diary, 19 June 1944, TNA, Royal Air Force, 37/784.

23 Roland G. Ruppenthal, *Logistical Support of the Armies*, vol. 1, May 1941 to September 1944(Washington, DC: Office of the Chief of Military History, Department of the Army, 1953), p. 460.

24 Field-Marshal Lord Alanbrooke, *War Diaries, 1939–1945*, Alex Danchev and Daniel Todman (eds) (London: Phoenix Press, 2002), p. 564.

25 Harry C. Butcher, *My Three Years with Eisenhower. The Personal Diary of Captain Harry C. Butcher, Naval Aid to General Eisenhower* (New York: Simon and Schuster, 1946), pp. 616–17.

26 E.G. Smith, Army Operational Research Group, 'Some Statistics of the North-West European Campaign, June 1944 to May 1945', October 1954, TNA, CAB 106/1580.

27 Wieviorka, *Normandy*, p. 292.

28 Brooke, *War Diaries*, p. 365.

29 Montgomery, *Memoirs*, p. 234.

30 Martin Blumenson, *Patton: The Man behind the Legend, 1885–1945* (New York, NY: William Morrow, 1985), p. 266.

31 Winston Churchill to Foreign Secretary, 10 May 1944, TNA CAB 102/244.

32 Quoted by François Kersaudy, *Churchill and De Gaulle* (London: Collins, 1981), p. 342.

33   Charles de Gaulle, *Discours et messages, 1940–1946* (Paris: Plon, 1970), p. 408.

34   W. Churchill to F.D. Roosevelt, 21 June 1944, TBA CAB 101/250.

35   Instructions retraçant les lignes générales des accords intervenus le 25 août 1944, Archives du Ministère des affaires étrangères, CPCLA/PM/1466.

36   Telegram from General Montgomery to Winston Churchill, 15 June 1944, TNA CAB 120/867.

37   Second British Army, Establishment of Cordial Relationship with the French, D-Day to 17 July 1944, NARA, RG 331 entry 54 box 292.

38   Civil Affairs Headquarters, 21st Army Group, Political Development in Normandy: Week ending 18 June 1944, 19 June 1944, NARA RG 331, entry 54, box 290.

39   Colonel W.F. Durbin, Report on Field Trip Made from 1 to 10 July 1944, Special Intelligence Bulletin no. 16, 26 July 1944, NARA RG 331 entry 54 box 282.

PART THREE

Remembering and Forgetting

Introduction

P.M.H. Bell

The third part of this volume concentrates on two main questions: first, how have Britain and France remembered the two World Wars? and second, how have these memories (and sometimes the forgetfulness which has gone with them) affected relations between the two countries and their peoples?

Looking first at the war of 1914–18, the French quickly established, and have largely maintained, a united memory of what was for a long time called simply the Great War. For the French, that war was necessary and moreover in a profound sense *right*, because it was fought primarily to drive the invading German armies out of north-east France, which they had conquered in 1914, and also to recover the lost French provinces of Alsace and Lorraine, annexed by Germany in 1871. The French casualties in this tremendous struggle were appalling, totalling some 1.4 million killed; but they were borne with remarkable fortitude and unity. This unity of memory has largely persisted, despite the passage of time and change of generations, and to this day 11 November is observed in France as a day of remembrance of the war and tribute to the dead.

The British experience has been very different, and the Great War has left the British people with complicated and divisive memories. Over time, the predominant impression has become one of a futile war which inflicted appalling and useless casualties, caused more by the blunders of British generals than by the fighting qualities of the enemy. The crude simplification of lions (the valiant British infantrymen) led by donkeys (the stupid commanders, with Haig at their head) dominates the popular mind, despite the revisionist efforts of a new school of historians, for example, Brian Bond and Gary Sheffield. Yet even at the height of the revulsion against the war and against Haig, the British people have maintained a respect for the dead of the Great War, who are still remembered by solemn ceremonies and by the wearing of poppies. It is also striking that the Royal British Legion, the ex-servicemen's organization which provides the impulse for commemoration, has recently chosen to name its new headquarters in London 'Haig House', reaffirming respect for Haig despite the many attacks on his reputation. Thus British memories of World War I remain divided and divisive; though the divisions have been softened by an increasing tendency to link the commemoration of World War I to World War II and to many other conflicts since 1945, so that the ceremonies of remembrance are now very wide in their appeal.

When we turn to World War II, the situation is almost totally reversed, with French memories bitterly divided and the British united in something of a warm glow. In France, the disastrous and sudden defeat of May–June 1940 divided people into opposing camps. Marshal Pétain and Vichy France confronted General de Gaulle and Free France. Inside France, a policy of collaboration with Germany was opposed by a growing movement of Resistance. Moreover, there were conflicts *within* these camps, notably for example between the various Resistance groups, which sometimes seemed to spend as much energy in fighting one another as in fighting the Germans. When the war was over, with a country to repair and a new political order to establish, most French people sought refuge in forgetfulness or in a myth that nearly everyone had always been on the side of the Resistance. The question of how to remember the war still haunts some Frenchmen and may be resolved only with the passage of time and the death of the wartime generation.

British memories of World War II stand in sharp contrast. The British recall it as a 'good war', fought in self-defence against German aggression, and to liberate Europe from a barbarous regime led by a man who personified evil and who has remained the yardstick by which all other tyrants are judged – some historians may compare Hitler to Stalin and not find much to choose between them, but in the popular mind Hitler remains unique. Britain fought to destroy this monster and his regime and eventually succeeded. The wide acceptance of this conviction has not been seriously undermined either by the passage of time or by the challenge of revisionist historical writing, for example, on the strategic bombing offensive or on the question of whether Britain could have done more to protect European Jews from persecution and massacre. Most of the British people (or at any rate those who think about such matters) remain convinced that they or their ancestors fought a just war, and they look back on it with pride.

In this broad picture, two points deserve to be singled out for particular emphasis. The first concerns the question of the futility or otherwise of World War I. In Britain, a sense of the futility of the war hangs heavily over public opinion. To the question of what the war was about and what it achieved, no clear and commonly held answer can be found. In France, the position is completely different. Jay Winter affirms that 'It is simply not possible to refer to a war of defence against the occupation of northern France as an act of futility . . . . In France . . . to refer to the war as a whole as an exercise in futility is to court bafflement or total incomprehension.' If there is one passage in this book whose meaning ought somehow to be brought home to the British public mind, this should surely be it, though it is by no means clear how this could be achieved.

The second point deserving particular emphasis is the contrast between the experiences of Britain and France in 1940, leaving very different memories among the two peoples. As David Reynolds points out in his chapter, Churchill called the second volume of his war memoirs, dealing with the events of 1940, *Their Finest Hour*, quoting from one of his most famous speeches. The French translation made no attempt to reproduce this title, but simply replaced it with *L'Heure tragique*. The difference between the two titles marked a parting of ways for the two countries, which has never been entirely restored or forgotten.

So far we have concentrated on the differences and divisions between the memories of the two countries. But this is not the whole story. Memory works at different levels and in different ways, and it is worth recalling some occasions when the memories of the two peoples moved in the same direction and brought France and Britain together.

The predominant element in the memory of the war of 1914–18 was found in two words: 'never again'. There must be no more battles like Verdun for the French, or the Somme and Passchendaele for the British. In both countries, war memorials, with their grim lists of the dead, stood as constant reminders that there must be no repetition of these events. In France, this revulsion against war was particularly strong among the peasantry, who had provided the backbone of the French Army and had borne the heaviest weight among its casualties. They were deeply conscious that they could not afford to repeat the experience. In October 1938, after a narrow escape from war in the Czechoslovakian crisis, an editorial in *La Revue des agriculteurs de France* declared that 'The blood-letting of another war would this time go together with the destruction of our peasantry, and without the peasantry what would remain of France? A war won would be almost as disastrous as a war lost.'[1] Another powerful body of anti-war opinion was to be found among the *instituteurs* (primary school teachers), whose main trade union, the *Syndicat national des instituteurs,* was strongly anti-war, and included a hard core of absolute pacifists. The organizations of *anciens combattants* were also generally anti-war and developed many contacts with their German opposite numbers. In 1936 there were over 200 'pacifist' organizations at work in France. The word pacifist was doubtless used loosely, but there could be no doubt that they shared the watchword 'never again'.[2]

In Britain the currents of opinion were very similar and every bit as strong. The largest group numerically among the British peace movements was the League of Nations Union, which was not strictly pacifist in the sense of totally renouncing the use of force, but sought to promote peace by international cooperation and disarmament. The main rallying point for unconditional pacifism was the Peace Pledge Union, founded in 1934–35 by Dick Sheppard, an influential Anglican clergyman. Among the political parties, the Labour Party was strongly anti-war and included a strong pacifist wing; indeed its leader from 1931 to 1935 was an absolute pacifist, George Lansbury. At the University of Oxford, the Union (a famous and much-esteemed debating society) passed on 9 February 1933 a motion that 'This House will in no circumstances fight for its King and Country', which attracted much attention, and was widely regarded as an expression of pacifism among a whole generation of undergraduates – though its precise significance was by no means clear.[3]

Thus in both countries the memory of the Great War produced the same reaction: 'Never again', and anti-war movements formed a current of opinion so strong that it was doubtful whether any French or British government could have led its country into war if this degree of opposition had been maintained. Yet by September 1939 this situation had been transformed. Memories remained, but they were overcome by a reluctant but near-unanimous determination that the advance of German power and of Hitlerism would have to be resisted. When the French Army was mobilized on 1 September 1939, the reservists joined their units almost to a man. There were no anti-war demonstrations and only a handful of individual protests. The leader of one of the pacifist organizations, Louis Lecoin, put out a leaflet headed '*Paix immediate*', but it had no impact, and it was even disavowed by some of those whose names were attached to it. Virtually all the French peace movements, including the peasants and *instituteurs*, which had represented such an apparently fixed cast of mind, reluctantly but resolutely accepted war in 1939. The same was true in Britain. The League of Nations had manifestly failed, and the League of Nations Union had lost its influence. The Peace Pledge Union gained more members on the outbreak of war, but only 2.2 per cent of those called up for military service in October 1939 registered as conscientious objectors, which was far from the general refusal of conscription that Sheppard had aimed at. In Parliament the Labour Party, once so strongly anti-war, reversed its views and did its best to force Chamberlain's government to declare war. At Oxford University, where the 'King and Country' resolution had created such a stir in 1933, no fewer than 2,362 out of some 3,000 students volunteered at once for military service.[4] Over the whole country, the British people went to war quietly but resolutely. The similarity in the patterns of opinion in France and Britain is very striking. In both countries the memory of the Great War remained powerful, but it was overcome by the sheer force of events.[5]

Peoples have memories. So do governments which keep records and consult them in order to learn from the experience of the past. This practical form of memory was much in evidence in Britain and France in 1939 and early 1940. In the course of the war of 1914–18, the British and French governments had moved only slowly to coordinate their policy and strategy. A Supreme War Council, bringing together the heads of government on a regular basis, was set up as late as November 1917. The need for joint action in economic affairs was recognized earlier, and in November 1916, on the initiative of Jean Monnet (then an official in the French Ministry of Commerce) and Arthur Salter (a civil servant in the British Ministry of Transport), a Wheat Executive was set up to make joint purchases of wheat in the United States. An Inter-Allied Maritime Transport Council was established in March 1918 to control shipping resources, and a whole string of joint organizations were set up in the next few months. When war against Germany was resumed in September 1939, the memory of the success of this machinery in Allied cooperation was still fresh, and the two governments moved quickly to pick up the threads. The Supreme War Council was revived at once, and it held its first meeting as early as 12 September 1939. Monnet and Salter resumed their cooperation in economic affairs with renewed vigour. Joint planning for food supplies was actually begun before war began. An Anglo-French Purchasing Board was quickly set up, under Monnet's guidance, to coordinate purchases of war supplies in the United States. The two governments concluded a financial agreement in December 1939, fixing the rate of exchange between their respective currencies. All this showed memory at work, in practical and far-reaching ways. In the event, the sweeping German victories of May to June 1940 effectively knocked France out of the war, and these long-term plans for cooperation in a long struggle came to nothing. But in our discussions of memory we should be careful to remember the practical use of governmental memories in 1939–1940.[6]

Occupying a middle ground between government policy and public sentiment are state visits and ceremonial occasions, when Britain and France set out to be on their best behaviour and to display the most favourable aspects of their past relations in order to strengthen their bonds in the present. On these occasions, the memories evoked were almost invariably those of one or other of the two World Wars – indeed, the watchword on these occasions appeared to be 'we *must* mention the war'! Let us recall a few examples.

In July 1938, at a time of intensifying crisis and the threat of another European war, King George VI and Queen Elizabeth made a state visit to France, at which the strongest theme of the programme of events and speeches was the memory of comradeship and common sacrifice during the Great War of 1914–18. The King inaugurated an Australian war memorial at Villers-Bretonneux, reminding the French that soldiers from the far corners of the world had fought and died in France. In response, an *Ode à l'Angleterre* was read on the French radio, recalling those killed at Vimy and La Bassée. One speech after another paid tribute to the dead and invoked the spirit of unity in battle, reflecting a growing sense that Britain and France were almost the last bastions of democracy and civilization in Europe and might have to fight to save themselves.

Many years later, during a state visit to France by Queen Elizabeth II and the Duke of Edinburgh in June 1992, the French Socialist Premier Pierre Bérégovoy made a moving speech, recalling that in the two World Wars young Britons and Frenchmen had died fighting for liberty: 'We do not forget that, Madame.' In June 1994 the Queen travelled to Normandy, along with thousands of ex-servicemen and their families, to mark the 50th anniversary of the D-Day landings. They were made welcome and warmly thanked for liberating France from a terrible regime which had reduced Europe to slavery. Yet just before the anniversary a French public opinion poll showed that 90 per cent of those questioned thought that the Free French had played a major part in the Liberation; and another poll revealed a belief that the Allies and the French Resistance had taken equal shares in driving the Germans out of France.[7] Neither view corresponded with the memories of the British and Allied servicemen who had fought in Normandy in 1944. Memories, especially faulty memories, could cut both ways.

When we return to the questions with which this discussion began, it is striking that the British and French have continued to remember the two World Wars and that their memories remain vivid and powerful after the passage of so many years. These memories themselves have sometimes brought the two countries and peoples together and sometimes divided them – which may be rather dull, but is nonetheless true for that.

Notes

1 Quoted in Mysyrowicz, Ladislas, *Autopsie d'une defaite: origines de l'effondrement militaire francais de 1940* (Lausanne : L'age d'homme, 1973), p. 337 (My translation).

2 There is a thorough review of all these organizations in Ingram, Norman, *The Politics of Dissent: Pacifism in France, 1919–1939* (Oxford: Oxford University Press, 1991).

3 See the detailed treatment in Ceadel, Martin, *Pacifism in Britain, 1914–1945: The Defining of a Faith* (Oxford: Oxford University Press, 1980); and Birn, Donald S., *The League of Nations Union, 1918–1945* (Oxford: Oxford University Press, 1981).

4 Figures for volunteers in Harrison, Brian (ed.), *The History of the University of Oxford, vol. VIII: The Twentieth Century* (Oxford: Oxford University Press, 1994), p. 281.

5 See Bell, P.M.H., 'Peace Movements', in Boyce, Robert. and Maiolo, Joseph A (eds), *The Origins of World War Two: The Debate Continues* (Basingstoke: Palgrave, 2003), pp. 273–85.

6 See Alexander, Martin. and Philpott, William (eds), *Anglo-French Defence Relations between the Wars* (Basingstoke: Palgrave, 2002), ch. 8, 'Preparing to Feed Mars: Anglo-French Economic Co-ordination and the Coming of War, 1937–1940', pp.186–208 and ch. 9, 'The Benefit of Experience? The Supreme War Council and the higher management of Coalition War', pp. 209–26.

7 The results of these two polls, commissioned respectively by *Le Figaro* and *Le Monde*, were reported in *The Times*, 31 May 1994. See Bell, P.M.H., *France and Britain, 1940–1994: The Long Separation* (London: Longman, 1997), p. 287.

CHAPTER SEVEN

Cultural Divergences in Patterns of Remembering the Great War in Britain and France

Jay Winter

Glory

In a talk broadcast by the BBC on 8 September 1940, the text of which he asked 35 years later to be placed in his coffin, the distinguished Republican jurist René Cassin recalled the villages in flames in which he had fought and his comrades who fell beside him near St Mihiel in October 1914. Herewith the French:

> Je vous reconnais bien, Capitaine Woignier, catholique lorrain à l'âme ardente, qui avez fermé les yeux en contemplant votre terre natale, et vous, Vandendalle et Pellegrino, sans peur et sans reproche, paisibles horticulteurs au sang vermeil, comme vos belles fleurs. Je te reconnais Garrus, humble journalier des collines du Var, toi le braconnier libre penseur, volontaire pour les patrouilles dangereuses, et vous, Samama, juge d'instruction qui aviez tenu, parce que juif, à ne pas rallier un poste moins exposé . . .[1]

My rendering of this passage in English is the following:

> I recognize you very well, Captain Woignier, Catholic from Lorraine with an ardent soul, whose last sight was that of your native soil, and you, Vandendalle

and Pellegrino, without fear or reproach, whose blood shone as red as your beautiful flowers. I recognize you Garrus, humble labourer of the hills of the Var, you the game poacher and free thinker, always ready to volunteer for dangerous patrols, and you Samama, examining magistrate who, because you were a Jew, would not accept a less dangerous position . . .

I start with this text because it illustrates my first point. Remembering the Great War in France frequently entails speech acts of a different kind and character from those attending remembrance in Britain. There is a florid, high-toned, romantic air in many French accounts of the war which, I believe, go beyond the Big Words of High Diction on which Anglo-Saxon writers from Robert Graves to Paul Fussell have focused. My claim is not that ponderous and plodding prose was unknown in Britain; on the contrary. It is rather that the language used to honour the living and the dead who went through the war is different today and has been different in France and in Britain ever since the war.

I have no settled views on why this is so, but offer several suggestions. The first is that while elites in both countries studied Latin rhetoric, they did so to different effect. The noble rhetorical posture of Cicero was reinforced by Corneille and Racine, producing French oratory in the grand manner of the kind René Cassin used in his BBC address to mark the Battle of the Somme 26 years after. In the British case, Cicero was there, but so was Tacitus and perhaps more importantly, the cadences of the King James version of the Bible, which has no equivalent in France. Separating the language of church and state in France produced Republican pomp that had a different timbre, operating in different registers, from British prose.

Let me try to make the point in another way. I want to suggest that the French word 'Gloire' is not the same as the English word 'Glory'. And here the difference may arise from the distinction between Catholic and Protestant notation. Here is a plaque from the village church at Auvers-sur-Oise, a church made immortal by Van Gogh's rendering of it. The plaque was written by the village priest:

Hommage d'affectueuse reconnaissance à mes chers enfants que j'ai élevés dans l'amour de Dieu et de la Patrie, ils sont tombés glorieusement au champ d'honneur.
Gloire à DIEU!
Gloire à notre France immortelle!
Gloire ici-bas et la Haut à ceux qui sont morts pour elle.
Ceux qui pieusement sont morts pour la Patrie
Ont droit qu'à leur tombeau la foule vienne et prie,
Entre les plus beaux noms leur nom est le plus beau !
Reposez en paix, mes chers enfants.
Dormez dans la gloire!!!
Votre vieux Curé bien fier de vous,
Qui n'a jamais désespéré de la victoire.

I hesitate to translate this passage, since my intention is to compare and not to ridicule. It is evident that the curé is drawing both on his faith and on Victor Hugo's poetry. Herewith his 'Chants du crépuscule' of July 1831, honouring those who died in the revolution of the previous year:

Ceux qui pieusement sont morts pour la patrie
Ont droit qu'à leur cerceuil la foule vienne et prie.
Entre les plus beaux noms leur nom est le plus beau.
Toute gloire près d'eux passe et tombe éphémère ;
Et, comme ferait une mère,
La voix d'un peuple entier les berce en leur tombeau.
Gloire à notre France éternelle !
Gloire à ceux qui sont morts pour elle !
Aux martyrs ! aux vaillants ! aux forts !
A ceux qu'enflamme leur exemple,
Qui veulent place dans le temple,
Et qui mourrons comme ils sont morts !
C'est pour ces morts, dont l'ombre est ici bienvenue,
Que le haut Panthéon élève dans la nue,
Au-dessus de Paris, la ville aux mille tours,
La reine de nos Tyrs et de nos Babylones,
Cette couronne de colonnes
Que le soleil levant redore tous les jours !
Gloire à notre France éternelle !
Gloire à ceux qui sont morts pour elle !
Aux martyrs ! aux vaillants ! aux forts !
A ceux qu'enflamme leur exemple,
Qui veulent place dans le temple,
Et qui mourrons comme ils sont morts !
Ainsi, quand de tels morts sont couchés dans la tombe,
En vain l'oubli, nuit sombre où va tout ce qui tombe,
Passe sur leur sépulcre où nous nous inclinons ;
Chaque jour, pour eux seuls se levant plus fidèle,
La gloire, aube toujours nouvelle,
Fait luire leur mémoire et redore leurs noms !
Gloire à notre France éternelle !
Gloire à ceux qui sont morts pour elle !
Aux martyrs ! aux vaillants ! aux forts !
A ceux qu'enflamme leur exemple,
Qui veulent place dans le temple,
Et qui mourrons comme ils sont morts ![2]

Twenty-two exclamation points in one poem; what could express better the cultural archive from which Cassin, the good priest of Auvers-sur-Oise, and others drew? My claim is that this mixture of revolutionary fervour and Catholic romanticism, lived in vigorous incompatibility together in the French language of 1914–18, and bore no resemblance to English usages in the war years and after.

Let me add some statistical evidence in support of my argument. Together with a consortium of universities, Google has created a unique statistical data base, composed of 6,000,000 books produced between 1800 and 2000, every page of which have been scanned in machine-readable form. These Google N-grams enable us to compare the frequency of the appearance of different words over time in a very large corpus of published books.[3] I have made two comparisons: one for the word *gloire* in French over the period 1900–1930, and a second for the word *glory* in British English books over the same period. The inflection in the recourse to *gloire* contrasts strikingly with the slow decline in the use of the word *glory* in British English. In the second set of graphs, the contrasts show the same pattern, though set against the years 1900–2000. The peak of *gloire* in French in the whole of the twentieth century came during the Great War; in contrast, *glory* in British English has declined in virtually a linear fashion from the Victorian years to the present.

To be sure the presence of a word in a book does not describe its weight or significance, but these data are consistent with my argument that language patterns vary and so do the way they encode widely disseminated messages about the Great War.

Another way to see the force of the cultural divide I want to explore is to compare this French inscription – one of thousands – with the inscription on the Cenotaph in Whitehall – the Glorious Dead. The term was chosen by Rudyard Kipling, a man who used language to talk about war in a much more ambivalent and subtle manner than usually he is given credit for. Why does the word *glorious* carry less heightened emotion than the word *glory* or its French equivalent *gloire*? Simply because the noun carries an attribute, something gained, and the adjective covers it perhaps a bit more delicately, like a shawl, leading to the word 'Dead', unmistakably something lost. In addition, by sticking to an adjective, Kipling subtly bypassed the realm of the religious, which was precisely what Edwin Lutyens had intended to do in designing the Cenotaph not as a Christian, but as an ecumenical site of memory. In a way, Kipling and Lutyens together showed how to glorify those who die in war without glorifying war itself. This suggests a paradox: Britain, with an established Church, may have had a somewhat more secularized language of remembrance than Republican France, which went to war in 1914 less than a decade after the end of a nasty battle over the separation of state and church.

And yet it is evident that the two cases – that of an assimilated Jewish Republican veteran born in Bayonne and raised in Nice, a man who almost died of his wounds in 1914, and that of a Catholic cleric from the rural hinterland of Paris – highlight one of the central contrasts of the cultural history of the Great War. The English language works differently from the

French language when it comes to heightened eloquence; consequently, memories expressed in the two languages may never be the same, and may always remain at a tangent to each other.

Let me try to add another nuance to this argument, using another image from the village of Auvers-sur-Oise. There is an unusual war memorial in the village church itself. It is literally next to the curé's paean to the dead, but it offers a very different message. The *bas-relief* shows a young woman kneeling down beside a cross with the laurel wreath of victory resting on the ground. In the background, a cock is crowing at the day of victory in November 1918. Her hand is on her head, presenting the classical pose of melancholy – her head is too heavy with grief, and her eyes have the eternal stare of the unconsolable.

I want to consider this plaque as a counterpoint to the noble rhetoric of the clergyman just to the right of it. The first point of difference is the gendering of mourning. The priest speaks to his fellow men about the nobility of their sacrifice, instilled in them in church and in school during their early years, and bearing its fruit in their wartime sacrifice. The woman speaks to other women, to her fellow mourners, wives, mothers, sisters, daughters, perhaps a majority of the *pratiquants* who gathered there in prayer or reflection. Gendering the message changes it radically. And here there may be more convergences rather than divergences in the representation of loss of life in the Great War in France and Britain. By this I mean that writing about the sacrifices of war showed striking cultural differences, whereas configuring the same theme in sculptural form may have enabled messages to cross language barriers. Writing war (or memories of war) and configuring war are not identical or even parallel acts.

I emphasize the tentativeness of this assertion. Mourning in prose or poetry and mourning in stone and colour follow different patterns. And when we consider monumental sculpture, we can see the huge variety of choices available to artists and artisans. Antoine Prost made the point 25 years ago in dealing with the range of messages in French war memorials.[4] There are those who try to configure glory and those who, like Lutyens, sidestepped the obvious or the clichéd and searched for symbolic indirection.

The Cenotaph undercut triumphalism; perhaps that is why it became the national point of reference for remembrance, and it fits well within the funerary category, one of the three Prost delineates in his typology of war memorials. There are other forms – classical, patriotic, to various degrees, but the funerary is there in both countries' sculptural repertoire. It is in this undercutting of triumphalism – vividly portrayed in the Auvers-sur-Oise *bas-relief* – that I believe point to some commonalities as between British and French ways of remembering the Great War and those who died in it.

Another French word rich with denominational associations and which seems to have no equivalent in English is *martyre*. Herewith a rhetorical gambit from a meeting of CIAMAC, the pacifist veterans' movement Cassin among others had built, in September 1935:

Réunie à Belgrade, cité martyre, victime en août 1914 d'une injuste agression, née de nouveau aujourd'hui du sacrifice de millions d'hommes, la CIAMAC rappelle quelle force puissante constitue la conscience du droit violemment offensé.[5]

Which I render in English as

Assembled in Belgrade, city of suffering, the victim in August 1914 of unjust aggression, today reborn through the sacrifice of millions of people, CIAMAC reaffirms the irrepressible force arising from the consciousness of a repugnant violation of the law of war.

Why is it so difficult to find a meaning in English for the phrase 'cité martyre' or 'Ville martyre', as Rheims is termed today in one online school textbook.[6] Yes, languages are defined as Rushdie said, by their untranslatable words, but what makes them untranslatable is still a problem historians need to address. To use the term 'martyred city' sounds too heavy, too grandiose, too sanctimonious in English. Maybe I am wrong, but there's the rub. Try translating that into French.

At this point, I would like to extend the linguistic turn into another interesting contrast between the cultural history of France and Britain during the Great War. Could it be that the rhetorical divide I have discussed so far may help us explain why war poetry took on a different character in the two countries? The purpose of the war poets, understood as a loosely constructed group of writers including Wilfred Owen, Siegfried Sassoon, Robert Graves, Edmund Blunden, Isaac Rosenberg, among others, was to puncture the rhetorical pretentions of the cult of glory and to honour the men who served and those who died in less pretentious ways than did the propagandists of the time. To do so required a major effort to scrape the hyperbole and euphemisms from descriptions of battle and the mayhem it caused. The corpus of these men has become part of English cultural history, possibly because it captured a more general sense within the British population that the word *glory* and all its associations did not survive the Somme and Passchendaele.

Without this allergy to the rhetoric of glory, French poets produced many kinds of verse, some ephemeral, some lasting. But it did not add up to a collective expression, a cultural moment, a resonant *cri de coeur* of the kind the British war poets provided. I would like to suggest that glory was still in the French rhetorical knapsack when the war of 1939 broke out, and in part through the efforts of the Resistance, and through de Gaulle's prose and political project, it may have survived even defeat, occupation, collaboration and the painful accounting which World War II precipitated. Whether or not *la gloire* is still alive and well in the Elysée palace, I leave to others. What seems important in our discussion is that the rhetorical differences in the register of remembrance in English and French extend to the canonization of the war poets of the Great War in English. Nothing like that exists in French or in France.

Perhaps a caveat here is necessary. To be sure, there were multiple ways by which soldiers spoke about the war in the post-war period. Henri Barbusse or Maurice Genevoix did not write of glory when depicting trench warfare. Perhaps there was a greater element of glory in civilian rhetoric than among *anciens combattants*. There was no one French discursive field, but a number of them. But even when we speak of multiple registers, there still seems to be a divide between the way in which most British and most French people spoke about war, and to a degree, that divide is still evident today. The difference is that of lexicon and rhetoric, the connotations, rather than the denotations attached to meditations on the Great War.

Futility

I want to emphasize the complexity of a comparison of the verbal or written and the visual or figurative evidence of commemorative forms and gestures in Britain and France following the Great War. Take the term 'futility'; here is a tough translation problem. 'Inutilité' is too functional to be a good equivalent, and 'sans valeur' makes no sense when it comes to the expulsion of the German army from Northern France. And that may be the point. It is not only linguistic barriers that separate French and British modes of remembrance, but also common and often unspoken assumptions about what the war was about, what it meant – the 'pour quoi?' in 'pourquoi?'.

It is simply not possible to refer to a war of defence against the occupation of northern France as an act of futility. It is perfectly acceptable to point to the futility of tactics or strategy, and no one thinks otherwise of the way in which General Robert Nivelle conducted the Chemin des Dames campaign after its failure to achieve its stated objectives in a limited time period. In France, though, to refer to the war as a whole as an exercise in futility is to court bafflement or total incomprehension; fighting on one's own soil to liberate it from occupation simply makes sense.

There may be other, less evident, historical remains behind this translation problem. Yes, most British soldiers did not die on British soil. But let us look at the matter in another way. Could the content of the term 'futility' to apply to a war reflect in part or indirectly a lack of militarism in British society, arising simply from the absence of compulsory military service prior to the war of 1914? Being a soldier in Britain was neither a necessary nor even a common *rite de passage* into adulthood. I would not call the other side of our comparative coin French militarism, though there are individuals and groups whose ideas do fit the term. I prefer to speak of an acceptance of military service as a sign of citizenship, which in the 2011 Bastille day parade made Frenchmen and women I was with accept as perfectly normal a *haka*, or Maori war chant, from Polynesian soldiers given pride of place in front of

President Sarkozy. Could you imagine anyone thinking the same in Britain if Maori soldiers performed a haka on Armistice Day or Remembrance Sunday? In Britain, such antics belong on the rugby pitch, not on solemn occasions; but going by the events on 14 July 2011, not so in France.

Following this, one MP, Eva Joly, a leader of the Green party, got into a lot of trouble when she suggested that maybe a non-military spectacle would be a better way to celebrate the French revolution. Go back to Norway, shouted outraged patriots: Joly is indeed Franco-Norwegian. Don't hold your breath for a change of the kind she advocated.

The naturalness of military service in France and the rocky road the French army trod from Dienbienphu in 1954 to Algiers a few years later may help account for another incident which highlighted the political stakes of the use of the term 'futility' or its equivalents when referring to the Great War in France. In 1957 Stanley Kubrick's film about the futility of the Chemin des Dames offensive, *Paths of glory*, was not submitted to French censors for approval due to French government pressure on United Artists not to release the film. Thus the film, with its savagely satirical portrayal of two French generals, one corrupt and the other incompetent, who send three innocent men to the firing squad to be shot for the 'failure' of the offensive they had ordered, was shown in France only in 1975. In Britain, the film was shown to general approval, and provided a kind of preparation for the more stylized version of the same theme, Richard Attenbrough's 1969 film adaptation of Joan Littlewood's 1963 stage play *Oh! What a lovely war!*, which in turn provided material for countless later comic renderings of the same theme from Blackadder to the History Boys to Monty Python and beyond.

I simply want to put the question: why is it not a good idea to make jokes about the Great War in France, while it is difficult, when teaching undergraduates, at least, to avoid them in Britain (and not only in Britain)? Here we come to the inevitable confrontation with that centerpiece of Great War cultural history – the centrality of irony in British narratives. Many other scholars have taken this claim apart, and I for one have tried to show how 'British' in style was a masterpiece of French writing on the war, Jean Giraudoux's *La guerre de Troyes n'aura pas lieu* (1935), a joke about the Great War in French, to be sure. Let us not draw distinctions too sharply in this domain; Giraudoux fought in Gallipoli, after all. And yet there is still something to be explained here, and it is not sufficient simply to refer to the screen memory of World War II, occupation, collaboration and humiliation, to appreciate the force of George Brassens's musical answer to his colonel's unstated question about his favourite war, 'Moi, mon colon, celle que je préfère/C'est la guerre de quatorze-dix-huit'. The Great War is sacred in France in a way that it is not in Britain. It is the Ur-Catastrophe of the twentieth century in Britain, but something different in France. When Jean-Baptiste Duroselle referred to the Great War as 'l'incompréhensible', he captured something very specifically French.[7] British irony makes the Great

War comprehensible, palpable, at times laughable. But in France, where the lists of the dead on war memorials are devastatingly long – twice as many French as British soldiers died in the war – this can never be a laughing matter.

Calendars of commemoration

Since language frames memory, then it is inevitable that different linguistic forms and conventions provide cultural boundaries separating *to some degree* acts of remembrance concerning the Great War in Britain and France. Differences abound: let us count the ways, just to set out the problem, rather than to pretend to have resolved it. Herewith a beginner's list, divided into two, one concerning forms of public remembrance and another focusing on scholarly differences. I invite all participants to add their own instances to this admittedly arbitrary framework.

1   The calendar: 11 November is a holiday in France but not in Britain. Why? More on this in a moment.

2   The Cenotaph: It was adopted in Britain by popular acclaim as the national war memorial; the catafalque constructed in Paris for the victory parade 5 days before was scrapped after the event, apparently because Clemenceau thought it looked too 'Germanic'. Why did it 'stick' in Britain and not in France?

3   The Imperial War Museum: There is no one national museum of the war in France with the standing and drawing power of the Imperial War Museum. France with a much more centralized state than Britain has a much more decentralized museum world. Why?

4   Funerary horticulture and design: War cemeteries reflect the difference between a conscript army fighting on its own soil and a volunteer army (until 1916) fighting and dying on foreign soil. That the Imperial (now Commonwealth) War Graves Commission chose small-scale cemeteries rather than the massive French or American equivalents requires explanation. Let me offer a few illustrations of this distinction from a less well-known venue, that of Gallipoli. This was a combined French and British operation, though, as I shall claim later, one with less than an indelible impression on French writing on the war. Just consider the contrast between these two cemeteries at Gallipoli. The first is a British and New Zealand cemetery at Suvla Bay in the north of the peninsula. The site is small, well tended even in these barren salt marshes. In this cemetery is the plaque to one man, Lance Corporal J.M. Brown of the Derbyshire

Regiment, who died there on 22 August 1915, as the inscription his family chose states, not for 'glory, but for a purpose'. What a contrast when we compare it with the French military cemetery right at the tip of the Gallipoli peninsula. The scale is grand and the individuality of each tomb is austere and limited to a name on a wrought-iron cross, easier to anchor in this soil than a stone. The serried ranks of the French dead present an entirely different narrative: in the French case, the man is embraced in the nation, whose army remains, as it were, at attention. In the British (or more precisely, Imperial) case, the individual stands apart, a civilian in uniform rather than a citizen-soldier.

6 Utilitarianism: If the voluntary nature of the initial military effort of Britain and her Dominions separates it from that of France, so does the utilitarian element in commemorative structures, gestures and acts. War memorials in Britain and in areas of white settlement include useful things, like water troughs, cricket pitches, scholarships, hospital wings, highways, gardens; French war memorials rarely follow the utilitarian path and stick to symbolic language. Both suggest that there is a debt to be repaid, but the French form of registering this debt is different from that of the British.

7 Veterans and Pensions: rights or charity? I want to extend the discussion to material matters. Soldiers' pensions mattered very much to veterans. Here was where the community expressed its sense of indebtedness. To Clemenceau, veterans, and especially disabled men, were 'the first creditors of the nation'. On many occasions he made it clear that we (civilians) were indebted to them (soldiers) and that that debt could not be forgotten.

In material terms, French veterans did better than British ones when it came to negotiating the bureaucratic straits and getting paid. This was certainly a matter of recognition, but it entailed a very different balance between the soldier and the state in the two countries. In France, from 1916, a very different approach from that of Britain was adopted to address the fundamental question of the presumption of origin of the condition for which a disabled man made his claim.[8] Here is the basis of the Pension Charter of 1919, in which it was affirmed that it was *not* the burden of the wounded soldier to prove that the army was responsible for his invalidity, but on the contrary, the state had to prove that his claim was unfounded. Hereby disabled men avoided the procedural difficulties of establishing the exact circumstances of their wounds. As soon as the army recognized a man as fit for service, any and all deterioration of his health, even without a direct link to combat, was imputable to his military service. A tubercular man serving in an army office could claim that his service was the cause of his illness: the army should not have taken him in the first place. This reversal of the burden of proof accelerated the pace of decisions granting men a pension. More important still was the establishment of the principle that the individual came before the state. In this way compensation for war-related injury or disability became a right.

Nothing could have been further removed from this approach than that of many British Pensions Tribunals. In Britain, it was the claimant who had to prove that his disability was war-related and not the result of a pre-existing condition. In Britain, disabled men, through their own associations, did not play an active role in the administration of the pensions system. In France, they demanded and got parity – that is 50 per cent of the boards managing the national office dealing with disabled men and with orphans, *les pupilles de la nation*, wards of the state. Private charities were much more central in this domain in Britain than in France. There is nothing in France remotely like the Royal British Legion.

This militancy with respect to pensions was matched by a much more powerful pacifist element in veterans' politics in France. The proportion joining veterans' groups in interwar France was four times as great as that joining such groups in Britain. It is hardly surprising, therefore, that many (but by no means all) veterans' groups had political clout in France and that many of them used it to lobby for disarmament, the League of Nations and the Kellogg-Briand pact.

At home, these groups had a particular style of commemorative activity, remote from their British colleagues. First there was the feast of the evening of 10 November, at times a very alcoholic and jolly affair, in which celebrating being alive and the simple pleasures of survival came first. Then came the solemn recalling of the names on the local war memorial the next morning. But the men who went to these events did not go there as soldiers; they went as civilians, as citizens who did not want their children to follow in their footsteps and have to go to war. Their pacifist dream was an evanescent one; but the way in which such men expressed it separates them from many, if not most, of their British counterparts.

Why? There is no one simple answer, but elements of it must be found in the pre-1914 conflict in France between the army and the state precipitated by the Dreyfus affair. The Radical coalition which came to power in the wake of this *cause célèbre* was an odd mixture of social conservatives, anti-clericals and internationalists. Briand, 11 times prime minister, was the *rapporteur* of the commission that worked out the modalities of separating church and state in 1905. He headed three wartime governments and devoted himself to international reconciliation. Militarism was simply not in his bones. He was one of millions of men who saw war as an abomination, deserving a pariah status, outside of international law. The fact that the Nazis and others exploded this dream in the 1930s does not render it a delusion. It was instead a great cause, a lost one to be sure, but a cause for which many veterans fought as hard as they could. The same cannot be claimed in the case of British veterans, a much more varied and less militant population. The army was less of a presence in the political life of the nation, and the navy had the advantage of not being present at home most of the time. Some towns did have a distinctive naval presence, but they were the exceptions. The interwar French veterans' movement had no precise equivalent in Britain or elsewhere.

Emphases, occlusions, omissions

These linguistic, cultural, ideological, administrative and political differences are evident. They were bound to have a bearing on the way in which historians – popular or academic – have written about the subject of the Great War in the century since its outbreak. Again, for purposes of opening a discussion rather than authoritatively concluding one, I list a series of striking imbalances in what British and French historians focus on when they write about the Great War.

The empire

Can any imagine a groundswell of support for 'une musée impériale de guerre' in Paris? There were such displays in Les Invalides and in the 1931 colonial exhibition, but they were always marginal to the domestic, 'hexagonal' story of the war. This was true when a group of us put together the Historial de la Grande Guerre at Péronne. The empire is there, but as a backdrop, extras in an epic film of European warfare.

Given the strength of family ties between Britain and her Dominions, the balance between home and imperial dimensions of the war was bound to be different. But this emphasis on Australia, Canada and New Zealand and on Gallipoli and the Western front has no equivalent in France. And the force of the British imperial narrative has occluded a recognition among British historians about the contribution of the French empire to the war.

The war at sea

The geographical setting of this distinction leads to a second contrast in historical foci. The history of the naval war is almost nonexistent in France. French capital ships went down alongside British ones in the failure to run the straits of the Dardanelles prior to the landing in Gallipoli, but this is a sideshow in French historiography. This is hardly surprising, given the proximity of Paris to the Western Front, but it still structures narratives of the war in different ways. The significance of the U-boat war in British historiography also has no counterpart in French writing on the same subject, meagre as it is.

Iconic Battles

It has taken 20 years and an awful lot of work to persuade French school textbook writers to give the Somme even a fraction of the coverage inevitably given to Verdun in accounts of the war on the Western front. And though there is more of an understanding in France now than ever before that the Somme was a Franco-British push and that there were 200,000 French casualties registered in the course of it, Verdun still holds centre stage as the iconic French battle of the war. Even less well known in France is Passchendaele, or Third Ypres, which was not coterminous with the failed campaign on the Chemin des Dames, but which followed it. The fact that the Somme began in the middle of the Battle of Verdun may help account for one occlusion, that of 1916, but the timing of combat in 1917 means we need to look for another explanation for the 1917 occlusion.

Mutiny

Perhaps that explanation lies in the significance of the mutinies of 1917 in the French army. Here there is a significant contrast, one I still stand by. The British army, I believe, was the only one which did not suffer a major and sustained revolt against discipline and failed tactics. The uprising at the base camp at Étaples in September 1917 did occur during the Battle of Passchendaele, but I prefer to see it as an act of loyal indiscipline, a reaction against the harshness of training and military policing in an anonymous mass of tents on sand dunes miles away from the front. Since 1967, when Guy Pedroncini first published his work on the mutinies,[9] their political and social significance has fascinated French scholars. Recent works in the Anglo-Saxon world, like those of Len Smith,[10] have by and large confirmed Pedroncini's early findings.

Why was there no British mutiny during Passchendaele is a difficult question to answer, but it does raise matters discussed indirectly in accounts of officer-men relations and strategies of establishing some degree of proportionality, as Sir John Keegan put it,[11] between ground to be gained and lives to be lost. And yet the question still remains as to whether the cohesion of the British army through thick and thin was a reflection of its civilian character, of its being made up of the most highly disciplined labour force in the world? I hope this matter will be explored further, in the close micro-history of individual units such as that of Helen McCartney's excellent account of the Liverpool Territorials.[12]

The Haig problem

Discussions of mutiny revolve around matters of failed leadership, and Nivelle has taken his rightful share of the blame for the misfiring of his offensive of 1917. But in the French historiography, there is nothing which even comes near the set battles which almost always erupt when the name of Douglas Haig is raised. There have been attempts to get beyond what I term the Haig problem. Robin Prior and Trevor Wilson have focused on General Rawlinson effectively, while never leaving anyone in the slightest doubt as to their contempt for his boss.[13] Exponents of the learning curve argument point to middle-level leadership as critical in moving from stalemate in 1916 to victory in 1918.[14] And the technicalities of the artillery war have become more central to a number of interpretations about the reason why the Allies succeeded in rolling back German lines in 1918 to the point where Ludendorff had to find a way to arrange an Armistice.

And yet these efforts, while valuable, still leave the central focus in the military history of the war on Haig. He still looms over much scholarship like a moored dirigible, impervious to the potshots his adversaries take time and again. Foch now has his Anglo-Saxon historian, and work is available on other French figures, but it all does not add up to the kind of focus or fixation on Haig.

One reason for the difference in French and British writing on military leadership is that in Britain, the civilian government was unable to maintain the kind of scrutiny and control of the high command that the French were able to do. Partly this was a function of financial controls, but it also reflected the fact that many parliamentarians in France were serving during the war and could muster the technical knowledge and authority Asquith or Lloyd George evidently did not have. Haig may not have won the war on the Western front single-handedly, as some of his admirers almost claim, but he certainly won the war against Whitehall. When the going got tough, it was Sir William Robertson, Chief of the Imperial General Staff, who had to resign, not Haig. This failure of civilian control in Britain may help account for the ongoing and profitable Haig industry in First World War studies.

The shell shock fixation

A final area of complete divergence as between French and British historical scholarship concerns the avalanche of work done in English, and not in French, on shell shock. Here too linguistic differences matter. The term 'shell shock' carries a punch which the multiple French variants of 'le choc traumatique' do not carry. I am still of the opinion that the term 'shell shock', first used (and then abandoned) by its inventor C.S. Meyers, for diagnostic purposes, slowly but surely turned into a metaphor for the war as a whole. It was an artillery war, and it destroyed the coherence of a British way of life based on prosperity, empire and naval power. Not only individuals suffered from shell shock; through the institutionalization of war poetry, generations of young people identified the condition of madness with the condition of England. The term, therefore, carries messages utterly different from those attached to shell shock or its equivalents in France. The term suggests an intolerable burden attached to military service, which a country with a system of military conscription cannot tolerate. Perhaps that is why French scholars, alongside the rest of their countrymen, do not appear to share the British (and more generally Anglo-Saxon) fascination with shell shock. Here medical traditions and their attitude to psychiatric illness must be taken into account, though I believe doctors follow, rather than determine, cultural trends. There are also the important gender issues imbedded in the study of hysteria, and the openness of British scholars to considering shell shock as the equivalent of female powerlessness or paralysis seems to have few French counterparts. My mind remains open to other explanations of this striking distinction, which to date (and to my knowledge) no one has studied in comparative perspective.

Memory or *la mémoire*?

Finally, there is a gap, at times a yawning gap, between the way in which the word 'memory' itself is deployed in the two languages and in the two cultures. The entire literature surrounding *la mémoire collective* was French in origin. Annette Becker has pointed to the paradox that the inventor of the term, Maurice Halbwachs, avoided applying it at any time to the Great War.[15] In addition, his usage of the term did not equate *la mémoire collective* with national patterns of remembrance, but rather with the remembrance practices of collectives which told their members who they were. And yet after years of effort, in trying to suggest that memory is a faculty and remembrance is a practice, I have had to admit defeat and recognize that the term memory is immovable and that there are national patterns in different memory cultures imbedded in language itself.

That leaves us with the question as to whether when we ask what is *la mémoire de la Grande Guerre* in France we are asking precisely the same question as when we interrogate people as to the memory of the Great War in Britain. The answer I have come to tentatively is yes and no. There seem to be three levels at which memory cultures operate when dealing with upheavals of the intensity and duration of the Great War. The first is family memories, and here I think French and British usages are just about the same. There are photographic albums and souvenirs and trophies, and caches upon caches of letters written from and to home by loved ones and soldiers. This bedrock memory culture is what drives forward a second level of memory activism, which is alive and well and shows no signs of abating. And that is the memory industry surrounding the war. This includes the production and consumption of books and journals and the products of internet sites. It extends to major and local museums from Auckland to London to Kansas City and beyond. And it fuels the buses, planes and boats that bring hundreds of thousands to pilgrimage sites like La Boisselle on the Somme, where a very large hole in the ground has been preserved by purchase. The proprietors are the families of Newcastle-upon-Tyne who gather there with their bagpipes and clergymen every 1 July; in the words of one of the inscriptions on a bench at the site: they offer homage from those who went home after that day to those who stayed behind.

The purchase of Great War motifs in popular fiction attests to the degree to which the demand curve for narratives about or set in the Great War has shifted to the right. My guess is that there are more detective novels of what Rosa Bracco termed a 'middle-brow' character[16] in the British market than in the French market, though films like *A very long engagement/Un long dimanche de fiançailles* (2004) suggest otherwise. On the other hand, there is a thriving market in *bandes dessinées* or comic strips for grown-ups which include vivid and at times gothic accounts of trench warfare. The French museum the Historial de la Grande Guerre presented as a temporary exhibition a series of works in this format by Jacques Tardi. He is not alone in this field.

Aside from family history and the memory industry, the third domain in which we can compare the two countries is in terms of institutional memory, imbedded in schools, universities, churches and state ceremonies. I still feel uncomfortable in identifying this level of remembrance with what might be termed 'national memory'; perhaps variations on 'official memory' might be a more accurate term to use, though the boundaries between official or state institutions and civil society is unclear. The best example of this blurring of boundaries is the Royal British Legion's sale of poppies every November before Armistice Day. There is nothing like this in France, where care for disabled veterans and their families is a recognized charge on the state. Private charitable activity reflects the robust character of the Protestant voluntary tradition in Britain, but buying a poppy for a few pennies is something millions of people do at the same time every year. Television presenters wear them, so do university lecturers like me. They are national symbols just as powerful as the flag and hence have a semi-official, national notation.

Similarly, there is a campaign, which has been gathering strength for some time, to turn Remembrance Sunday back into Armistice Day. That is, to make the 11th hour of the 11th day of the 11th month of the year the moment for reflection on the Great War, as it was before 1939. I do not know if this effort will succeed, but it does show a concern with nationalizing a practice – that is putting it back into the rhythms of the nation's daily life – which now has a church affiliation, at a time when church attendance is dwindling rapidly. Ironically, should this occur, then British and French 'official memory' would draw closer together, at least in a formal sense.

In both countries, the Great War is associated with sacred stories, and these stories have been and will continue to be configured in different ways, with different gestures, and different terms. Language matters, here as elsewhere, and language, while locally inflected, is a national resource, through which groups of people tell stories about their past. As such, my conclusion is that the phrases *la Grande Guerre*, alongside *the Great War*, are national speech acts, and remain among those untranslatable terms which tells us who we are, French, British, other, or *un cosmopolite, intellectuel, déraciné, comme je suis.*

Notes

1   *Cahiers de l'Union Fédérale*, no. 377, November 1987, «René Cassin au Panthéon», Archives Nationales, Fonds Cassin, 382AP185.

2   Victor Hugo, *Œuvres complètes:* Les Feuilles d'automne. Les Chants du crépuscule. Les Voix intérieures. Les Rayons et les Ombres (Paris: Ollendorf, 1909), vol. 17, pp. 203–4.

3   Jean-Baptiste Michel, et al., 'Quantitative analysis of culture using millions of digitized books', *Science*, 331, 2011, 176ff.

4   Antoine Prost, 'Les monuments aux morts', in Pierre Nora (ed.), *Les lieux de mémoire*, vol. I (Paris: Gallimard, 1984).

5   Archives nationales, Pierrefitte-sur-Seine, 382AP10, conférence de Belgrade de la CIAMAC, 24 sept. 1935.

6   'Classe de Première S. / Histoire / Epreuve majeure type bac_dossier documentaire / 2007' http://crid1418.org/doc/pedago/etude_docs_reims.pdf.

7   Jean-Baptiste Duroselle, *La Grande Guerre des Français: l'incompréhensible* (Paris: Perrin, 1994).

8   *Loi créant des allocations temporaires spéciales pour les réformés no. 2 (réformés à titre temporaire).* See the discussion in Antoine Prost and Jay Winter, *René Cassin et les droits de l'homme. Un projet d'une génération* (Paris: Fayard, 2011), ch. 2.

9   Guy Pedroncini, *Les Mutineries de 1917* (Paris: Presses Universitaires de France, 1967).

10 Leonard V. Smith, *Between Mutiny and Obedience: The Case of the French Fifth Infantry Division during World War I* (Princeton, NJ: Princeton University Press, 1994).

11 John Keegan, *The Face of Battle* (London: Penguin Books, 1976).

12 Helen B. McCartney, *Citizen Soldiers: The Liverpool Territorials in the First World War* (Cambridge: Cambridge University Press, 2005).

13 Robin Prior and Trevor Wilson, *Command on the Western Front: The Military Career of Sir Henry Rawlinson, 1914–18* (Oxford: Basil Blackwell, 1992).

14 G.D. Sheffield, *Leadership in the Trenches: Officer–Man Relations, Morale and Discipline in the British Army in the Era of the First World War* (Basingstoke: Macmillan Press in association with King's College, London, 2000).

15 Annette Becker, *Maurice Halbwachs: un intellectuel en guerres mondiales 1914–1945*; préface de Pierre Nora (Paris: AgnèsViénot, 2003).

16 Rosa Maria Bracco, *Merchants of Hope: British Middlebrow Writers and the First World War, 1919–1939* (Oxford: Berg, 1993).

CHAPTER EIGHT

The Second World War through French and British Eyes

Robert Frank

In France, the memory of World War II is immeasurably more fractured and fragmented than that of World War I. There is a broad consensus about World War I that reflects the national unity of the time. But there is little in the way of consensus surrounding the memory of World War II which is characterized by divisions, tensions and a general sense of unease. Numerous books and articles have been written about 'the Vichy Syndrome' and France's 'poisoned' and 'divided' memory, which contrasts with the consensual British memory of this war.[1] These arguments are now well known and it is not my intention to rehearse them again here. Instead, I want to examine the memory of the relationship between the two countries during the conflict. This will naturally entail a consideration of joint memories and, to a lesser extent, the rather different narratives of the war that have developed on either side of the Channel.

The primary focus, then, will be on the image of the 'other' – of the French and France in Britain, and of Britain and the British in France. When dealing with the question of representation, it is worth reminding ourselves of three key methodological points. First, the image of the other is intimately related to the perception of the self, of which it is a mirror image. The same is true of the image of the other in the past, which depends on present – or even future – images of the self. Second, the issue of temporality plays a crucial role in determining the contours of memory and representation: the perception of the present is conditioned not only by the present, but also by that of the past and the future. Likewise, memory is conditioned not only by the past, but also by the present and the future.[2] Finally, the act of forgetting is an integral part of memory. Without repression, silence and amnesia, no viable memory can be created.

In order to understand Franco-British memories of World War II, we must, therefore, identify the mirror images that defined the self-perception of the two powers, highlight the weight of the present and future in the construction of memory and assess the French and British capacity to forget. We will look at six key moments: the 'phoney war'; the French defeat in 1940; the relations between the British, Vichy, de Gaulle and the other powers; the role of the British in the liberation of France in 1944; the Yalta conference; and de Gaulle's *de facto* capitulation to Churchill over the Syrian question on 30–31 May 1945. These examples will allow us to make tentative conclusions about France and Britain's conflicting interpretations of events, as well as to consider the various ways in which forgetting has helped structure the Allied memory of the war.

The 'phoney war' or the forgotten recovery

The period from September 1939 to May 1940 is called 'drôle de guerre' in French. The English translation uses the word 'phoney' rather than 'funny'. This reflects the fact that 'there was nothing intrinsically 'funny' about it. For many soldiers, waiting patiently to fight, the war did indeed seem 'phoney'. Inevitably, because we know what happened next, this period has left many negative memories, but this has obscured some of the more fundamental questions that historians need to ask of this period. Why were the armies so passive? Why did they refuse to fight? What led to the demoralized resignation that looked so much like defeatism?

In fact, memories of the 'phoney war' have remained imperfect and fragmented. Paradoxically, it is the positive aspects of this period that have been forgotten. Historians have uncovered numerous examples of recovery during those eight and a half months. The 'phoney war' was a 'strategy' and not simply a situation to which the Allies passively acquiesced.[3] The reason for this was simple: if the balance of immediately available forces favoured Germany, the British and French clearly held the advantage with respect to long-term potential. It was, therefore, merely a matter of time before this potential was transformed into reality. The French slogan from the beginning of 1940 – 'we will win because we are the strongest' – seems ridiculous to us now, but it was a fair assessment of the balance of power at the time. The aim was to hold off war until the summer of 1941, by which point France and Britain's military potential would be realized.

Despite occasional disagreements, this strategy was broadly shared between the two allies, who even managed to put together a framework for economic, financial and monetary cooperation. The agreement signed on 4 December 1939 created a full solidarity between the two countries and made it possible for transactions to be conducted in either currency, even though they were not convertible. For the purposes of importing goods, both currencies were freely recognized on either side of the Channel and across the French and British empires. This encouraged mutual trade and ensured that both powers could build up dollar reserves that could be used to purchase goods unavailable in either country. It was not only in financial terms that the French and British were well prepared, but also the production of weapons and machinery in the two countries – particularly in the aviation sector – surpassed that of the Germans, first in the rate of growth and later in absolute terms. At the time of the German attack, Franco-British war production had reached impressive heights. The number of French tanks was equal to the number of German tanks and the gap in aircraft numbers was on the point of being closed. Indeed, in May and June, more planes were built than destroyed and, at the time of the French defeat, it would have taken only a few more days to get much more completed aircraft ready for combat.[4]

All of these positive facts have been forgotten, especially on the French side, for reasons that are perfectly understandable. After all, they did not alter the end result, which was the fall of France in 1940. Moreover, they have been lost between two grand symbolic disasters: the diplomatic capitulation of Munich in 1938 and the military defeat of 1940. But to forget this last-minute recovery during the 'phoney war' is to reinforce the idea that the French defeat had its roots in material deficiencies. This was far from true. Rather, France's military capabilities on the eve of its downfall lead us to a much more uncomfortable conclusion, namely that the causes for defeat lay, not in force of arms, but in what Marc Bloch described at the time as an 'intellectual defeat' in terms of strategy, tactics, deployment of forces and management of time.[5] However, this forgotten narrative of the 'phoney war' is almost certainly less significant than others; it is first and foremost an indication of the extent to which this period has remained subservient to subsequent traumas.

From the shock of defeat to the '1940 syndrome'

The most long-lasting of these traumas was the fall of France in 1940. This left a difficult memory of military, intellectual, political and moral collapse. To paraphrase the words of Henry Rousso, it created a 'syndrome' – a heterogeneous set of symptoms – that resulted in an intense and durable trauma in French society. In this case, it was not so much forgetting that was the problem, but a surfeit of memories. For the most part, this did not lead to the kind of blurred memory we saw in relation to the 'phoney war', but there was still a tendency to downplay activities before the defeat at the expense of later events. For a long time, the standard view of the military debacle of 1940 was a linear and teleological narrative that emphasized cowardice, flight, chaos and material inferiority. But historical scholarship since the 1980s has shown that the French defeat was not inevitable. Many soldiers fought bravely and the casualties were considerable, while the number of German planes shot down over France was greater than the number shot down during the Battle of Britain a few months later.[6] Nevertheless, these 'positive' narratives were rapidly eclipsed. France's defeat marked an end; what came before appeared to be of negligible importance.

The British did not forget the positive elements of 1940 quite so readily – a point made especially clear in the attitude towards the Dunkirk evacuation in June 1940. For the French, the evacuation was remembered almost entirely negatively. The events were absorbed into a linear narrative of defeat and fed into images of a 'perfidious Albion' that gave priority to its own soldiers. It is worth remembering, though, that this Anglophobia only emerged a few weeks after the event with the sinking of the French fleet at Mers-el-Kébir in early July. At the time of the evacuation, both parties stressed the exceptional achievements of the two fleets. But this positive reading was quickly confined to British national memory alone: the evacuation showed the resilience of British forces and marked the beginning of opposition to German dominance. This so-called 'Dunkirk spirit' was incomprehensible to the French. After the war, when Dunkirk was chosen as the site for the signature of the 1947 Franco-British alliance, it evoked mixed memories: for some, it was the beginning of the long march to victory; for others, the new alliance was the opportunity to exorcise the ghosts of abandonment and defeat.

There can be little doubt that, for the French, the '1940 syndrome' dominated national memory after the defeat. One might even argue that it was more significant than the famous 'Vichy syndrome', although it operated along different lines and followed a different trajectory. Most importantly, the '1940 syndrome' appeared immediately and was quickly instrumentalized by the Vichy regime in its attempt to gain legitimacy. The 'Riom trial' of 1942, in which the Vichy regime tried vainly to blame pre-war republican politicians for the defeat, added a further (negative) dimension. After the Liberation, the 1940 syndrome returned again as the French looked for people to blame for the defeat. The Vichy regime was put on trial at the same time, which naturally led to a conflation of the two syndromes. In the 1950s and 60s, these memories were repressed: the desire for national unity meant that both Vichy and the memory of the fall of France were put aside. The repression of the latter was, however, less intense. It was expressed in political and cultural terms through the phrase 'plus jamais ça!' ('never again!'), but its influence was far-reaching. Thus, decolonization after 1945 seemed to reactivate the fear of losing territory that was so central to the 1940 syndrome. Similarly, post-war economic modernization was driven by an intense desire to transcend the humiliation of defeat, seen to be a direct consequence of France's industrial 'backwardness'. Already under the Fourth Republic, France was obsessed with restoring its 'rank' through the construction of Europe or, later, under the auspices of Gaullist grandeur. And, of course, there was an umbilical link between the 1940 syndrome and the post-war consensus surrounding the development of France's nuclear capabilities. The French atomic bomb had not only the well known functions of dissuasion vis-à-vis USSR and of independance vis-à-vis the United States; it was also meant to rebuild national identity and wash out the French humiliation of defeat.

It is interesting, in this respect, to compare de Gaulle's varying degrees of success in dealing with these two post-war 'syndromes'. By declaring the Pétainist regime null and void, downplaying state collaboration and maintaining that the French were all 'résistants', he failed to ease the weight of the 'Vichy syndrome'. Rousso has clearly shown the extent to which his departure from power in 1969 opened the lid on a wide range of repressed memories. The effects of 1968 and the 'Paxton revolution' (generated by historical work on Vichy by the American historian Robert A. Paxton)[7] brought the issue abruptly into the foreground: public opinion now urgently sought new insights into the relations between the French government, the French people and the occupying forces during the war. By contrast, de Gaulle's tendancy of exaggerating the role of France in the final victory of 1945 and his politics of grandeur aimed to heal the wounds of the "1940 syndrom" and, over time, de Gaulle's successors continued to champion the policy of independance as a way of mitigatioin the shame of 1940.

The British had their own version of the '1940 syndrome'. Obviously, it was not based on a collective sense of humiliation since 1940 was, in Churchill's words, Britain's 'finest hour'. But, alongside the French defeat, the British constructed a syndrome that combined a sense of glory and pride with a growing uncertainty about French motives. There was an initial period of compassion, but the real shock was the realization that the French had defected. This gave rise to a sense of abandonment that mirrored French reactions to the Dunkirk evacuation. The British could no longer rely on the fragile agreement of the 1904 *entente cordiale*; their erstwhile ally had become far too unreliable. Indeed, one might even argue that the British treated all of Europe with suspicion such was the fear of Nazi contamination. In this changed environment, there could be no redemption without the forging of a 'special relationship' with the United States. Churchill's alliance with the Americans from the summer of 1940 onwards made the British position clear – but it was one that the French found hard to understand. After the war, these fears of an untrustworthy Europe were eclipsed by the glory of victory. It was this that enabled the British to begin a relatively peaceful process of decolonization: unlike in the French case, it was not perceived as profoundly damaging to the country's national identity. On the other hand, perceived success in the war prevented the British from accurately assessing their declining geopolitical status. They belonged to the 'Big Three' and thus largely ignored the possible benefits of European integration. This was not an option for the French, the Italians and the Germans, all of whom had been chastened by their defeats in 1940, 1943 and 1945, respectively.

In short, then, there were two incompatible variants of the '1940 syndrome', neither of which acknowledged the existence of the other. They both implied distinct interpretations of the post-war world and drew on fundamentally different historical experiences of the period from 1940 to 1944. The British and French have each remembered their own experiences but have singularly failed to place these alongside those of the other.

The British, Vichy and de Gaulle: Remembering and forgetting

The interactions between the British and the Free French – and between Churchill and de Gaulle – have been well documented. Both the actors themselves and numerous observers have published memoirs, historians have written weighty tomes on the subject and many television and film documentaries have been produced. De Gaulle himself used his *Mémoires de guerre* (1954–59) to build a remarkable image of himself as an upstanding and punctilious man, capable of defending French interests against a predatory Anglo-Saxon whose aims threatened to compromise France's position. This vision – which was widely instrumentalized – contributed to the forging of the Gaullist legend and reinforced the legitimacy of de Gaulle's oppositional foreign policy after 1958, much of which was directed against the very same Anglo-Saxon force he had distrusted during wartime.

Almost entirely forgotten in this picture are Britain's relations with Vichy. These were not, ultimately, very significant, but they demonstrated the extent of British uncertainty and the uncomfortable balance of power between Pétain and de Gaulle. Meetings in Madrid between the French and British ambassadors, Count Renom de La Baume and Sir Samuel Hoare, began on 30 August 1940; in October, Prof Louis Rougier, an unofficial envoy from Vichy, was received in London; and, at the end of the year, the Canadian diplomat Pierre Dupuy was pushing the possibility of cooperation with Vichy.[8] Rougier, who was a Professor of Philosophy at the Faculty of Letters at Besançon, later exaggerated the importance of his 'mission' to London: for instance, his claim that he had brokered a deal between Pétain and Churchill was a fabrication. These lies were a way of defending Vichy and suggesting that Pétain was playing a 'double game' with the Allies and Hitler. Nevertheless, contacts between Vichy and London did take place. The former hoped that any mutual agreement would result in the easing of the blockade that was having a detrimental impact on the standard of living in France. The latter hoped for a declaration of neutrality and indications that Pétain might return to the Allied camp in due course. This mutual exchange did not last long, however. The British called off all contact in January 1941 when it became clear that Pierre Flandin, the Vichy Foreign Minister, was passing information directly to the Nazis, who were encouraging contact in the hope that a lighter blockade would make it easier to supply Germany.[9] A year later, in 1942, Churchill once again succumbed to the temptation to negotiate with Vichy, although he met with strong opposition from the Foreign Secretary, Anthony Eden, over the issue. Not that he wanted to disown de Gaulle: on the contrary, he had contempt for Vichy and its leaders. But his pragmatism led him to believe that Pétain would embrace the British once he realized that Hitler was losing the war. In the event, he underestimated Pétain's ideological commitment. Still, Churchill's vacillation demonstrated the extent to which there was scepticism towards the Free French who had been unable to rally the majority of the French people to their cause.

These events are now well known to historians, but they have had little impact on France and Britain's national memories. They fit uncomfortably with the myths surrounding de Gaulle and Churchill and they highlight the contradictions of these two 'great men'.

The forgotten role of the British in the Liberation of France

There has always been a good deal of admiration in France for British conduct during the war. The French remember the British fighting against Hitler alone, acknowledge the British victory in the Battle of Britain and, of course, recognize British support for de Gaulle and the Resistance. These sympathetic memories were perhaps best dramatized in the highly popular 1966 film comedy, *La grande vadrouille*, in which British parachutists find themselves stranded in occupied France and seek French help in order to escape the Germans.

Once the Americans entered the war, however, their presence eclipsed that of the British. This change of orientation had long-lasting consequences for French national memory, particularly in the case of the 1944 D-Day landings. This was confirmed in a 1984 survey by Louis Harris for the French magazine *L'Histoire*. When asked which army had played the most important role in the liberation of France, those who replied gave a startling response. 44 per cent answered that the Americans had played the most important role, but a mere 4 per cent of respondents opted for the British. This was far behind the 34 per cent who chose France (15 per cent for the Free French and 19 per cent for the *maquisards* of the Resistance). These results suggested that, even 40 years later, the Free French in London were seen to be three or four times more significant than the British in the Liberation of France! This amnesia was yet another symptom of the '1940 syndrome'. For the most part, it has been easier for the French to recognize the role played by the American giant than acknowledge Britain, a power of similar rank. British successes have continued to hold up a mirror to French humiliations.[10]

Yalta: A French victory without de Gaulle

From 1940 to 1944, de Gaulle's political tactics consisted almost entirely of elevating the role of France so that she might participate in – and reap the rewards of – victory. He was, therefore, angry to discover in January 1945 that there would be a meeting of the 'Big Three' the following month at Yalta from which France was excluded. De Gaulle already knew that Franklin Roosevelt was hostile to a French presence at the negotiating table, but he used the visit of presidential advisor Harry Hopkins to Paris on 27 January to enquire as to the causes of the poor relations between the two countries. The reply the French leader received – which he later transcribed in his *Mémoires de guerre* – showed that there was also an American dimension to the '1940 syndrome':

> The reason [for bad relations], he replied, lay above all in America's extreme disappointment at seeing France collapse, then capitulate, in 1940. The image we had of her vitality and strength was turned upside down in an instant . . . We realised that France was no longer what she had been and we could no longer trust her to play a major role.[11]

When the Yalta summit began a few days later, de Gaulle warned in a radio broadcast that, when it came to any peace settlement, 'France would not, of course, be bound by any decision that she had not discussed and approved alongside others'.[12]

After the summit, de Gaulle found himself marginalized once again: he received a message from Roosevelt, who asked to see him in Algiers. The fact that the American president had 'invited' the leader of the French Provisional Government to a meeting on French territory appeared to be another example of 'misplaced' hubris. Predictably, de Gaulle refused: he was not able to make an 'impromptu' visit to Algiers and 'regretted' that it would, therefore, be impossible to meet.[13] However, the French leader was forced to admit that the outcome of the Yalta summit was not entirely negative. While he continued to deplore the lack of French participation, and denounce certain 'irritating' recommendations, he recognized in his *Mémoires de guerre* that 'on a number of key points, the agreement was very satisfactory'.[14]

In fact, what de Gaulle did not (and did not want to) say was that France was one of the major winners at the Yalta summit. Despite having no representation, the French were granted privileges about which both Roosevelt and Stalin felt uneasy: a zone of occupation in Germany, a place at the Interallied Control

Commission in charge of the administration of the German territories and the possibility of a fifth seat on the United Nations Security Council (the Americans had planned to create only four). A number of these gains were promised immediately in the autumn of 1944, without necessarily being implemented; but the seat on the Security Council was officially announced a few months later at the United Nations conference in San Francisco. The Yalta summit and especially Churchill were instrumental in this process. This is not to underestimate de Gaulle's ability to create a favourable context for these developments: his intransigence in negotiations, his desire to rebuild the French army and his intention to use this army at the end of the war forced the Allies to consider seriously the idea that France deserved to come back in the international arena. Nevertheless, French gains at Yalta were mostly due to the British. Churchill had no great love for de Gaulle. But there was mutual admiration between the two men and the British Prime Minister knew that he could be a useful ally in a hostile post-war context. Britain was stranded between two superpowers, both of whom were anti-colonial. The addition of a fourth player – with converging interests and a similar commitment to empire – might allow Britain more room for manoeuvre.

It is not hard to understand why the French so quickly forgot Britain's role in securing a favourable compromise at Yalta. At the time, de Gaulle did not want to acknowledge his debt to Churchill, in part because of the continued disagreements between the two men over other issues, but also because he mistakenly feared that it would be interpreted as a sign of weakness. As time passed, Britain's role at Yalta was almost entirely excised from French national memory. To some extent, this had to do with a strong commitment to a Gaullist narrative: to minimize de Gaulle's role would have been to minimize the role of the French people in their liberation and recovery. More than this, however, it reflected the same processes of forgetting we saw earlier. Thus, any event that elevated Britain was repressed. This was not a consequence of latent Anglophobia for the British were widely admired. Rather, the French feared that the positive attributes of the British would hold up a mirror to the humiliations of the French. The French memory of Yalta was, again, defined by a powerful '1940 syndrome'.

A forgotten French capitulation: Syria in May 1945

Churchill's sympathetic position at Yalta in February 1945 gave way in May to a much more intransigent attitude towards French involvement in the Middle East. Inevitably, the German surrender on 7–8 May dominated the news in that month but this meant that numerous other significant events were forgotten, most of which have since been rediscovered by historians. These included a massacre by French soldiers in eastern Algeria after a demonstration in Sétif on 8 May – a tragedy that had long-term implications for Algerian nationalism. Likewise, at the end of the month the French army was involved in violent clashes with civilians in Syria. The crisis was so acute that the British had to intervene in order to stop the bloodshed. Significantly, the Syrian debacle was accompanied by a sharp but now largely forgotten confrontation between Churchill and de Gaulle. The quarrel did not go unnoticed at the time since the French leader angrily narrated his own interpretation of events in his *Mémoires de guerre*.[15] But it has not persisted in French national memory, both because it was concealed by apparently more significant events and because it reveals an uncomfortable strategic short-sightedness.

It had been clear since 1941 that Syrian independence was imminent. De Gaulle himself had not denied the principle of self-determination. However, in the absence of a negotiated treaty, he sought to maintain a French presence in the region by every means possible – including by force. He was convinced that the English intended to oust the French from the Middle East and, as a result, underestimated the strength of opposition to imperial rule. The Minister of Foreign Affairs, Georges Bidault, tried in vain to explain to de Gaulle that the 'conflict' between the Syrian people and the colonial administration 'long predated' British intrigues in the region. He added: 'If we want to avoid permanently alienating the goodwill of the people, we must abandon our backward-looking attitude and develop a grand political strategy'.[16] Instead, de Gaulle chose to send reinforcements to Syria and use force against anti-French demonstrations in Damascus and Aleppo. On 29 May, the capital was bombarded and the city became the site of fierce street fighting. On 30 May, Churchill summoned the French ambassador, René Massigli, and informed him that Britain was now obliged to intervene in order to relieve the situation. Truman had agreed to this operation and the Commander-in-Chief of Middle East Command, General Paget, was preparing the necessary measures. Predictably, de Gaulle was incensed, but Bidault pressed him to back down and he agreed to a ceasefire. Even so, on 31 May there were further clashes, with Senegalese troops ransacking Damascus amidst a veritable orgy of violence. In reply, Churchill decided the same day to set an ultimatum: he made the Secretary of State for Foreign Affairs, Anthony Eden, read out in the House of Commons a message sent by Churchill to de Gaulle that the French had not yet received:

> In view of the grave situation which has arisen between your troops and the Levant States, and the severe fighting which has broken out, we have, with profound regret, ordered the Commander-in-Chief, Middle East, to intervene to prevent the further effusion of blood in the interests of the security of the whole Middle East which involves communications for the war against Japan. In order to avoid collision between British and French Forces, we request you immediately to order the French troops to cease fire and to withdraw to their barracks. Once firing has ceased and order

has been restored, we shall be prepared to begin tripartite discussions here in London.[17]

De Gaulle was furious: this seemed to be another attempt to humiliate him. He refused to reply to the ultimatum since in any case a ceasefire had already been declared the day before, even if this hardly reflected the situation on the ground. In addition, he ordered French soldiers to remain in position and ignore any orders given by the British army. Nevertheless, he instructed them to moderate their actions and tolerate the latter's presence. This was enough to restore stability to the region but, in truth, it was the beginning of the end. France's international image was badly tarnished by the universal condemnation of its brutal repression in May and, in the following weeks, the French were forced to relinquish control of a number of state functions to the Syrian and Lebanese authorities.[18] In April 1946, European forces withdrew completely – conclusive proof that the British had no intention of supplanting the French, as de Gaulle had feared. Of course, in the *Mémoires de guerre*, the French leader glossed over his errors of judgement, while still making it clear that his actions were met with disapproval in France. Regarding the ultimatum, a wounded de Gaulle was forced to admit a few days afterwards to the British Ambassador, Duff Cooper, that 'we are not currently able to wage war with you . . . but you have offended France and betrayed the West. This will not be forgotten'.[19] But, if de Gaulle did not forget, the French people did, and the Syrian episode has disappeared from French national memory.

Conclusion: The politics of forgetting

Not every form of forgetting has the same meaning. In the case of the positive results of the Franco-British alliance during the 'phoney war', the absence of memory was due to an inability on the part of subsequent generations to 'fix' a narrative of these events. After all, whatever happened in 1939–40 appeared negligible alongside the catastrophe of defeat. In other cases, there is an active process of forgetting and repression. This is especially true when memories threaten the image of a 'great man'. Thus, Churchill quietly 'hid' his flirtation with Vichy and de Gaulle rewrote the narrative of the Syrian debacle. Finally, the act of forgetting can be induced by a wider and more complex trauma. For the French, this came in the form of the 'Vichy syndrome' and the '1940 syndrome'. The latter was clearly expressed in the French desire to exorcise the memory of defeat through economic modernization and post-war grandeur, while both syndromes worked together to marginalize Britain's role in liberating France and securing French interests at the Yalta summit: everything that elevated Britain was – there is a mirror effect at play – a reminder of France's humiliation, loss of status and shameful Vichy interlude. It is still easier to celebrate the United States since it does not hold up a mirror to French failings in the same way. Moreover, as we have seen, these forgotten episodes of World War II are instrumental, not simply in shaping French national memory, but also in determining visions of the future. Since 1945, Franco-British disagreements over Europe, the United States, the Atlantic world and global foreign policy have not all been based on a rational calculation of competing and diverging interests. Many of them are the result of each country's profoundly different experiences and memories of the period from the fall of France in 1940 to the Allied victory in 1945.

Translated by Emile Chabal

Notes

1 Henry Rousso, *Le syndrome de Vichy* (Paris: Le Seuil, 1987); Robert Frank, 'La mémoire empoisonnée', in Jean-Pierre Azéma and François Bédarida (eds), *La France des années noires*, vol. II: *De l'Occupation à la Libération* (Paris: Le Seuil, 1993), pp. 483–514; Olivier Wieviorka, *La mémoire désunie: Le souvenir politique des années sombres, de la Libération à nos jours* (Paris: Le Seuil, 2010).

2 See the important methodological discussion in Pierre Laborie, *L'opinion française sous Vichy* (Paris: Le Seuil, 1990).

3 François Bédarida, La stratégie secrète de la Drôle de guerre: *Le Conseil suprême interallié, septembre 1939-avril 1940* (Paris: Éditions du CNRS, 1979).

4 Robert Frank, *La hantise du déclin: Le rang de la France en Europe (1920–1960): finances, défense et identité nationale* (Paris: Belin, 1994).

5 Marc Bloch, *L'étrange défaite* (Paris: Société des Éditions Franc-Tireur, 1946).

6 Jean-Louis Crémieux-Brilhac, *Les Français de l'an 40*, vol. I: *La guerre, oui ou non ?*; vol. II: *Ouvriers et soldats* (Paris: Gallimard, 1990); Karl-Heinz Frieser, Le mythe de la guerre-éclair. La campagne de l'Ouest de 1940, Paris, Belin, 2003.

7 Especially *La France de Vichy* (Paris: Le Seuil, 1973), originally *Vichy France: Old Guard and New Order* (New York, Knopf, 1972).

8 Robert T. Thomas, *Britain and Vichy. The dilemma of Anglo-French Relations 1940–1942*, (London: Macmillan, 1979); Jean-Baptiste Duroselle, *Politique étrangère de la France. L'Abîme 1939–1945* (Paris: Imprimerie nationale, 1983).

9 Robert Frank, 'Vichy et les Britanniques : double jeu ou double langage ?', in Jean-Pierre Azéma and François Bédarida (eds), *Vichy et les Français* (Paris: Fayard, 1992), pp. 144–163; Robert Frank, 'Pétain, Laval, Darlan', in Azéma and Bédarida (dir.), *La France des années noires*, vol. I, pp. 297–332.

10 Robert Frank et Henry Rousso, 'Quarante ans après: les Français et la Libération,' *L'Histoire*, 67 (1984).

11 Charles de Gaulle, *Mémoires de guerre*, vol. III: *Le salut, 1944–1946* (Paris: Plon, 1949), p. 102.

12 Ibid, p. 106.

13 Ibid, p. 110.

14 Ibid., p. 109.

15 Ibid. pp. 221–38.

16 Anne Bruchez, 'La fin de la présence française en Syrie: de la crise de mai 1945 au départ des dernières troupes étrangères,' *Relations Internationales*, 2005/2, no. 122, p. 20.

17 House of Commons Debates, 31 May 1945, vol. 411, cc 378–80. For de Gaulle's account, see *Mémoires de guerre*, vol. III, pp. 229–30.

18 Bruchez, 'La fin de la présence française' pp. 22–25.

19 de Gaulle, *Mémoires de guerre*, vol. III, p. 233 (4 June 1945).

CHAPTER NINE

France, Britain and the Narrative of Two World Wars

David Reynolds

France and Britain were allies in the world wars of 1914–18 and 1939–45, history's most appalling conflicts. In both cases they ended up on the winning side. Yet the two countries approached those wars in very different ways, they extracted divergent policy lessons from each conflict and they developed distinctive patterns of remembrance. These are the themes that I want to explore here. I shall argue that how France and Britain came to terms with the two world wars helps explain some of their contrasting attitudes to the second half of the twentieth century. In the process I shall emphasize the need to weave together diplomatic history and cultural history, to connect policy and memory.

Constructing a narrative of the two world wars is obviously sequential: 1914–18 generated lessons and created cultural memories which in turn shaped the experience of 1939–45. But it is important to note that this process also worked in reverse because, conceptually, World War II came before World War I. In Britain in the 1920s and 1930s the conflict of 1914–18 was referred to as the 'Great War'. In France the term *la grande guerre* also predominated, though with some exceptions, such as the academic journal *Revue d'histoire de la guerre mondiale*, inaugurated in 1923 under the editorship of Pierre Renouvin, and the series of paperbacks issued in the 1930s by the Paris publisher Jules Tallandier under the title *La Guerre Mondiale: pages vécues*. In Germany, however, the conflict was from the start referred to as *Weltkrieg* because it centred on a struggle for world power (*Weltmacht*) against Britain, a global empire (*Weltimperium*). Once the United States entered the conflict in 1917 Americans likewise called it the 'world war' because it was fought outside the Americas and because of President Woodrow Wilson's globalist ideology to 'make the world safe for democracy'. This was how Adolf Hitler and Franklin Roosevelt also conceptualized the next war, the American president dubbing it 'the Second World War' as early as May 1941, 6 months before Pearl Harbour. But only after 1945 did 'World War' become the norm in France and eventually in Britain, thanks in part to its use by Winston Churchill as the title of his war memoirs. At the official level the issue was finally settled in 1948 by the formal decision of a Cabinet Committee, endorsed by Prime Minister Clement Attlee.[1]

These observations about discourse serve to illustrate a simple but significant point: the war of 1914–18 looked very different after 1939–45. I want to explore how Britain and France developed their overarching narratives of the first great conflict and then reframed these in the light of the second war. Let me start with 1914–18, proposing three broad contrasts between the ways in which France and Britain reacted to the Great War.

First, the war had an existential meaning for the French that was lacking in Britain. In France it was a war for national territory, both to protect the *patrie* against German invasion in the northeast and to recover Alsace and Lorraine which had been lost to Germany in 1870. Britain, by contrast, was never invaded, though German warships did shell some towns on the East Coast, and there was little aerial bombing even of London. So, territorial issues were not salient for the British in the Great War. For diplomats and policy makers what counted in the July Crisis of 1914 was the continental balance of power – the danger that Germany would pose to Britain if its troops controlled Belgium and northern France, opening up the Channel to the German navy. Frequent allusion was made to the titanic struggle against Revolutionary and Napoleonic France a century before; indeed, the British term 'Great War' was borrowed from that struggle. 'German policy', declared the Foreign Secretary Sir Edward Grey in August 1914, 'is that of the great European aggressor, as bad as Napoleon'. Among politicians, however, morality was more potent, especially the German invasion of Belgium whose neutrality Britain was pledged by treaty to protect. 'A German attack on France involved British interests', observes historian Zara Steiner, but the Liberal Cabinet 'had resisted this conclusion for many years; now ministers cloaked their final choice in moral terms. The treaty obligations to Belgium provided the necessary justification'.[2] What solidified public opinion were the German 'atrocities' that autumn, with the burning of Louvain University and the shelling of Reims Cathedral having a particularly profound effect. From them emerged the dominant image of 'the Hun' as a brutal, militaristic race which, if not contained, would trample on freedom, families and property in the name of Germanic *Kultur*. As one poem in the *Daily Mail* put it in August 1914:

You seek excuse in 'Die Kultur'
For every stratagem and lure . . .

For Hunnish Code and Mongol lust,
For violated pledge and trust;
For women raped and children slain
For Malines, Termonde, Rheims, Louvain . . .[3]

The idea that the war was being fought to uphold the values of civilization against Germanic barbarism was, of course, also axiomatic in France. This consensus, shared by Republicans and Catholics alike, has been described as 'one of the more remarkable cultural achievements of the Union sacrée'.[4] The patriotic backlash against all things German, which even damned 'Kubisme' as 'Boche art', demanded 'a return to order', to classical models in art and architecture, and it affected even the most individualist avant-garde artists such as Picasso. The 'iconography of classicism', to quote art historian Kenneth Silver, became 'the language of national defence in the face of imminent extinction'.[5] This French self-image was reinforced by propaganda from the Central Powers insisting that they were engaged in a struggle between Germanic *Kultur* and French *civilisation*, a claim famously articulated in Thomas Mann's *Reflections of a Non-Political Man* (*Betrachtungen eines Unpolitischen*), in which he contrasted the literary, politicized ethos of France – rooted in the *philosophes* and the Revolution – with the poetic, musical culture of Germany that his countrymen were heroically defending against 'the imperialism of civilisation'.[6]

Having acknowledged all that, I would, nevertheless, argue that the British were fighting *mainly* for abstractions such as civilization, liberty and honour rather than for national defence. 'The Prussian Junker is the road-hog of Europe', declared David Lloyd George in September 1914. 'If we had stood by when two little nations [Belgium and Serbia] were being crushed and broken by the brutal hand of barbarism, our shame would have rung down the everlasting ages.'[7] To put the point more abstractly: the headstones in great French cemeteries such as Verdun state that the soldier 'died for France' (*mort pour la France*). British war graves do not make a similar claim.

My second contrast follows from this first point about the centrality of national defence for France: after 1918, the dominant theme of French foreign policy was to avoid a repetition of 1870 and 1914 by keeping Germany firmly under control. 'My life hatred,' Clemenceau declared shortly before his death in 1929, 'has been for Germany because of what she has done to France'. At the Paris peace conference he and Marshal Ferdinand Foch pressed for substantial reparations to help rebuild north-eastern France and for a frontier on the Rhine to enhance French security. In Britain, however, such policies were seen as repressive and counterproductive. Without a strong international system, observed Arthur Balfour, the Foreign Secretary, caustically, 'no manipulation of the Rhine frontier is going to make France anything more than a second-rate Power'. The Cabinet Secretary Maurice Hankey found the French delegation at Paris 'full of chicanery of all kinds, without any idea of playing the game'.[8] That feeling, at least, was mutual: 1919 confirmed many French leaders in their convictions about *l'Albion perfide*. Clemenceau, though a lifelong anglophile, regarded Lloyd George as 'a cheat' and, according to one biographer, got so carried away in one of their flaming rows that he offered the British premier a choice of pistols or swords.[9]

As enforcement of reparations became harder and the Rhineland occupation came to an end, French governments opted for a defensive strategy in the west based on the Maginot Line. This was backed in the east by alliances with Poland, Czechoslovakia and other new states, though these constituted a pale shadow of the Franco-Russian axis of 1914. For the British, by contrast, the German challenge had been naval rather than on land and this threat had disappeared, thanks to the scuttling of the German fleet in 1919. Fears that a harsh peace would provoke Germany into another war prompted British efforts in March 1919 to moderate the proposed terms: 'if she feels that she has been treated unjustly in the peace of 1919,' warned Lloyd George, 'she will find means of exacting retribution.'[10] At times there was even talk in the Foreign Office of France not Germany being the real enemy because of the former's apparently hegemonic ambitions in Europe and its imperial rivalry with Britain, especially in the Middle East after the Ottoman collapse. 'I am seriously afraid that the great power from whom we have most to fear in future is France,' Lord Curzon told Cabinet colleagues in 1919: 'their national character is different from ours, and their political interests collide with ours in many cases.'[11] In 1926, when French opposition to British policy prompted a Foreign Office official to ask if the French were mad, Eric Phipps at the Paris Embassy replied: 'I do not think that the French are really mad, but they are very feminine' – though, he added, one might consider that 'the two things are almost identical'.[12]

On both sides, there were, of course, exceptions to this process of mutual alienation. In the mid-1920s after France's abortive occupation of the Ruhr, a few policy makers and officials in Paris such as Aristide Briand and Jacques Seydoux moved beyond the traditional concept of a Franco-British pact directed *against* Germany to one that *included* Germany and its neighbours. Such an interlocking system of guarantees, Briand predicted, would 'aid German democracy, prepare the return of Germany to the community of nations and thus have a stabilising effect on Europe'.[13] In Britain Austen Chamberlain and elements of the Foreign Office believed that Britain had to make serious commitments to French security. 'We cannot afford to see France crushed, to have Germany or an eventual Russo-German combination supreme on the continent,' Chamberlain noted in January 1925, as he bent his energies to a Franco-German rapprochement guaranteed by Britain. Later in the year he wrote angrily to the British Ambassador in Berlin: 'Your Germans – I use the possessive pronoun as one says to one's wife: your housemaid – are very nearly intolerable . . . At every stage the Germans sow distrust in my mind. At every stage Briand disproves the common assertion that the difficulty is now with France.'[14]

But the 'spirit of Locarno', of renewed *entente cordiale*, soon evaporated. French policy in the 1920s and 1930s was predominantly designed to keep Germany down, while Britain, even after Hitler's *Machtergreifung* in Berlin, sought to move beyond the treaty of Versailles and create a new and more flexible architecture for European security. When German troops reoccupied the Rhineland in 1936, Stanley Baldwin, Britain's Prime Minister, airily dismissed Hitler's demarche as just the latest round in a long-running dispute – 'a historical cleavage which goes back to the partition of Charlemagne's Europe' – in which sometimes France had been the problem, sometimes Germany.[15] On both sides of the Channel in the mid-1930s the rhetoric of a few publicists verged on hysteria. 'France has recovered the military predominance she enjoyed under the first Napoleon,' boomed the Labour journalist H.N. Brailsford, while the French polemicist Henri Béraud was so exercised by the endless examples of 'violence, perfidy, implacable selfishness and disloyalty' that sullied English history that he wondered whether 'England must be reduced to slavery'.[16]

My third theme relates to the public memories of 1914–18. Here the divide is less stark. France lost 1.4 million dead (about 14 per cent of men between the ages of 15 and 49, Britain 720,000 (about 6 per cent of the same age group).[17] In both countries the slaughter was sanctified as 'sacrifice' and memorialized in Christian language and imagery. In France, again bridging the divide between religious and secular, commemoration fused the ideas of civilization versus barbarism, Good versus Evil, the soldier dying for France and also emulating Christ's passion.[18] There was also a powerful tradition of anti-war writing – French novelists such as Henri Barbusse and British poets such as Siegfried Sassoon – but in neither country did a tone of criticism become dominant, even after the flood of books and films in the late 1920s, cued by the tenth anniversary of the Armistice. There was, however, a profound sense in both countries of 'never again' – 1914–18 must be the war to end wars. That, after all, was the message of Barbusse's grisly final chapter of *Le Feu*, set in a flooded wasteland of mud and corpses but entitled *L'Aube* (Dawn), which ends with the sun finally coming up as the survivors talk about democracy, equality and no more wars. Sassoon, who on Armistice Day in 1918 decried 'the loathsome tragedy of the last four years', was deeply influenced by Barbusse's vision and looked to the League of Nations as the basis for a new world order.[19] The dominant mood in Germany, except on the left, was of course very different: the *Dolchstosslegende* – the idea that the German army had been stabbed in the back by leftists and pacifists on the home front – encouraged the view that 1918, far from being a genuine defeat, was a lost victory that had to be redeemed. Here were the seeds of another war, for which the British and French peoples would have little appetite.

In terms of cultural memory the main difference between Britain and France lies, I think, in the nature of the perceived future threat. British opinion in the 1930s was seared by the new horror of aerial bombing, sensationalized in films, novels and political pamphlets. After only one air raid, predicted the philosopher Bertrand Russell in 1936, London would be 'one vast raving bedlam, the hospitals will be stormed, traffic will cease' and the government 'will be swept away by an avalanche of terror. Then the enemy will dictate its terms'. Russell, of course, was a radical pacifist, but his apocalyptic vision was shared at the heart of government. Whitehall planners anticipated 150,000 casualties in London in the first week of an air attack. (This was, in fact, more than the total civilian casualties for all the United Kingdom during the whole of World War II.)[20] The French public, especially Parisians, entertained a similar 'obsession' about bombing. In the words of one journalist:

> People have never thought so much about war and about its future horrors, real or imaginary – towns destroyed in a few hours by a rain of bombs, poison gas capable in a few minutes of killing every living thing in a city as big as Paris, millions of men, women and children dying together.[21]

But Britain was detached from the continent by geography and that divide had become central to its national narrative, with the Channel – the country's 'moat defensive' in Shakespeare's felicitous phrase – guarded by the Royal Navy against would-be invaders such as Philip II of Spain, Napoleon and the Kaiser.[22] From that perspective, the threat from the air had a novel potency because war planes could now fly over the Channel to pulverize Britain's cities and citizens. For the French in the 1930s the German menace was essentially an intensification of historic anxieties, with the Luftwaffe accentuating the Wehrmacht's threat to north-eastern France, whereas, for Britain, the new terror of airborne destruction turned Neville Chamberlain's policy of appeasing Germany into a desperate bid to avert Armageddon.[23]

I have tried to sketch, albeit in highly simplified terms, some contrasts in the ways that France and Britain reflected on the war of 1914–18 at the level of both government policy and public attitudes. For the French but not the British, this was a war of national territory; afterwards, France sought to prevent a repetition of 1914, whereas the British wanted to move on from 1919. 'Never again' was the watchword for both peoples, but British dread of war was intensified by the novel threat of aerial bombing. Before moving to analyse attitudes in the two countries to the second war, I want to highlight the significance of 1940 for Franco-British relations. That momentous year was to see both a remarkable cross-Channel rapprochement and then a durable rupture.[24]

First, the rapprochement. In the Czech crisis of September 1938, Chamberlain led and Daladier followed. But after Hitler marched into

Czechoslovakia in March 1939 a shaken British government moved rapidly into a new entente with France and then, from September, a wartime alliance. The extent and depth of this rapprochement in 1939–40 should be emphasized because it was then eclipsed by the fall of France and has consequently been neglected in public memory and even by historians. In early 1940 British policy makers admitted, at least in private, that they had been naïve about the threat from Germany. Determined not to repeat that mistake again after the current war was over they envisaged the kind of peacetime alliance with France that leaders in Paris had vainly sought after 1918. This would go much further than simply military affairs. Sir Orme Sargent, a senior official at the Foreign Office, suggested in February 1940 that the only alternative to another punitive peace would be to show the French that they could 'count on such a system of close and permanent cooperation between France and Great Britain – political, military and economic – as will for all international purposes make of the two countries a single unit in post-war Europe'. Sargent meant close inter-governmental cooperation rather than any federal structure, but even this would require a revolution in British thinking. He, therefore, proposed a major propaganda campaign for the public at large and a special effort to promote understanding of France in British schools. 'I entirely agree,' noted Chamberlain. Behind the scenes, an inter-departmental Whitehall committee was established to identify areas of administration in which the experiment of union could be tried. The Board of Education established two committees – one for primary schools, the other for secondary schools – to promote greater understanding of France, liaising with the BBC about special radio talks. Similar planning was initiated in Paris. And on 28 March 1940 the two countries publicly pledged that 'after the conclusion of peace' they would maintain 'a community of action in all spheres for as long as may be necessary to safeguard their security and to effect the reconstruction, with the assistance of other nations, of an international order which will ensure the liberty of people, respect for law, and the maintenance of peace in Europe'.[25]

Situated in the long history of Franco-British rivalry such comments and commitments were remarkable. What they might have portended if the war on the Western Front had followed the pattern of 1914–18 is fascinating to imagine. Fascinating yet pointless, because of the even more astonishing events in the summer of 1940 which, I have suggested elsewhere, should be seen as 'the fulcrum of the twentieth century'.[26] In 40 days a jumped-up Austrian corporal achieved what the Kaiser's best generals had failed to accomplish in 4 years, namely to break the Western Front and eliminate the French army. In the campaign of 1940 only 92,000 French soldiers were killed (perhaps far fewer), but 1.8 million trekked off to German prisoner-of-war camps.[27] The reasons for the Fall of France remain a matter of debate, but whether this was a 'strange defeat', in Marc Bloch's famous phrase, or a 'strange victory', as historian Ernest May has argued, it was unquestionably a massive humiliation for France. And the collaboration of the Vichy government with the Nazis would leave enduring scars in French politics and society.[28]

With regard to Franco-British relations, the French collapse abruptly ended the remarkable rapprochement of 1939–40: Britain turned away from a now alien and hostile continent. As Lord Halifax, the British Foreign Secretary, observed in July 1940: 'it may well be that instead of studying a closer union with France we shall find ourselves contemplating the possibility of some sort of special association with the U.S.A.'[29] This 'special association' or 'special relationship', in Churchill's later and more famous phrase, became the watchword of British policy during the war and afterwards. As the 1940s progressed British leaders acknowledged the shift of power across the Atlantic, with America clearly the more powerful partner, but privately they believed that they had the experience and skill to guide the neophyte superpower in the ways of international politics. 'We . . . are Greeks in this American empire,' declared Harold Macmillan expansively in 1943 while serving as political liaison with Eisenhower's Allied Force Headquarters in North Africa. 'We must run A.F.H.Q. as the Greek slaves ran the operations of the Emperor Claudius.' To quote an anonymous verse penned during Britain's negotiations in 1945 for a post-war American loan:

> In Washington Lord Halifax
> Once whispered to Lord Keynes:
> 'It's true *they* have the money bags,
> But *we* have all the brains.'[30]

To a large extent the European war was won on the Eastern Front – unlike 1914–18 – in brutal and bloody fighting by millions of Soviet soldiers. In the 3 years between Barbarossa and Overlord (June 1941 to June 1944) over 90 per cent of the Wehrmacht's battle casualties (killed, wounded, missing and prisoner) were inflicted by the Red Army.[31] But Britain played a vital part in the eventual Allied victory, first by holding on in 1940–41 and then by acting as the essential base for liberating continental Europe. Yet Britain could not have done this without the support of the United States: for instance, American financial aid covered more than half of Britain's balance of payments deficit during the war.[32] Equally important was the contribution of Britain's empire as a source of food, raw materials and manpower. The Canadian navy played a crucial role in escorting convoys during the Battle of the Atlantic, while troops from Australia, India, South Africa and New Zealand were essential for victory over Rommel in North Africa. At the battle of El Alamein in October 1942 only about 40 per cent of Montgomery's infantry was British.[33]

Britain's global turn to what Churchill called the 'English-speaking world' reflected deeper disenchantment with France after the debacle of 1940. 'It is almost a relief to be thrown back on the resources of the Empire and of America,' wrote Hankey, who in the spring of 1940 had headed the committee examining closer union with France. And, he added, 'if we are successful we shall expose the fallacy of the glib statement that Britain is no longer an island' and disprove 'the strategical theories on which our policy has been based in recent years' because there 'will be no strategical object in seeking alliance with France and other continental States that have proved so unreliable'.[34]

France, of course, fought on after 1940 under the leadership of Charles de Gaulle but it did so essentially as a client of Britain and America, not as an equal partner as in 1914–18. From this de Gaulle drew sharp and enduring lessons. 'Anglo-Saxon domination in Europe was a growing threat,' he told Jean Monnet in 1943, 'and if it continued after the war France would have to turn to Germany or Russia.' De Gaulle's dependence on Britain and America was humiliatingly demonstrated in June 1944, when he learned only at the last minute that the liberation of France was going ahead. There ensued a furious row with Churchill, during which the British Prime Minister made it clear that his primary allegiance was to the United States. According to de Gaulle's colourful account in his memoirs, Churchill declared: 'each time we must choose between Europe and the open sea (*le grand large*), we shall always be for the open sea. Each time I must choose between you and Roosevelt, I shall always choose Roosevelt.'[35]

British policy was not quite so simple or simplistic as de Gaulle claimed: in the 1940s, as in the 1920s, cross-currents may be discerned. 'It has always seemed to me', wrote Foreign Secretary Anthony Eden in late 1944, 'that the lesson of the disasters of 1940 is precisely the need to build up a common defence association in Western Europe' in order to forestall 'another Hitler, whencesoever he may come'. Eden argued that the 'best way of creating such an association would obviously be to build up France'.[36] Contrary to the French myth that the Yalta conference represented the division of Europe between Stalin and the Anglo-Saxons, Churchill and Eden succeeded, against the preferences of Roosevelt and Stalin, in securing for France a zone of occupation in post-war Germany. And after 1945 the Labour government consolidated Franco-British defence cooperation through the Treaty of Dunkirk and the Brussels Pact. But these efforts were always subordinate to Britain's central post-war goal which was the construction and maintenance of an Atlantic alliance. 'Our policy should be to assist Europe to recover as far as we can', concluded a meeting of top Whitehall officials early in 1949. 'But the concept must be one of limited liability. In no circumstances must we assist beyond the point at which the assistance leaves us too weak to be a worth-while ally of for U.S.A. if Europe collapses.' Nor, they added, 'can we embark upon measures of "co-operation" which surrender our sovereignty and which lead us down paths along which there is no return'.[37]

In foreign policy, therefore, 1940 was both a false dawn and a great divide for Britain and France. Let me now explore how World War II was understood in both countries and how it affected their attitudes to World War I.

To take France first. This is familiar ground and I will move quickly. De Gaulle was one of the first to incorporate 1939–45 into a larger narrative of a modern 'Thirty Years War', stretching from 1914 to 1945. This had the value, for him, of 'de-ideologizing' the recent conflict by locating it within the long history of Franco-German antagonism and also reaching back over the dark barrier of 1940 to link the victors of 1944–45 with the heroes of 1914–18.[38] The Gaullist myth of *résistancialisme* – originating during the war itself – held sway in the 1950s and 1960s. It asserted that the Resistance represented the real France and was incarnated in de Gaulle and his followers, thereby casting a veil over both Vichy and collaboration. Although dominant during de Gaulle's presidency, this political myth was never universal. Communists, of course, elevated their own role in the Resistance. And the equation of Vichy and treachery was hard to square in the 1950s when many wartime Pétainists became ardent supporters of *Algérie française* – a cause that de Gaulle would eventually betray.

In the 1970s, as Julian Jackson observes, 'the glacier of official memory began to break up', with the 1969 film *Le Chagrin et La Pitié* starting the avalanche. The central issue was French complicity, hitherto hushed up, in the deportations of Jews to Nazi death camps. The end of Gaullist domination of French politics in 1974, when Valéry Giscard d'Estaing was elected president, also opened up a debate on the wartime past, so much so that Vichy became almost a national 'obsession', to quote historian Henry Rousso. Major trials in the 1980s and 1990s of those who had assisted in the deportations – notably Klaus Barbie, Paul Touvier and Maurice Papon – generated furious controversy. Rousso even complained about the 'Judaeo-centrism' of current memorialization which obscured other victims of the Nazi regime, including the Resistance itself: the duty to remember, he argued, should not become an obsession with the past. The title of Rousso's 1994 book *Vichy: un passé qui ne passe pas* mimicked the notorious essay by German philosopher-historian Ernst Nolte (*Vergangenheit, die nicht vergehen will*) that sparked the German *Historikerstreit* over Nazism in the 1980s. Critics claimed that Rousso, like Nolte, was in danger of relativizing the Holocaust; supporters argued that the rosy story of France united in resistance had been replaced by a 'black legend' of general collaboration and opportunism. The acrimonious debate still rumbles on, influencing Nicolas Sarkozy's recent attempts to revive the Gaullist grand narrative, both about the war itself and about the grandeur of French history as a whole. Although the study of the resistance is now a flourishing field of scholarly history, embracing questions of gender and immigration, nevertheless the story of France on the home front in the war of 1939–45 remains politically contested and highly ambiguous – *la mémoire désunie*, to quote the title of Olivier Wieviorka's book – in a way that is not true of the grand narrative for 1914–18.[39]

In foreign policy, however, France *has* been able to move on from World War II – though this took time. France's wartime dependence on America and Britain continued after victory, even more acutely than in the years after

1918. And French post-war security policy had initially many echoes of the 1920s – especially the yearning for a Rhineland frontier, the desire to control the industrial resources of the Ruhr and vigorous opposition to a strong German government. 'Consider this', de Gaulle told a press conference in October 1945, 'that we are neighbours of Germany, that we have been invaded three times by Germany in a single lifetime, and you will conclude that we want no more of the Reich'. Nor, mindful of 1919 and after, did he expect serious help from Britain and America. 'You are far away and your soldiers will not stay long in Europe', he told a US diplomat. 'The British . . . are worn out. We can expect nothing from them in the way of facing the Russo-German combination.'[40]

But the late 1940s saw a dramatic French shift towards rapprochement with the old enemy. This partly reflected the pressure of events: America and Britain were moving ahead on German reconstruction, both economically and politically, and France had little choice but to follow suit. But this period also saw the emergence of a new and remarkable policy of European integration, fostered by Christian Democrats in France, Germany and Italy. The key political figure in France was Robert Schuman, architect of the Council of Europe, whose life story personifies the history of Franco-German relations in the first half of the twentieth century. Schuman was born in Luxembourg in 1886; his French father grew up in Lorraine but became a German citizen after Bismarck's annexation in 1871. Schuman's mother tongue was Luxembourgish; he learnt German and French only at school and always spoke French with a pronounced accent. Most of his higher education was in German universities and he set up as a lawyer in Metz, the capital of Lorraine. In 1914 he was, therefore, called up for service in the German army and might easily have died fighting for the Kaiser at Verdun or on the Somme but for the good fortune of being transferred to civil service work on medical grounds. After the war Lorraine reverted to France and Schuman served as a deputy in the French Assembly for most of the 1920s and 1930s. He helped organize opposition to the Nazis in Lorraine in 1940 and was arrested by the Gestapo, eventually escaping in 1942 to work with the Resistance in occupied France. Untainted by Vichy but at arm's length from de Gaulle, he became a leading figure in the post-war *Mouvement Républicain Populaire*, as Foreign Minister in 1950 sponsoring the Schuman Plan for a European Coal and Steel Community.

Given such a life story, few in France had greater authority to speak out on Franco-German relations. 'If we don't want to fall back (*retomber*) into the old errors in dealing with the German problem', Schuman declared in 1949, 'there is only one solution, that is the European solution.'[41] This was, of course, the approach prefigured by Briand and Seydoux a quarter-century before. Progress on European integration was tortuous and uncertain: momentum stalled in 1953–54 when an unholy alliance of Gaullists and Communists dominated the French Assembly. But eventually in 1957 France and Germany signed a pact that would have been utterly inconceivable in 1945. It embraced the Benelux countries, traditionally caught in the jaws of the Franco-German antagonism, and also Italy which, like Germany, sought rehabilitation from fascism and the war. The Treaty of Rome was effectively the peace treaty that finally drew a line under World War II in Western Europe.

And not just under World War II but also centuries of Franco-German antagonism, as de Gaulle made clear when welcoming Adenauer to France in 1962. Perhaps the most richly symbolic venue was Reims Cathedral – sacred coronation place of French kings but also, as we saw, site of one of Germany's most notorious cultural atrocities of 1914 – where the two leaders attended Mass at the High Altar. Later, at the Elysée Palace, de Gaulle spoke movingly about how the endless rivalry between France and Germany had led only to a cycle of victories and defeats marked by countless graves. But now, he declared, their two countries were finally able to realize the dream of unity that had haunted the souls of 'our Continent' for twenty centuries back through Charlemagne and the Holy Roman Empire to Imperial Rome itself.[42]

This historically astounding rapprochement, therefore, opened a new perspective on the past. It helped to generate a progressive Franco-German narrative about the era of the two world wars, about a saga of ruinous nationalism eventually transcended in internationalism as the bloody first half of the twentieth century gave way to a second half characterized by peace and prosperity. This is, of course, a vast simplification of the past, but I am describing myth not history. The survival of the European Union and its gradual enlargement across Europe, especially since the end of the Cold War, has served to enhance that heroic integrationist narrative.[43]

Across the Channel in Britain by the 1960s there emerged a very different national narrative to connect the two world wars. 1914–18 now represented merely the horrific and futile prelude to the next round of the struggle, whereas 1939–45 seemed to the British both meaningful and triumphant. In 1940–41 British cities were heavily bombed and the country was threatened with invasion, so this war, unlike 1914–18, clearly became a struggle for national survival. Yet victory was achieved at roughly half the human cost of 1914–18 – 350,000 dead instead of 720,000. Moreover revelations of the Nazi death camps served to confirm the justice of the Allied cause, while this time Germany was categorically defeated and placed under Allied occupation. So World War II was seen as resolving the unfinished business left over from 1918 – this was a knock-out blow, not the prelude to another round. Within this new narrative the jagged contours of 1939–45 were smoothed out. The contribution of the Commonwealth and Empire to British victory was gradually obscured in popular memory, in official accounts and in many histories. Instead 1940 was enshrined as the heroic moment when the island fortress of Britain defied a hostile world, alone. This perspective owed much to Churchill's presentation of the conflict in his war memoirs: the volume on 1940 took as its title *Their Finest Hour* from the climax of one of his hortatory speeches that summer: 'Let us therefore brace to our duties, and so bear ourselves that, if the British Empire and its Commonwealth last for a thousand years, men will still say: "This was their finest hour."' That phrase has become British shorthand for 1940 – very different from the resonance of *l'année quarante* in France. Revealingly when Churchill's memoirs were published in French, his publishers, Plon, deviated only once from his own volume titles: the Paris edition of *Their Finest Hour*, which appeared in 1949, was called *L'Heure Tragique*.[44]

This process of 'nationalizing' the British war effort – marginalizing the role of the United States and even the Empire – was reinforced by a succession of war films that featured Britain's soldiers, sailors and airman taking on the Germans with little help from any allies. Their heroes – actors such as Jack Hawkins, John Mills and Richard Todd – usually displayed stereotypical British male attributes of gritty courage, understated humour and a stiff upper lip. More than 100 of these war films were made in Britain in the two decades after 1945, mostly during the 1950s, and they gained a new lease of life when recycled on television in the 1960s and 1970s. These movies helped contract the whole focus of the war down to 1940, when the heroic island fought on alone after the continentals had wimped out, and suggested that 'only the British male character could have seen it through'. Cumulatively these films have left an enduring imprint on popular British conceptions of the war.[45]

While 1939–45 became mythologized in a positive sense, British views of 1914–18 became overwhelmingly negative. In 1964 the 50th anniversary of the outbreak of war was marked by the path-breaking BBC TV series *The Great War*, in 26 episodes. About one-sixth of the potential viewing population, 8 million people, watched each episode on BBC1. Strikingly *The Great War* received an almost completely uncritical response, not only from its audience but also from reviewers. Approval ratings put it in on the same level as an FA Cup Final or a Royal Wedding. Although the producers and writers were not avid debunkers and drew on the latest military history, it was not the script but the archive footage and sound effects that stuck in people's minds – conveying the horror of the trenches to a new generation whose images of war came mostly from 1939 to 1945. During the 1960s the anti-war poets of the trenches were reprinted and also circulated in new anthologies. Wilfred Owen, previously a minor figure, was now elevated to the canonical voice of the conflict, with his 'Anthem for Doomed Youth' summing up the prevailing impression of the war. At a time when the British Establishment was under attack from students and radicals, Field Marshal Haig and other generals of World War I were easy targets – castigated for aristocratic aloofness and almost criminal stupidity in endlessly throwing their men into battle. This became the subject of satire, notably in the 1963 musical *Oh! What a Lovely War!* and the subsequent film starring Richard Attenborough. Even more biting was the 1989 TV series *Blackadder Goes Forth* in which British strategy seems to revolve around periodic, homicidal efforts by Haig to 'move his drinks cabinet six inches closer to Berlin'. In one episode Captain Blackadder's superior, the crazy sadist General Melchett (played by Stephen Fry), announces that 'Field Marshal Haig has formulated a brilliant tactical plan to ensure final victory in the field.' Blackadder wonders if this brilliant plan would 'involve us climbing over the top of our trenches and walking slowly towards the enemy?' Asked how he knew, because this was 'classified information', Blackadder replies: 'It's the same plan we used last time, sir. And the seventeen times before that.'[46]

This vein of satire exposes a sharp difference between British and French memorialization of 1914–18. In both countries there is profound recognition of the horror and the cost of that war, but for the French, the conflict remains a tragic sacrifice and has not become a subject for black humour, as Jay Winter observes in Chapter 7. French directors have made comic or satirical films about World War II and the Resistance – *La Grande Vadrouille* (1966), for instance, or *Papy fait de la résistance* (1983). But the Great War seems to be sacrosanct.

Against what the British now see as the dark tragedy of 1914–18, the conflict of 1939–45, therefore, stands out in bright and heroic colours. This has shaped not only British cultural attitudes but also the country's foreign policy. Here, for instance, is Ernest Bevin, Labour's down-to-earth Foreign Secretary in 1950, explaining Britain's reservations about the Schuman Plan to US diplomats: 'The people in this country were pinning their faith on a policy of defence built on a Commonwealth-USA basis – an English-speaking basis. People here were frankly doubtful of Europe. How could he go down to his constituency – Woolwich – which had been bombed by the Germans in the war, and tell his constituents that the Germans would help them in a war against Russia.' Similarly, Bevin continued, 'in regard to France, the man in the street, coming back from a holiday there, was almost invariably struck by the defeatist attitude of the French.' In short, exclaimed Bevin, 'it must be realized that Great Britain was not part of Europe; she was not simply a Luxembourg.'[47]

In 1962 Dean Acheson, the former US Secretary of State, declared in 1962 that 'Great Britain has lost an Empire and has not yet found a role.' The outcry in London indicated that Acheson had struck a raw nerve. Prime Minister Harold Macmillan delivered a schoolmasterly rebuke but, revealingly, he pointed to ancient history rather than present realities, accusing Acheson of having 'fallen into the error which has been made by quite a lot of people in the last four hundred years, including Philip II of Spain, Louis XIV, Napoleon, the Kaiser and Hitler.'[48] In fact Acheson had offered an apt depiction of Britain in limbo. During the 1960s the colonial empire crumbled very rapidly. Between 1948 and 1960 only 3 British colonies had gained independence; over the next 4 years, 17 did so – many of them African territories previously judged incapable of standing on their own for several more generations.[49] At the end of the decade, as the Sterling Area disintegrated, Harold Wilson's Labour Government decided to withdraw

British troops from east of Suez (apart from Hong Kong). And the British, having ignored European integration in its early days, were forced to come to terms with the existence and success of the European Community. 'If we try to remain aloof', a Cabinet committee warned in 1960, 'bearing in mind that this will be happening simultaneously with the contraction of our overseas possessions, we shall run the risk of losing political influence and of ceasing to be able to exercise any real claim to be a world Power'.[50] But although Britain tried to negotiate membership from 1961, two Olympian vetoes by President de Gaulle kept the country outside Europe's magic circle until 1973. By then the club rules had been set in ways inimical to basic British interests, particularly on agriculture and the budget.

France, of course, was also losing its empire in the 1960s: for both countries, decolonization has been traumatic and its legacies, at home and abroad, endure into the twenty-first century. But, arguably, France found a new role within the process of European integration, whereas Britain has remained on the periphery of this new Europe, centred on the Franco-German entente. Whereas French foreign policy has moved on from World War II, British diplomacy has found that less easy to do so.

In conclusion, we can say that the French cherish a positive if tragic remembrance of 1914–18, whereas the public memory of 1939–45 is fragmented, edgy and pained. The British have become bleakly negative about World War I, but they have celebrated World War II, especially 1940, in ways that made it hard for policy to move on, whereas the French developed an integrationist narrative that helped ease them into the second half of the twentieth century. For Britain, however, the European Union has been a necessary evil rather than a positive good. Back in 1939, as war dawned again, Lord Halifax spoke of Britain being 'on the fringe of this mad continent'.[51] In the twenty-first century, despite the Channel Tunnel and Easyjet, many British people would still agree with him. Geography has shaped these attitudes but so, too, has history, especially the legacies of the two world wars.

Notes

1   For a fuller discussion see my essay 'The Origins of "The Second World War": Historical Discourse and International Politics', in David Reynolds (ed.), *From World War to Cold War* (Oxford, Oxford University Press, 2006), 9–22.

2   Zara S. Steiner, *Britain and the Origins of the First World War* (London, Macmillan, 1977), 237; Keith Wilson, *The Policy of the Entente: Essays on the Determinants of British Foreign Policy, 1904–1914* (Cambridge: Cambridge University Press, 1985), 252.

3   *Daily Mail*, 26 September 1914, quoted in Adrian Gregory, *The Last Great War: British Society and the First World War* (Cambridge: Cambridge University Press, 2008), 57.

4   Leonard V. Smith, StéphaneAudoin-Rouzeau and Annette Becker, *France and the Great War* (Cambridge: Cambridge University Press, 2003), 58.

5   Kenneth E. Silver, *Esprit de Corps: The Art of the Parisian Avant-Garde and the First World War* (London: Thames and Hudson, 1989), 297.

6   Thomas Mann, *Reflections of a Nonpolitical Man* (1918), trans. Walter D. Morris (New York: Frederick Ungar, 1983), 32–4.

7   'Empire's Honour', *The Times*, 21 September 1914, 12.

8   Margaret MacMillan, *Peacemakers: The Paris Peace Conference of 1919 and Its Attempt to End War* (London: John Murray, 2001), 35, 39, 205.

9   Christopher M. Andrew and A.S. Kanya-Forstner, *France Overseas: The Great War and the Climax of French Imperial Expansion* (London: Thames and Hudson, 1981), 189, 197.

10 Alan Sharp, *David Lloyd George* (London: Haus Publishing, 2008), 83.

11 Andrew and Kanya-Forstner, *France Overseas*, 172.

12 Robert Boyce, *The Great Interwar Crisis and the Collapse of Globalization* (London: Palgrave Macmillan, 2009), 139.

13 Peter Jackson, 'French Security and a British "Continental Commitment" after the First World War: A Reassessment', *English Historical Review*, 126 (2011), 345–85, quoting p. 357.

14 Stephanie C. Salzmann, *Great Britain, Germany and the Soviet Union: Rapallo and After, 1922–1934* (London: Royal Historical Society, 2003), 56, 64–5.

15 R.A.C. Parker, *Chamberlain and Appeasement: British Policy and the Coming of the Second World War* (London: Macmillan, 1993), 63.

16 Robert and Isabelle Tombs, *That Sweet Enemy: The French and the British from the Sun King to the Present* (London: Heinemann, 2006), 522.

17 Jay Winter, *The Great War and the British People* (London: Macmillan, 1985), 75.

18 Smith, Audoin-Rouzeau and Becker, *France and the Great War*, 162–3. See also Jay Winter, *Sites of Mourning, Sites of Memory: The Great War in European Cultural History* (Cambridge: Cambridge University Press, 1995), ch. 4.

19 Henri Barbusse, *Le Feu*, ed. Pierre Paraf (Paris: Flammarion, 1916), 375–6; John Stuart Roberts, *Siegfried Sassoon* (London, 2005), 132, 134.

20 Uri Bialer, *The Shadow of the Bomber: The Fear of Air Attack and British Politics, 1932–1939* (London: Royal Historical Society, 1980), 47, 130.

21 Gugliermo Ferrero (1931), quoted in Ladislas Mysyrowicz, *Autopsie d'une Défaite: Origines de l'effondrement militaire français de 1940* (Lausanne: L'Age de Homme, 1973), 319 (editors' translation); see also Peter Jackson, *France and the Nazi Menace: Intelligence and Policy Making, 1933–1939* (Oxford: Oxford University Press, 2000), 271–4.

22 See Linda Colley, *Patriots: Forging the Nation, 1707–1837* (New Haven: Yale University Press, 1992).

23 David Reynolds, *Summits: Six Meetings That Shaped the Twentieth Century* (London: Penguin, 2007), 44–5, 78–80.

24 A story first told in the pioneering monograph by P.M.H. Bell, *A Certain Eventuality: Britain and the Fall of France* (Farnborough, Hampshire: Saxon House, 1974).

25 Minutes by Sargent, 28 February 1940 and Chamberlain, 1 March 1940, FO 371/24298, C4444/9/17 (The National Archives, Kew – henceforth TNA); 'Schools in Wartime' memo no. 18, 'France and Ourselves', April 1940, Board of Education papers, ED 138/27 (TNA); House of Commons Debates, 2 April 1940, vol. 359, cols 40-1.

26 David Reynolds, '1940: Fulcrum of the Twentieth Century?' *International Affairs*, 66 (1990), 325–50.

27 Sarah Fishman, *We Will Wait: Wives of French Prisoners of War, 1940–1945* (New Haven: Yale University Press, 1991), 27. The exact death toll remains in dispute and a much lower figure of around 50,000 or 60,000 has been suggested: see Jean-Jacques Arzalier, 'La campagne de mai-juin 1940: les pertes?', in Christine Levisse-Touzé (ed.), *La campagne de 1940* (Paris: Tallandier, 2001), 439–40.

28 The most detailed study is Jean-Louis Crémieux-Brilhac, *Les Français de l'an 40* (2 vols, Paris: Gallimard, 1990); see also his essay '1914 dans 1940', in Jean-Jacques Becker, et al. (eds), *Guerre et Cultures, 1914–1918* (Paris: Armand Colin, 1994), 287–93. More recent works include Ernest R. May, *Strange Victory: Hitler's Conquest of France* (New York: Hill and Wang, 2000) and Julian Jackson, *The Fall of France: The Nazi Invasion of 1940* (Oxford: Oxford University Press, 2003).

29 Halifax to Hankey, 15 July 1940, FO 371/25206, W8602/8602/49 (TNA). The letter was drafted by Sargent, prime mover in the earlier Anglo-French entente.

30 Richard Crossman, 'The Making of Macmillan', *Sunday Telegraph*, 9 February 1964, 4; Richard N. Gardner, *Sterling-Dollar Diplomacy in Current Perspective: The Origins and the Prospects of our International Order* (3rd edn, New York: Columbia University Press, 1980), xiii.

31 Jonathan R. Adelman, *Prelude to Cold War: The Tsarist, Soviet and US Armies in the Two World Wars* (London, 1988), 128.

32 R.S. Sayers, *Financial Policy, 1939–1945* (London: H.M. Stationery Office, 1946), 498–9.

33 James J. Sadkovich, 'Understanding Defeat: Reappraising Italy's Role in World War II', *Journal of Contemporary History*, 24 (1989), 46. On the general importance of the empire for British power, see David Edgerton, *Britain's War Machine: Weapons, Resources and Experts in the Second World War* (London: Penguin, 2011), chs 2–3.

34 Hankey to Sir Samuel Hoare, 19 July 1940, Templewood papers, T/XIII/17 (Cambridge University Library).

35 Jackson, *Fall of France*, 241; Charles de Gaulle, *Mémoires*, Marius-François Guyard (ed.) (collected edition, Paris: Gallimard, 2000), 488. On de Gaulle's war, see the essays in Philippe Oulmont (ed.), *De Gaulle, Chef de Guerre: De l'Appel de Londres à la Libération de Paris, 1940–1944* (Paris: Plon, 2008).

36 Eden to Churchill, 29 Nov. 1944, PREM 4/30/8, p. 453 (TNA).

37   Minute of meeting on 5 January 1949, printed in Richard Clarke, *Anglo-American Economic Collaboration in War and Peace, 1942–1949*, Alec Cairncross (ed.) (Oxford: Clarendon Press, 1982), 208–10.

38   Olivier Wieviorka, *La Mémoire désunie: le souvenir politique des années sombres de la Libération à nos jours* (Paris: Seuil, 2010), 28.

39   Julian Jackson, *France: The Dark Years 1940–1944* (Oxford: Oxford University Press, 2001), epilogue, quoting p. 613; Henry Rousso, *The Vichy Syndrome: History and Memory in France since 1944* (Cambridge, MA: Harvard University Press, 1991), 168. See also Pierre Laborie, *Le Chagrin et le Venin: La France sous l'Occupation, mémoire et idées reçues* (Paris: Bayard, 2011).

40   Quotations from John W. Young, *France, the Cold War and the Western Alliance, 1944–1949: French Foreign Policy and Post-War Europe* (Leicester: Leicester University Press, 1990), 82.

41   Quoted by Raymond Poidevin, 'Le facteur Europe dans la politique allemande de Robert Schuman', in Poidevin (ed.), *Histoire des debuts de la construction européene (mars 1948-mai 1950)* (Brussels: Bruylant, 1986), 326.

42   Hans-Peter Schwarz, *Adenauer: Der Staatsmann, 1952–1967* (München: DeutscherTaschenbuchVerlag, 1994), 759–60.

43   For a trenchant critique of the heroic integrationist narrative see Alan S. Milward, *The European Rescue of the Nation-State* (London: Routledge, 1992), 1–20.

44   David Reynolds, *In Command of History: Churchill Fighting and Writing the Second World War* (London: Penguin, 2004), 204–8. The speech was broadcast on 18 June 1940.

45   Malcolm Smith, *Britain and 1940: History, Myth and Popular Memory* (London: Routledge, 2000), 122–3, and generally John Ramsden, 'Refocusing "The People's War": British War Films of the 1950s', *Journal of Contemporary History*, 33 (1998), 35–63.

46   Dan Todman, *The Great War: Myth and Memory* (London: Hambledon Continuum, 2005), esp. 28–35, 116–17.

47   Pierson Dixon, memo of meeting of 23 August 1950, FO 800/517 (TNA).

48   Harold Macmillan, *At the End of the Day, 1961–1963* (London: Macmillan, 1973), 339.

49   David Reynolds, *Britannia Overruled: British Policy and World Power in the Twentieth Century* (2nd edn, London: Longman, 2000), 208.

50   N. Piers Ludlow, *Dealing with Britain: The Six and the First UK Application to the EEC* (Cambridge: Cambridge University Press, 1997), 32.

51   Halifax to Lord Lothian, 27 September 1939, FO 800/324 (TNA).

INDEX